Jungian Art Therapy

Jungian Art Therapy aims to provide a clear, introductory manual for art therapists on how to navigate Jung's model of working with the psyche. This exciting new text circumambulates Jung's map of the mind so as to reinforce the theoretical foundations of analytical psychology while simultaneously defining key concepts to help orient practitioners, students, and teachers alike. The book provides several methods, which illustrate how to work with the numerous images originating from the unconscious and glean understanding from them. Throughout the text readers will enjoy clinical vignettes to support each chapter and illuminate important lessons.

Nora Swan-Foster, MA, LPC, ATR-BC, NCPsyA is a Jungian Analyst and Jungian Art Therapist in private practice in Boulder, Colorado. She is a Board Certified and Registered Art Therapist and a senior training analyst with the Inter-Regional Society of Jungian Analysts (IRSJA). Nora teaches at Naropa University, where she was on the faculty for several years. Her art therapy research and publications opened the door for using art therapy as early intervention with childbearing-related issues related to medical trauma, PTSD, anxiety, and depression. Nora is on the editorial board for the *Journal of Analytical Psychology* and her chapter "Jungian Art Therapy" was included in Judith Rubin's *Approaches to Art Therapy*. She continues to investigate the Jungian path of creativity through teaching, painting, dreams, and active imagination.

Jungian Art Therapy

A Guide to Dreams, Images, and Analytical Psychology

Nora Swan-Foster

Routledge
Taylor & Francis Group

NEW YORK AND LONDON

First edition published 2018

By Routledge
711 Third Avenue, New York, NY 10017

and by Routledge

2 Park Square, Milton Park, Abingdon, Oxon, OX14 4RN

Routledge is an imprint of the Taylor & Francis Group, an informa business

Library of Congress Cataloging-in-Publication Data
Names: Swan-Foster, Nora, author.
Title: Jungian art therapy : a guide to dreams, images, and analytical psychology / Nora Swan-Foster.
Description: New York, NY : Routledge, 2018. | Includes bibliographical references.
Identifiers: LCCN 2017047220 (print) | LCCN 2017047575 (ebook) | ISBN 9781315457017 (ebk) | ISBN 9781138209534 (hbk) | ISBN 9781138209541 (pbk)
Subjects: LCSH: Art therapy.
Classification: LCC RC489.A7 (ebook) | LCC RC489.A7 S92 2018 (print) | DDC 616.89/1656—dc23
LC record available at https://lccn.loc.gov/2017047220

ISBN: 978-1-138-20953-4 (hbk)
ISBN: 978-1-138-20954-1 (pbk)
ISBN: 978-1-315-45701-7 (ebk)

Typeset in Goudy
By Keystroke, Neville Lodge, Tettenhall, Wolverhampton

Printed in the United Kingdom
by Henry Ling Limited

In memory of Pepper

Contents

Illustrations

All images in Chapters 9 and 10 are supplied in a color plate section between pp. 132–133

Acknowledgments

I would like to thank all the students of Jungian psychology and art therapy who have crossed my path—this book was quietly seeded by your curiosity and enthusiasm for Jung's work, and your own daring quests with the unconscious. The gifts were numerous and made this possible. I am honored and eternally grateful to those who generously agreed to share snippets from their personal journeys with images to clarify theory and application—this book would not exist without each and every one and the text is greatly enriched as a result. I am appreciative of the analysts and participants of the Boulder Jung Seminar—the gifts of community were essential. To Stephen Foster, my companion in everything meaningful: thank you for devoting hours of discussing, reading, and technical computer support at a time when you'd rather be hiking. Your loving patience and unending faithful encouragement and theoretical knowledge were ever present. To Jennifer Phelps: your positive enthusiasm, persistent dedication to the content, and unwavering focus in the valley of details as an editor brought greater clarity and flow for those new to Jung. It would have been impossible to complete this on schedule without you both working to prune the summer growth.

To Sondra Geller for opening the gate wide one evening for the idea to come through, to Judith Rubin for holding the gate open in an important moment (and for your years of inspiration), and to Michael Franklin, Mimi Farrelly-Hansen, and Dottie Oatman for your various creative acts of devotion to art therapy. To Laury Rappaport, Bruce Moon, and Shaun McNiff for bushwhacking creative paths forward. For Jordan Potash for your grace and generosity in sharing the work.

To the following who were influential in unique ways—your depth and breadth challenged me to find my own way: Joan Joan Anderson, Wynette Barton, Gus Cwik, Ethné Gray, Deborah Herman, Bernice Hill, Tom Kelly, Margaret Johnson, Don Kalsched, Ronnie Landau, Mary Sue Moore, Ann Murtha, Judith Savage, David Sedgwick, Mark Winborn, and Don Williams. Thank you. To Joe McNair for tending the alchemical fires with stories, imagination, and walking your own creative path. To Sam Kimbles and Suzy Spradlin for your graceful leadership in Jungian group trainings— each one offered an unforgettable perspective. To the original Denver Jung Seminar: the monthly discussions laid an important foundation. To Laurel Howe, I'm grateful for your professional generosity along with Matt Christie—both of you shared the goodness found in daily life. When times were bleak, your calm was a buoy in the storms. To Kathleen Goldblatt for your generosity and poetic friendship that renewed, inspired, and reminded me to gather what had been lost. To Annette: your deep connection to nature and meditation rooted me. And to you both for the hours of collegial adventures that fertilized. To Susan Roberts—your knowledge and presence in the right moments made space for the project to breathe. To Leona Furnari, Denise Meyer, Teresa Robertson, and Doug Tyler for unfettered moments of valued connections. To Kellie Murphy— your endless heartfelt gifts nourished my soul. To Anne and George—your spirits guided me from start to finish—and Cynthia Swan for believing in the possibility of change. And most importantly, to Fiona Foster and Hamilton Foster: your steady encouragement reminded me how to imagine the world anew. Thank you. To all those whose paths I crossed but are not listed here: you gave me what I needed to endure the many required labors.

I am indebted to all those at Routledge/Taylor & Francis. Some I know by name and they have become a kind of second family, but many are like angels who work tirelessly behind the scenes. Chris Teja, who carried the idea forward. Anna Moore, Elizabeth Graber, and Amanda Devine, who each played a significant role, especially with support for so many colored, and black and white, images. Emma Starr was unwavering as she enthusiastically stepped forward to fill in the gaps and maintain oversight and communication. And to the production manager, Amy Kirkham, who seamlessly carried the project to completion—I have utmost admiration. Appreciation to Jean Pierre Jerome for marketing and Tom Hussey for his creative cover design. To those who worked deep into the details: I'm appreciative of Maggie Lindsey-Jones, Managing Director at Keystroke, and the fantastic team, for their stellar job of keeping me on schedule and pushing for the best, including Kelly-Jayne Winter for her attention to details, including her investment in the best pictures possible. And Fiona Wade for her graceful copy-edits that invisibly stitched and mended individual pieces into a whole book, and Andrew Melvin for taking a final lap with proofreading. Any remaining omissions or mistakes are my own responsibility.

I'm grateful to all those who have directly or indirectly provided permission to quote their works, including:

From *The Collected Works of C. G. Jung, Vol. 8: The Structure and Dynamics of the Psyche* by C. G. Jung. Copyright © 1970 by Princeton University Press. Published by Princeton University Press. Reprinted by permission. Copyright Clearance Center ODI: 70591504
From *The Collected Works of C. G. Jung, Vol. 16: The Practice of Psychotherapy* by C. G. Jung. Copyright © 1985 by Princeton University Press. Published by Princeton University Press. Reprinted by permission. Copyright Clearance Center ODI: 70591505

CHAPTER 1

Introduction

Images are all around. We are bombarded daily with images from various sources, but what we neglect most in these times is to attend to the images that come from within, from the unconscious. These images are often left unattended, let alone remembered, and yet through personal images such as pictures, dreams, poetry, and other creative expressions we are secretly fed. These images carry their own consciousness; they become our guides on the path to transformation.

Our own deep nature is reflected in the living nature around us—it is a mirror of our own inner possibilities. Jung built his psychology around principles from nature: psyche is image, psyche is nature. Image and nature are joined in psyche. Jung's psychology is both simple and complicated, and filled with paradox. It's made up of opposites that join together to mobilize eventual sparks of insight, change, and possible transcendence. Jung makes us work hard at learning his psychology, to take up the same struggle with the shadow that he did, and to seek meaning in our lives and our times. When we step onto our own path, we step into a fully lived life.

Contrary to popular belief, Jungian psychology is not simply an intellectual endeavor of interpretation and analysis. Rather it is truly a path of seeking consciousness, through experience and sacrifice, because we release what encumbers us so we can live more fully. We relinquish what we believe we know and invest in our true path, which does not avoid the depth of life, but embraces the unavoidable trials and suffering where a new light may be found. When we embrace the human experience through our various images, we discover the hidden gate that opens us to our life. Life initiates us.

As the late Jungian analyst Elizabeth Ruff said in her "Sacrifice and Initiation" lecture:

> The creative challenge of our time is to take our own path of individuation under our feet because if we do not, no one will do it for us and we will be forever undone. To live one's own life is to take these steps of creativity.
>
> (Ruff, 1988)

Jungian art therapy is a catalyst to *take our own path of individuation* and embrace the paradoxical found in all creative processes. We gather our visceral and sensory experiences that come with thoughts and feelings and mix them into conscious images that will change not just our individual lives, but potentially also the world around us.

So, as Jung advised us, choose a beautiful blank book and make it yours. Place in it your soul's longings, thoughts, and free expressions. With unbridled spontaneous love and compassion, you will discover a new way to attend to the psyche, to work with the unconscious. Let the critical voice take a rest and run from those who devour you. Steal away a few moments for yourself so you can have time to get lost in the creative journey of your life. There is only this one moment and then it's gone.

Honoring the soul through image-making is fundamental to Jungian art therapy. This book was greatly inspired by those who have come into my life, engaged with psyche, and offered their images, including those students who registered for an introductory class called Jungian Psychology: Transpersonal Foundations and Central Concepts, which I teach at Naropa University.[1] I'm grateful for their participation as their sacrifice has meant an early Monday morning class and having to relinquish other coursework. Their questions and musings were invaluable to me and allowed us to join together in the study of Jung's material.

The purpose of the course is to teach the fundamentals of Jungian psychology, or what is known as analytical psychology. In addition, the course includes several written and art assignments in response to the readings as well as an analysis of a chosen movie using Jungian principles. And finally, each person is required to create his or her own visual "Red Book" over the course of the semester centered around a chosen contemplative practice.

There is a wide range of possibilities for how their books are created; what organically emerges is often consistently reflective of Jung's structure of the psyche and the archetypal pattern of individuation. Pictures, images, writing, dreams, daily practice notes, class notes, and poetry are all included in the books. Students sometimes hand-make their books, or transform purchased blank books into creative binders. What is consistent is their enthusiasm for the project. The discoveries students make about themselves as individuals sustain them, and they begin to listen to what is most meaningful in their daily lives. They wrestle with their fear of the unconscious, the images that haunt them, and the messages they receive from the images. The fire grows and both the inner life and the life around them collaborate in the enterprise of individuation. When students are given free rein to explore their own creative process with unbridled spontaneity and very few rules, they are motivated by something far greater than expectations, grades, and outside perceptions. Their motivated engagement is authentic because it comes from within. By taking their path of individuation "under their feet" and making their own "Red Book," their souls are undoubtedly deeply moved. I am forever grateful to be an ally and witness to so many inner adventures, and to be touched by such enthusiasm and dedication to the gifts provided by the unconscious.

My Journey into Jungian Psychology

In one of my journals, I found a reference to a working title and the outline of chapters for this book. However, that was before I trained as a Jungian analyst, where I deepened my own interests in Jungian art therapy as well as my growing disappointment with how little Jungian psychology is included in the curriculum of a general psychology degree. It perplexed me. My early idea slipped into the background, or back into the unconscious, as Jung might have said, while other tasks took precedence. Yet, my passion for Jung's ideas and Jungian art therapy remained close to my heart.

As the reader of this book, your story, similar to mine, likely contains the incredibly memorable stages of awakening that arises from suffering, deepening, and an emergence into a new state of consciousness, all of which is aided by images and symbols that continue to live and expand in meaning and reference for future directions you may travel. In coming to understand how individuation is innately expressed through our unique lives, it is only reasonable to share briefly a few of my own encounters with Jungian psychology and images that have quietly helped to form this book long before I knew of its existence.

My first encounter with Jung was when I was about 12 years old, flopped out on my mom's side of the bed on a hot humid day in the Midwest. I was bored, in a state that, if pursued, often leads kids to curiosity and discovery. In this case, I sorted through her stack of books, looking for something of interest. One of them was by the Jungian analyst June Singer, *Boundaries of the Soul*. The title was intriguing as was the author's name. The word

"Singer" had music and rhythm. At that age, I knew what boundaries were, but I wasn't sure what *soul* meant—I thought I might try to read the book to find out. I remember working at it. I'm not sure how far I got at that age, but I now like to think that some seed was planted for later life.

My next encounter was at age 20 when I rode a bus, known then as the *Magic Bus*, from Athens to London for four long days to reconnect with my now husband, the Jungian analyst Stephen Foster. The *Magic Bus* traveled north through the various winter climates of Europe. We experienced crisp mornings with dappled sunlight on the bus windows, fog, snow, thunderstorms, and then relentless, blinding rain. Each time we unloaded from the bus for a bathroom break and a bite to eat, there were new sounds, smells, and a different language being spoken. Unbeknownst to me at the time, I was traveling through a liminal world, on an archetypal journey, that laid the path for my future. How we ever made it to our London destination, I'm not sure.

Partway through the trip a young woman with short black hair, who sat in the seat in front of me, turned to tell me about pearl diving in Greece and the overwhelming amount of shit in the streets of India that was continuing to haunt her dreams. At one point, she handed a book over the seat and said, "Have you ever read this? You're welcome to it—I picked it up at the hostel in Athens." The book was *Memories, Dreams, Reflections* (*MDR*) and reading Jung's memoir set me on a trajectory.

All of us needed a distraction from the anxiety we shared as the bus lurched along small winding mountain roads in the former Yugoslavia and swerved through tumultuous weather on the highways of Germany and France. Our driver took breaks on the side of the road to drink and later needed help from one of the passengers in the front seat to navigate the blinding rain. Jung's book led me inwards and quieted my mind; I soon was immersed in his life story and the role of psyche and the importance of dreams. Before I knew it, we were pulling into London's Victoria Station. Of course, it was still raining and cold. I had become sick with a relentless chest cold and I had only a few English pounds in my pocket—the days before credit cards. Despite the conditions in the outer world, I had found confirmation from reading Jung's reflections and memories that the unconscious was a reliable resource and that my early interest in art, dance, music, astrology, psychology, spirituality, and various occult topics was not so unusual. Moreover, it became clear that these interests were doors into the collective unconscious where I could find meaning and connection to the transpersonal world that had fascinated me for many years.

The black-haired woman who had been pearl diving in Greece was a kind of vision, a dream figure, who appeared in my life under the triangular glow of the bus's reading light during the liminal bus ride between my past and my future. She was a shadow figure who connected me to what Jung referred to as the "higher intelligence" of the unconscious, and to the metaphorical and psychological process of diving for pearls. She handed me a task and I completed it. It was a symbolic and mysterious moment in my life, an image that has stayed with me and continues to carry me forward.

Shortly after this, as a young 20-year-old, I left England, and returned home. I registered for the first of several process painting classes at the University of Wisconsin–Madison with Professor Larry Junkins. On the first day, he introduced the class to the idea of painting not from the ego but from the unconscious. This was a new approach for me, but reading Jung's work had prepared me. Previous teachers had focused on the formal qualities and techniques of painting and drawing. Because Jung's work had influenced Junkins, he was passionate about teaching painting as a tool for accessing unconscious material. He'd often ask us to stop painting and step back and get quiet, to listen to what was before us. He'd tell us to "sit with the image." Then he'd circumambulate the room and visit each student's painting; in those moments with him, we would consider what had been delivered from psyche, what the soul was speaking to us, where it took us, or what repelled us. Did we find particular images interesting or distasteful? Did it arouse our passion for the process?

I found this time deeply contemplative and meaningful. My painting practice took on new purpose, and my interest in image making was enlivened by the mystery of the moment-by-moment process and the unknown that I might paint into visibility. As Jung named it, we were "making pregnant" (as cited in Chodorow, 1997) the images found on the canvas, fertilizing and nourishing the lines, shapes, and colors into an expressive and aesthetic cohesive image that represented something meaningful for us. This was Jung's idea of libidinal energy—psychic energy that touches and revives what is purposeful, making it possible, resulting in constructive forces expressed through images of all sorts. At the time, I did not realize I was working with my personal complexes or archetypal patterns.

To have someone value the "accidents" in a painting class, the areas where color and line worked well or didn't quite hold any possibility, was a fresh outlook on art and psychology. I could see my painting in a different light. I could also see myself. Not so interested in formal skill building, Junkins had us discover, uncover, and recover. He required us to experiment with canvas size and various materials, including kitchen tools, fruits and vegetables, odd brushes, sponges, and then to consider mixing media. He asked us to play and be curious. At the same time, he asked us to be discerning and to differentiate what worked and what didn't work and to consider why.

These classes took me away from *thinking* about the formal aspects of painting to *feeling into* the process of painting. I felt a kind of weaving process occur, a formation of my identity, as I cultivated a visual voice and a connection to soul. *This is what soul feels like*, I thought as the connection was made between body, soul, and spirit. *A kind of coming home to myself.* I felt the boundaries as well as the stretching beyond them, and so I recovered a connection to that young child, flopped out on the bed, who had innately sensed these mysteries and was searching for answers in this song of life.

Art (art museums, art galleries, and art making) had always been a major part of my family life. I grew up in a household that was under construction and in constant process. Both my parents were artists; my mom had her block printing studio in the living room area and my dad would draw or paint with watercolors when he wasn't completing his architectural projects or working on carpentry tasks within our unfinished houses. We moved often to follow the architectural jobs that mirrored the economy, so from an early age I lived as an outsider within the collective, which led to feelings of being isolated and disoriented or having feelings of missing out. These complexes gave me empathy for the marginalized kids because I often felt like one myself. The complexes related to loss were inevitable. Several times we sacrificed our familiar routines and friendships within our community for the adventure into the unknown.

When I've described this artistic, organic, gardening lifestyle to some, they've remarked on how it sounds unique, and maybe even idyllic. Although this lifestyle had some wonderful benefits, it was not always easy or ideal. The complicated feelings of uncertainty whitewashed with messages of adventure or courage were spiced with periods of intrusive authoritarian parenting and interspersed with neglect and emotional abandonment. I cultivated a private underground path to follow because relationships and emotions were poorly regulated and unpredictable, and occasionally traumatizing. The eruptions of violence in the collective that I recall, such as President Kennedy's assassination, followed by protests and hard political divisions marked by the pivotal 1968 riots and assassinations of Martin Luther King Jr. and then Bobby Kennedy, fueled the emotional conflicts inside our home. The tension grew as my older siblings broke boundaries of all sorts, came of age, and entered the fiercely changing world. I escaped to my room with art materials or found places in nature to play and sing the songs that comforted me. I searched for some verification and articulation of what I witnessed and felt inside. Because art was the accepted way to communicate, the arts in general became my resource to connect with my body and soul and cross boundaries into the imagination.

After completing my degree at UW-Madison, I found Lesley University's Expressive Arts Therapy program from a random meeting with a professor who handed me a pale purple mimeographed sheet that I could hardly read. Today, with the internet and widespread access to almost anything we want or need, we forget how we used to find (or not find) information. It was a synchronous event that led me to the program, founded by Shaun McNiff, where I further explored my interests at the interface between psychology and art. I entered Jungian analysis with Ethne Gray and began to work with my dreams—to make sense of the images that had haunted me for years. When I had the dream directing me to "sing the mole's song" (Chapter 9), she encouraged using art materials to track my unconscious and illustrate my dreams. At Lesley, McNiff's (1992) emphasis on the imagination through the expressive arts and process painting allowed me to pick up some of the dropped threads in my life; it invigorated the role of sound and dance along with the use of image, not from an interpretive diagnostic way, but within an engaged personal practice that promoted image and movement of all kinds, large or small, individually or in groups. While not defined as such, the Expressive Arts Therapy program inherently valued the transpersonal aspect of the psyche—discovered through this multi-modal approach—so that the various images could speak, sing, and pulse from within.

In the 1980s, Massachusetts was a leader in the country for promoting early intervention programs; the state advocated emotional support for young children and mothers. As I worked with "at-risk" children at a major Boston psychiatric hospital and therapeutic nursery, the children not only led me to reflect upon my own upbringing but also taught me about the developmental stages, learning and attachment styles, the effects of trauma, and how the psyche organizes and makes sense of a world when living under stress in high-risk environments where safety and food is a primary concern. There were those children who were extraverted, purposeful, and intent on constructing change through play and there were others who were introverted, withdrawn, and protected, unable to find enough freedom from their hurts and worries to trust, let alone access, their own spontaneous playfulness.

Academically, I was learning about expressive therapy, but it was the children who taught me about psychology. They affirmed that we all have an innate yet diverse expressive knowing available to us, where the pain and poison can become the healing agent. The children showed me how one art medium fluidly moved to another, allowing them to find what they needed to soothe or resource themselves and master the unsolvable dilemmas by using music, image, art materials, and storytelling. They were often without inhibitions. As living expressions of psychic energy and the image, the children became master teachers on the formation of the psyche from a young age.

As adults, we often deny ourselves these sorts of opportunities to engage with our creative nature; with our complexes in place, we resist the time to paint, to write, to dance. I know that reaction well—the difficulty I sometimes have to carve out time for what I love to do. The resistance to making time is common amongst artists. In *MDR* (1961) Jung advocated play as a way to unearth one's sense of wholeness. He also found resiliency in his own play, art making, and writing. Indeed, as time unfolded for me, Jungian analysis recovered my enjoyment of playing with the symbolic material of dreams and expressing the images through art projects, small paintings, or even sketching in my journal.

Eventually I built a private practice, conducted independent art therapy research with pregnant women, and had woven marriage, parenting, and motherhood into my life and identity. What I had learned in my graduate training became ever more relevant for my professional life and my daily family life with two children and two dogs. Living a symbolic life, as Jungians often refer to it, was definitely growing more layered, complex, and intricately patterned. Jungian analysis and expressive therapy was cultivating an attitude, fertilizing a way of life. It was a philosophy, an appreciation for the daily mystery as well as the demand to be adaptable, spontaneous, and creative in many different areas of my life.

At a later juncture, I joined the art therapy faculty at Naropa University in Boulder, Colorado. Once again, an interest in theory and process expanded and deepened within me. For several years I taught graduate-level art therapy courses and formulated several picture indicators for prenatal depression and anxiety (1989; 2003; 2012). Subsequent research in other fields offered evidence that post-partum depression was more likely to follow prenatal anxiety and depression, which validated that emotional prenatal support through art therapy actually benefitted a mother's maternal adaptation and fostered healthier attachment styles. Art therapy group work also fascinated me as I noticed the continuous tension of opposites between the talkers and the non-talkers, the conscious and the unconscious, and the ways that art making could defend against the life of the group and the unconscious; paradoxically I noticed how art making can be a place to hide from our emotions (2001). Jung's ideas on complexes and typology and the push from the unconscious became visible and relevant both academically and clinically.

And, ever more present was my work with the unconscious through dreams and art. It was on fire. During one of the studio classes that I taught, I painted a large picture of a seed planted in the earth with light in the center, and only a thread of it emerging. It came from some unknown place within me, flowing easily, without much effort, out of the unconscious. I felt enlivened—connected to the depths of my inner world as well as

Figure 1.1 Seed in the Earth

poised for something beyond me. The image (Figure 1.1) expressed both my being-ness and my becoming at once. As I worked with the image, the seed expanded from the image into an important symbol.

At this point, analytical psychology was calling me. Within a short period of time, I came across several books that offered a compelling direction for me to integrate my interests in art therapy with Jungian theory and application: Furth's *The Secret World of Drawings* (1988) and Schaverien's *The Revealing Image* (1992) brought together the essential language of art therapy and Jungian psychology in exciting ways. Kalsched's book *The Inner World of Trauma* (1996) described the power of the "self-care system" that develops from early childhood trauma in an imaginal way I had yet to encounter, but it explained what I knew with my work with children and adults as well as my own reactions of growing up in a family and historical time period filled with traumatic events and major transformation. Undoubtedly, I was being led back around the circle to incorporate Jung's theoretical ideas on the image, and fill in language for traumatic memories.

As if standing at a gate, I could see a path open before me that integrated my clinical training with my personal experience of Jungian analysis. At the same time, my dreams were showing repetitive signs of descents into dark tunnels and dream conversations with women who lived and worked with Jung, along with directions associated with an educational training process. As settled as I felt with my professional work, the unconscious was pushing on me. I was being called away from teaching art therapy; the dreams urged me to follow the stairs down to the metaphoric train track, to get on the train, and to deepen my academic knowledge of Jung's structure of the psyche as a clinical orientation. I longed to understand the psyche from a deeper theoretical perspective, with more acumen and confidence. Reading Jung's *Collected Works* provided the initial handholds for me as I immersed myself in the archeological work with the unconscious. I eventually applied and was accepted into analytic training with the Inter-Regional Society of Jungian Analysts (IRSJA).

We all receive calls from the unconscious; some calls we respond to and others we do not. Some calls are major events while others are small pivots that we take to adjust our stance. But each calling signifies a new journey, a new initiation process, and the potential for change, growth, and development. Jung named this whole process *individuation*. If we resist the opportunity, we may receive the information in another format. Some say that if we resist the call, then we will find ourselves suffering the consequences. It's not always easy to know which call is right for us and later in life we may realize that the opportunity was a major step we wish we had taken.

For me, there was the crucial call to temporarily turn away from art therapy, at least art therapy as I knew it. It was a world where I had built a decent professional reputation with publications, presentations, and teaching that could have continued to sustain me for the rest of my life. One morning I woke up from a dream with the words on my lips to discontinue all of my teaching commitments. It was a huge and frightening leap of faith into the darkness. The call was persistent and it did not give up. Not until I applied for training as a Jungian analyst with the IRSJA was there a calming of the unconscious. The push was not an ego-driven need to fulfill—in fact, my ego resisted the idea for a long time—but it came from something greater than myself that could not be ignored, a deeper instinctual truth or perhaps the organizing principle of my psyche, which Jung referred to as the *Self*.[2]

Several years ago, after my chapter on Jungian art therapy was included in the third edition of *Approaches to Art Therapy* (2016), another push from the unconscious was making itself known. I was having dreams about a pregnant woman. She represented for me a shadow figure in my psyche who held something unknown. In one dream she was dressed in yellow, the colour of intuition (Figure 1.2), and sat on a couch rubbing her belly.

The woman reappeared in various locations within subsequent dreams, until several weeks later she was nursing a baby and sitting next to other

Figure 1.2 Woman in Yellow

women on a couch. Who was she? What was she doing in my dreams? At the time, I had no idea. She arrived several months before a book contract with Routledge was even discussed. It seemed as if through the process of teaching and writing about Jungian art therapy, this book had been conceived and was now incubating, becoming real, and being nursed by a part of my psyche. Within time, a book outline emerged. Perhaps the yellow was suggesting the intuitive leaps and the persistence that would be needed to bring this project into life.

After I submitted the book proposal, I dreamt of another female figure dressed in layers, but the image of her was peculiar. I wasn't sure what the figure was so I drew it in hopes of sorting it out (Figure 1.3). When I did an active imagination with the figure, she said, "I'm the seed that took you into training . . . I'm a woman of many layers. Your work is to uncover and bring the layers into the light." When I returned to the original seed painting, I noticed the similarities between the two images. Now the yellow that had been within the seed had moved to surround the Layered Woman.

Why This Book?

As I hope my story reveals, Jungian art therapy is a method that emphasizes the imagination and the underlying path of individuation. Through the use

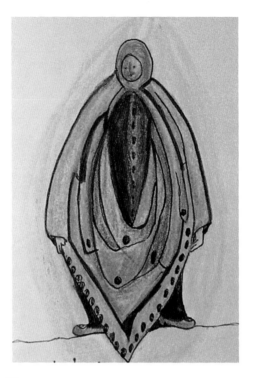

Figure 1.3 Layered Woman

of personal images and symbols, a unique theoretical model of the psyche can be accessed and worked with. Jung's theory is best learned through lived experience, and the combination of the two (the personal and the theoretical) leads us to recognize an epistemological foundation. Over the years I have come across too many texts that reference Jungian psychology and the arts, yet contain inaccurate historical or theoretical statements, leave out complex theory, or are overly simplistic regarding Jung's principles as well as his model of the psyche. I felt charged to explain what was left in the shadow, and focus on retrieving some of the Jungian history and theory of art therapy that had been left behind or misconstrued. Jung is most often credited for the concepts of the archetypes and the collective unconscious, while the advances he made in personal and relational psychology remain mostly unacknowledged. Conversely, some texts are overly complicated and verbose; students complain that the material is too intellectual or "heady" so they become intimidated by Jungian psychology and the gate shuts.

Maybe this is because many art therapists are strong visual learners and come into the field because of personal trials and tribulations; they view the world not just through words but through images. The goal of this book is to fill some of the theoretical holes for Jungian art therapy, in particular Jung's pivotal statements regarding libidinal energy (psychic energy); the relationship between energy, emotion, and image; the role of the body in Jungian art therapy for both analysts and analysands; the importance of complexes; and how the image and symbol become known and transform consciousness. In addition to basic theory, Jung had a great many interesting reflections on the therapeutic role of the creative process, which makes his model of the psyche even more pertinent to Jungian art therapists. He developed several methods and had ideas about developmental stages of therapy and consciousness (see the Appendix for more). I believe his ideas deserve to be part of the foundation in all basic art therapy training, but that is quite a task and inevitably something will be left behind. What will fill those gaps are images that illustrate his structure of the psyche with its key concepts and principles that make it a dynamic living model. This book is an invitation for art therapists, Jungian-oriented psychotherapists, Jungian candidates and analysts, and anyone else interested in Jungian psychology, to open the gate and explore their imagination through some of the most fundamental concepts of Jungian art therapy.

Navigation: Two Centuries, Two Paradigms

Words and images are a natural duo in Jungian psychology. Perhaps this reflects how Jung straddled two centuries—he was born in 1875 and died in 1961. Shamdasani (2009) noted that this had a significant influence on Jung's personal and professional work. However, Jung didn't just straddle two centuries, he also saw himself as both a scientist and a philosopher, and we can sometimes become disoriented within his theoretical landscape because of these two different perspectives. Evers-Fahey (2017) investigated the role of the ego in Jung's theory of the unconscious and offered some structure and clarity by framing Jung's work within an energic paradigm and a symbolic paradigm:

> While the energic paradigm focused on mechanistic dynamics, the symbolic paradigm is more mythopoetic and views the operations and experiences in the psyche as having a teleological intention beyond psychical balance or compromise. The integrative functions of the ego, for example, would have an underlying purpose beyond personal growth and development and lead to greater consciousness and relatedness in the world.
>
> (2017, p. 6)

Thus, from assumptions based on the time period in which Jung lived, where the world was observed objectively and quantifiably outside the person, the energic paradigm arises from objective scientific observation of a person living in the outside world. Yet, as Evers-Fahey explained, Jung turned this inside out and used these scientific ideas to map and study the inner world of the psyche. On the other hand, the symbolic paradigm contains the ineffable material, or the creative phenomena of the psyche that holds contents that are not quantifiable; it embraces the transpersonal psyche, which is often unknowable, or only partially known. The symbolic paradigm is found in personal experiences and emotions, the imagination, and the symbol, and has roots in the Romantic period.

By understanding that Jung's approach to the psyche held the tension between these two opposing paradigms, we gain greater clarity regarding the process in which unconscious contents come into consciousness. While his theory evolved from the interaction between these two paradigms, Jung also bridged a world where old ideas and concepts no longer worked with a new world that had not yet been created (Evers-Fahey, 2017). When we can recognize that Jung was carving out new territory, then we have a framework that holds the theoretical tension of opposites (the mechanistic aspect and the imaginative aspect) inherent within Jung's model, both of which participate in a dialectical conversation that furthers consciousness. When we encounter Jung's shifting or contradictory definitions that amplify the structure of the psyche as *both* energic (empiricist voice) and symbolic (romantic voice), Jung's model of the psyche is more easily comprehended and navigated.

The question remains: How do we attend to the theoretical principles and key concepts without becoming overly concrete or lost in the imagination? This balancing act is a legitimate concern in Jungian art therapy. Without a basic understanding of Jung's model of the psyche, much theoretical orientation is lost or misunderstood in terms of clinical work. With an overabundance of imagination, our theoretical ground can become muddled and we can lose our way (Edwards, 1987). Certainly the imaginal aspects are vital principles of Jung's philosophy, but within popular culture today, Jungian psychology seems to be solely identified by archetypes and the collective unconscious. In some cases, Jung's original ideas have become sanitized and inaccurate, thus losing their rich veracity, or his principles have been seamlessly integrated into other theories and practices with the mechanical maneuvering of predefined images and symbols that we "attach to" without a lived experience. Uncovering the images and symbols that *find us* from the "bottom up" requires a heartfelt and deeply meaningful personal relationship with the unconscious. Our daily lives are invigorated by these complexes and the archetypal patterns that awaken us to the transpersonal content of everyday life.

It's good to keep in mind, too, that if we've spent much of our lives numb and asleep, or plugged into the collective, waking up to the individuation process may be frightening or painful. It's understandable if we resist the work. Jung said it best:

> The development of consciousness is the burden, the suffering, and the blessing of mankind. Each new discovery leads to greater consciousness, and the path along which we are going is merely an extension of it. This inevitably calls for greater responsibility and enforces a great change in ourselves. We must draw conclusions from what we know and discover, and not take everything for granted.
>
> (Jung as cited in McGuire & Hull, 1977, p. 248)

My return to Jungian principles is not a regression to the essentialist views of the past, nor is it a rejection of the evolutionary unfolding of contemporary developments in Jungian psychology. Certainly there are areas where Jung was caught in his generational and cultural complexes and his thinking and language benefit from clarifications, particularly with contemporary clinical issues associated with broad diversity issues, gender and multicultural challenges, as well as the socioeconomic disparity and political unrest that now expresses itself in our consulting rooms. I am inspired and delighted to see the diversity of publications that integrate Jung's concepts. This sustains the life of Jung's ideas that remain ever prescient and relevant. Still, we benefit from a more deliberate understanding of Jung's theoretical model.

Circumambulating the Stages

Circumambulation is a useful term and approach to uncover the layers of Jungian art therapy, especially when confronting Jung's vast body of work. The psychologist Jerome Bruner[3] insisted that motivation for learning is based on interest and not external competition. He advocated for learning structure over facts, and outlined the idea of a *spiral curriculum*: "A curriculum as it develops should revisit these basic ideas repeatedly, building upon them until the student has grasped the full formal apparatus that goes with them" (Bruner, 1960/1977, p. 13). Using this idea, the pattern of this book spirals around Jung's model of the psyche and revisits the general principles that make up an image of the psyche. As a natural movement, the circumambulation will uncover what has yet been learned and deepen what we already know. Paradoxically, while we uncover and make the invisible visible, we will also discover how the basic principles express themselves for each of us personally so that we can grasp Jung's theory and philosophy in an embodied, experiential way. Three major sections provide a structure for this circumambulation: Gateway, Attending, and Passage.[4] As stages based on feminine initiation, these three parts encourage a layered and spiraled curriculum for learning Jungian psychology as well as a structural model that supports the learning brain so that it can relax and trust in the gradual deepening that comes with an inherent archetypal structure. The three stages provide us with visual markers for the learning process, and for acknowledging an individuation journey that can become visible through unconscious contents within Jungian art therapy. These stages are not rigid or linear. They are meant to nourish our imagination about our inner journey.

Gateway

The gateway stage is the initial stage of visiting and contemplating something before us. The root meaning of *gate* suggests a "door-like structure," or "hole, opening" (Ayto, 1993, p. 250). The term also describes the state of expectancy and urgency that we feel with the movement of some unknown energy within us. We may feel frightened or hopeful, anxious or enlivened. In a state of anticipation, we may also feel all of these things at once. The image of a gate denotes a formally defined space that is not yet accessible; there is the possibility of moving through into another world not yet encountered, but still imagined. Similarly, when we have a blank piece of paper or a ball of clay, we are before a psychological gate, anticipating what is beyond it that has not yet become known.

Attending

Attending is the middle stage of this process. *Attend* means "to stretch, listen or direct the mind toward something" (Ayto, 1993, p. 42). Its Latin root is *attendere*, meaning "to stretch and to wait," that eventually led to the Latin verb *tenere*, which means "to hold and contain" (Ayto, 1993, p. 42). Eventually *attend* took the meaning of "caring for and to be present with," suggesting a *waiting* and *stretching* that could be applied to the idea of the softening ego consciously extending towards a relationship with the unconscious. The allowance for an expansion evokes the totality of the personality while simultaneously recognizing the numinosity of the moment. This is an example of when the energic and the symbolic paradigms are working in tandem and when the major elements of Jungian art therapy are in play. The attending stage is where we focus on the therapeutic work, create the sacred space to allow the unconscious content to enter, and recognize that psyche has its own perfect timing.

Passage

The passage stage is the point when we move into a post-liminal phase and begin to integrate aspects of the new state of consciousness associated with a personal journey. The word *passage* denotes a hallway, a passageway, or a way to arrive at the destination. The image of a passageway is as varied as each of our personal journeys. While we rarely, if ever, arrive at a set destination in Jungian art therapy, there is a point when the conscious material reaches symbolic form through our investment in an image and we may find ourselves deeply touched by both its powerful clarity and its mystery. We will consider the methods deepening our relationship with the unconscious material—art therapy, dreams, and active imagination—as the passage into a state of new consciousness.

The Map of the Book

The three primary parts described above create an archetypal structure for the ten chapters of this book. In the first part (*Gateway*), Chapter 2 introduces the basic concepts and principles of Jung's map of the psyche. Chapter 3 provides a concise history of analytical psychology as the bedrock on which art therapy was founded. The evolution of Jungian art therapy in United States and the United Kingdom is also presented. An explanation of directed and non-directed thinking is included in Chapter 4, as well as an introduction to Jung's basic formulations of energy and its movement between conscious and unconscious. Chapter 5 introduces the synthetic method and the transcendent function, Jung's conceptualization for how psychic energy facilitates the birth of symbols into consciousness.

In the second part (*Attending*), Chapter 6 highlights the role of imagination in Jungian art therapy, while Chapter 7 orients the reader as to the basics of complex theory, the structure and impact of complexes on the ego, and how they are visible in Jungian art therapy. Chapter 8 investigates archetypes as the bedrock of Jung's psychological map.

The third part (*Passage*) consists of Chapters 9 and 10, which consider the application of Jungian art therapy through dreams and active imagination, respectively. These final chapters illustrate the intersection of theory and application with further examples from Jungian art therapy; these lived experiences of Jung's methods expand the role of the creative unconscious.

The Appendix includes Jung's ideas on the stages of therapy, which remain relevant in contemporary times, especially in Jungian art therapy.

Terms

Jungian Art Therapy

The term *Jungian art therapy* was deliberately chosen as an umbrella term for art therapists who want to tune into both Jung the philosopher as well as Jung's theoretical map of the psyche. This term embraces both the energic/scientific as well as the symbolic/imaginative process of Jung's model and allows art therapists to adjust their style to best suit their own individual process or particular work site. I've continued to use *Jungian art therapy* with the awareness that others before me have chosen a variation on this term such as *Jungian analytic art therapy* (Edwards, 1987), or *analytical art psychotherapy* (Schaverien, 1992). However, since students of art therapy often find themselves grappling with how to best name their theoretical orientation, and because the purpose of this book is to simplify and clarify, *Jungian art therapy* will be used with the intent of maintaining distinctly recognizable terminology.

Images and the Interpretation of Images

Jung used the word *image* throughout his work to describe the psychic situation as a whole. He was interested in symbols, but a primary focus was on the spontaneous image that arose from the unconscious to express both personal and primordial elements. Image was paramount to his idea that *psyche is image*. The use of the word *image* gracefully sidesteps the discourse and expectation that is assigned to the word *art*. For Jung the image was the dramatic and sacred voice of the unconscious.

This book is not concerned with the developmental stages of drawings nor with specific interventions that facilitate art therapy from an ego-oriented perspective. There are many excellent art therapy books where the stages of drawings, art materials, and interventions for treatment plans with various populations can be found. However, Theodor Abt's *Introduction to Picture Interpretation* (2005) is the single most reliable English text for a Jungian approach to picture interpretation. This work consolidates the essential elements of how to respectfully approach pictures using Jungian picture interpretation while considering the underlying purposive archetypal patterns. Schaverien (1992; 1995) has also made significant contributions expanding upon Jung's ideas to formulate terminology that has remained true to his work but modernized some of his ideas to suit the field of art therapy, including the embodied image and specific issues associated with transference/countertransference. Both Edwards (1987; 2010) and Wallace (1987) were influential in their early declarations of integrating Jung and art therapy. Their investment in the creative process was evident and I have aimed to remain true to their creative spirits and dedication to the unconscious and the Self.

Building on these remarkable foundations, there remains a need for students to understand the basic elements of Jungian psychology. Beginning students of Jung will find that this book is framed in simple, direct language and uses vignettes that elucidate Jung's unique model of the psyche. The interspersed images amplify basic principles and concepts so that the reader also has a visual theoretical model. It is my hope that this book will clarify and illuminate those theoretical basics of Jungian psychology that have a profound relationship to the image, art therapy, and clinical applications.

Affect, Emotion, and Feeling

In his "Psychological types: Definitions," Jung (1921/1990) stated that he used *affect* and *emotion* interchangeably, but that by *affect* he meant "a state of feeling characterized by marked physical innervation on the one hand and a peculiar disturbance of the ideational process on the other" (CW 6, p. 411). Affect has been associated with physiological unconscious states that are roots for emotions. Jung associated emotions with complexes and the image. Feeling, on the other hand, is associated with conscious well-defined expressions that are also easily released and less gripping than emotions and affect. In other words, "Affect is the biological/archetypal root that combines with lived experience to form complex emotion, which in turn can be introspectively distilled into feelings through conscious awareness" (Dougherty, 2011, p. 2). I will primarily refer to emotions and affect rather than feelings, unless it is warranted.

Client/Patient/Analysand

Although *client* is a popular name used for someone in psychotherapy, it lacks the relational aspects that evolve from deeper psychological work. Consequently, I will use *patient* and *analysand* interchangeably. The word *patient* has root origins associated with *patience* and *attending to* (as in one of the three stages of the circumambulation process). The Latin *patī* means "suffer" (Ayto, 1993, p. 370), and so "waiting" and "submitting to suffering" depicts the Jungian method as a process of acknowledging our suffering and not trying to fix it—or make it go away. The word *analysand* demarcates a psychoanalytic orientation that preferences the relationship with the unconscious. As an analysand, we attend to the inner process by spiraling around our complexes, recognizing and enduring the suffering, until a new view opens. Rather than an ego-oriented process that outlines specific goals (a method associated with counseling, psychotherapy, and solution-oriented coaching), the words *patient* or *analysand* remind us that the unconscious has its own timing and plays a vital part in transforming our personality. Finding an emotional home where we engage in such deep psychological discoveries through Jungian art therapy is the work of a patient or an analysand who is willingly and curiously engaged in the inner journey.

Ego

The term *ego* is used throughout to represent the center of consciousness. Even though Jung acknowledged *ego complex* in order to explain the deeper dynamics of the psyche because it is "as much a content as a condition of *consciousness* [original emphasis]" (CW 6, 1921/1990, p. 425), for simplicity this book uses the primary term *ego*. Evers-Fahey's (2017) in-depth investigations concluded that Jung had four separate ego attitudes within his model (discussed in Chapter 2).

He/She

In order for the narrative of the text to flow easily, *she* will be used throughout. The masculine gender is not intended to be left out as it has a significant role and voice in Jung's psychology. Jung's view of the collective unconscious is associated with the feminine principle; therefore, the pronoun *she* encourages a greater visibility to the feminine aspect of the psyche. The masculine tends to already have its own innate visibility and is more fully conscious within all of us, as well as within many of our cultural structures. Moreover, both the masculine and the feminine principles are vulnerable to the patriarchal structures that define and hold power throughout history and within contemporary cultures.

Masculine and Feminine Principles

It is a biological fact that we are all conceived from the joining of these opposites (male and female) and that for most living creatures this remains a fact. Jung based his pioneering ideas of the masculine and feminine principles on the energies found within nature. It is a common mistake to confuse the masculine and feminine principles with the male and female genders. These are two different things and are not what Jung meant, although some confusion does ensue in his writing. From a theoretical standpoint, masculine and feminine are universal structures and concepts used to describe *psychological principles*, or archetypal energies, with particular patterns associated with *Logos* and *Eros* that are rooted in the collective unconscious. So as to avoid the confusion with gender, sometimes *Yin and Yang* or *Sun and Moon* are used instead.

The feminine and masculine principles also relate to the concepts of *anima* (soul) and *animus* (spirit), the feminine and masculine principles of the psyche. Jung used these terms to identify the contra-sexual aspect within the psyche. Best understood, anima/animus are the furthest point away from the ego, or the least known or familiar to the ego. Some of Jung's explorations and formulations reflect his cultural and generational biases yet these have been adjusted over time to suit our more modern ideas. While alchemical images of the *syzygy* (a yoking of masculine and feminine) offer an archetypal reference to this long-standing issue, the current contemporary discussions around sexual orientations and gender transitions/identity/fluidity will not be addressed in this book.

Genius Loci: *Sacred Space*

The Greeks and Romans associated every place with a specific deity or *genius loci*. Places that were considered sacred or needed protection to maintain balance within nature such as fountains, gates, doors, valleys, caves, and trees were honored. The *genius loci* as a sacred place was also referred to as having a soul. Nature images that illustrate the many expressions of the *genius loci*, which spontaneously emerged during difficult emotional times and major transitions, are also included in this book.

Figure 1.4 illustrates how this sacred place may spontaneously emerge from dreams or active imagination. The image depicted the analysand's deceased dog that was swimming at the center of a pond. The dream carried a numinous message for the dreamer regarding his need for increased play within nature.

The beauty and the complication of teaching Jungian psychology is that everything is interconnected—touch one idea and it impacts something else—the Jungian-oriented psyche is dynamic and electrically charged. When we add the idea that Jung's work was far-reaching and encompassed a range of images, ideas, concepts, and disciplines that were not often laid out in a straight line, then this book is but one small gateway into the study of Jungian art therapy and Jungian psychology. Without a doubt, much has been left unsaid. My hope is that this offering will show you to future gates and passageways, and support both your personal adventures as well as your clinical work. This text covers a miniscule part of Jung's ideas and philosophy, and so I recognize the impossibility of doing

Figure 1.4 *Genius Loci* Pond

justice to such an innovative and creative mind that gave us not just a depth psychology, but a philosophy to live by.

Endnotes

1. *The Handbook of Jungian Psychology* (Papadopolous, 2006) has been our central text.
2. Jung developed the psychological concept of the Self to describe what he saw as an ordering principle in the unconscious that influences the psyche throughout our lives, drawing us to expand our lived experiences, and promoting balance and wholeness. He saw the Self as the transpersonal aspect of the psyche.
3. Dr. Jerome Bruner (1915–2016) was an American psychologist and pioneer of cognitive psychology who made significant contributions to educational psychology, cognitive learning theory, and memory with a particular emphasis on the appreciation of the process of education and curriculum development that enhanced learning and memory development in children.
4. Originating in the natural creative process, these stages are derived from my research using Jungian art therapy with pregnant women and they provide a framework based on Lincoln's (1981/1991) feminine model of initiation (Swan-Foster, 2012).

Part I

Gateway

Preparing to Engage

When we start a new adventure, the psyche naturally goes through a range of emotional and mental preparations in anticipation of that experience. We typically experience anxiety or excitement, and perhaps we can't separate the two or know the difference. We anticipate, plan, and wonder. It is as if we are approaching a gateway without knowing what is on the other side of the gate. The gateway stage is the first step of the process before we enter into a liminal or timeless space where we lose our orientation to regular life but become more aware of our interiority and our connection to the unconscious. In the next three chapters, the Gateway portion of this book, we will explore the basic concepts and principles of Jung's model and consider a brief background and history of Jungian art therapy; this will include the work that Jung undertook before his confrontation with the unconscious. It is the gateway work of analytical psychology before it was named, and stems from Jung's work at the Burghölzli hospital, and his collaboration with Freud. Jung's gateway would lead him to his journey into the unconscious, which was captured at the time and later published in *The Red Book* (2009a). Jung's model of the psyche, and his discovery of the Collective Unconscious, complexes, and archetypes is briefly considered as the groundwork for creative work, which allows us to be prepared for entering deeper into the space where we actively attend to these images in Jungian art therapy.

23

CHAPTER 2

A Jungian Landscape
for Theory and Practice

Landmarks: Conscious, Unconscious, and the Symbolic

For many years prior to and alongside Freud, other philosophers, doctors, and psychiatrists had been tilling the fertile ground of the unconscious; it was, however, Freud who planted the psychiatric structure of the unconscious, put psychoanalysis on the map, and took the promotion and leadership of psychoanalysis as a major movement of the twentieth century (Ellenberger, 1970).

The basic psychological structure of the psyche that had been developing over the years consisted of two primary spheres: the *conscious* and the *unconscious*.[1] As Frey-Rohn (1990) explained:

> What Freud had initiated, Jung continued. Freud had demonstrated empirically the role of affect-toned disturbances in the unconscious, and Jung *experimentally* [original emphasis] confirmed these factors. Both investigators contributed to making the unconscious (formerly only a philosophical concept) accessible to empirical exploration.
>
> (p. 18)

Jung was well aware of the unconscious through his experimental research with the word association experiment (WAE) with Eugen Bleuler at the Burghölzli. The research provided Freud's firsthand observations of the unconscious in his Vienna patients with an empirical and theoretical boost. Jung's enthusiasm to further validate the unconscious was beneficial to Freud as psychoanalysis faced tremendous criticism. Freud and Jung along with other psychoanalysts banded together to defend the role of the unconscious and the work of psychoanalysis. At the time this was somewhat of a subversive position, and yet there was tremendous interest coming from creative and progressive individuals. As much as Jung respected Freud's contributions, Freud's view of the psyche was overly mechanistic and reductive for Jung with its limited emphasis on repression, projection, and the sexual drive theory to explain psychological conflicts. Jung diverged from Freud's idea of repression because Jung conceived unconscious material as having a purpose and direction that was carried by the image.[2]

Jung was concerned with not just the innate psychological healing and wholeness of the psyche, but also how the natural dissociability of the psyche, with its many parts, expressed the dynamism that could facilitate new consciousness. By revealing the multiple psychic images through painting or active imagination, Jung discovered a differentiation between the ego that holds conscious reality and the activity in the unconscious. Jung believed that there needed to be a relationship between the ego and the unconscious in order for the psyche's wholeness to become known.

For instance, *sublimation* was a great mystery to Jung. Rather than viewing the figures or contents as merely repressed material or content that could be redirected or sublimated into tasks deemed worthwhile by the ego, Jung thought it was not a "*voluntary and forcible* channeling of instinct into a spurious field of application, but an *alchymcal* transformation for which fire and the black *prima materia* are needed [original emphasis]" (Jung, 1973, p. 171). Jungian art therapy acknowledges the mysterious unfolding of the personality through the creative process. Rather than art activities and interventions where the ego is dominating the psychological work, the ego and Self (a deep guiding aspect of the unconscious) are in collaboration. When this attitude is in place, the unconscious content is valued as symbolic material that drives the psyche towards wholeness. Jung had ideas about this process that will be discussed in later chapters, but for now Jungian art therapy ascribes to a very different attitude regarding how the ego approaches the unconscious, the role of the unconscious, and the purpose of dynamic tension that is created between the conscious (ego) and the unconscious (Self). Post-Jungian authors may refer to the relationship between the two as the Ego–Self axis.[3] Rather than the images being reduced to defined pictures or repressed content that is interpreted, the attitude towards pictures is centered around the inquiry, "How does this image, in this moment, further consciousness, or facilitate individuation? What is its purpose and voice?" Thinking symbolically, rather than literally, is an essential tool in the art of all depth psychotherapies and psychoanalysis.

Jung, Signs, and Symbols

Throughout psychoanalysis, symbolic thinking has been integral to working with the unconscious no matter what our theoretical orientation. The engagement brings meaning and purpose to our daily lives and emerges as we do our psychological work, or spend time with a particular image. Images are meant to be played with and listened to, not defined. This is when the most creative psychological work happens. We may pursue an image through the use of art materials that asks for amplification and investigation. Our willingness to be destabilized by the process infuses the image with meaning (symbol) and then the attitude of the ego is changed. Symbolic thinking is an integral part of psychic energy, Jung's synthetic method, and imagination (Chapters 4, 5, and 6).

Jung differentiated between signs and symbols. Signs are known communication while symbols are layered and only partially unknown. For example, when we drive we read the road signs that tell us where to stop or indicate safe driving speeds, or we may have learned to read the "signs" in our family to keep ourselves safe, whereas a symbol "reveals itself in a concrete, unique situation, is surprising, uncontrollable in all its implications and personal in nature" (van den Berk, 2012, pp. 48–49). An image has the power to transform the psychic climate because it carries the energy from the unconscious to the conscious—this generates a personal relationship with the unconscious as we project meaning and psychic energy into the image. In so doing, it becomes a "living symbol."

Jung said we make a symbol "pregnant," meaning that we bring it alive by paying attention to it, circumambulating its various attributes, and working on cultivating a relationship with what is becoming known. Building on Jung's ideas, Schaverien (1992) named the first stage of the art-making process "the life in the picture," which could result in a *diagrammatic image* as linear and flat (sign) while the *embodied image* (symbol) carries life and energy. The picture may come from a preconceived idea or from simply playing with the materials, but there is the willingness to embrace the ineffability of the process through both a conscious and unconscious collaboration leading the maker to "relinquish the attempt to reproduce the preconceived image" (Schaverien, 1992, pp. 86–87). Dougherty (1998) furthered this discussion by suggesting that:

> the symbolic function of a work of art is based on the *attitude* [original emphasis] of the maker towards the artistic production both during

and after the making process. A work of art has the potential to function symbolically for the community when the artist has tolerated the holding of the opposites in order to allow the making process to act as a channel for the "wordless occurrence" to incarnate into form. (pp. 489–490)

In other words, pictures that halt our judgment, loosen our imagination, and force us to reflect contain symbolic material. By remaining open to the unconscious content, both the maker and the viewer of the image (patient and therapist) are faced with choices and possible psychological change. While Jung saw the symbol as the transformer in the psyche, Dougherty (1998) also pointed out that the creative work cannot always change the artist's sense of self. As a misconception it perpetuates the idea that artists can work in isolation and make psychological changes (p. 484). Consequently, the elements that go into the conscious process of transformation will be explored in future chapters.

Circumambulation: An Attitude for the Inner Journey

Circumambulation originally referred to the devotional practices of religions all over the world where there is a circling of the altar, of moving through levels of consciousness, of getting closer to the center. *Circumambulation* has Latin roots: *circum*, which means "around," and *ambulation*, which means "to walk." Psychologically, Jungian art therapy is a devotional practice, not to a particular religion or god but to images from the unconscious. The images that are offered through dreams or spontaneous artwork pique our curiosity and invite us to decipher. We circle around what is offered, attend to it, and consider various approaches through lines, shapes, colors, and material choices. The idea of circumambulation is personalized through our own relationship with the unconscious, and our attitude is paramount.

Relaxing our linear and rational thinking may sound simple, but it remains a challenge when we are confronted with the collective and have to adapt to everyday life. One of Jung's contributions to depth psychology was his insight that an actively creative and contemplative attitude towards the unconscious through imagination and play is invigorating, while being a slow cooking process. Joe McNair, a Jungian analyst from Los Angeles, led his seminars on Celtic mythology and alchemy with this attitude. He metaphorically opened the gate for us and we entered into a liminal space that was timeless, slow, and gentle. The mysterious images and stories touched us, moved us, and changed us in unfathomable ways. As we contemplated and circumambulated the ingredients, we only realized how the imaginal had seeped into our souls once the weekend was over.

Jungian art therapy may consider the images from the unconscious as sacred objects that sit within the temple, perhaps on an altar, that we call our psyche. When we attend to the altar, we begin to piece together the fairy tale or myth of our life. At first these dusty shards are in the shadow, disavowed and forgotten, meaning they are:

> chaotic and interminable . . . and only gradually do the signs increase that our path is leading anywhere. The way is not straight but appears to go round in circles . . . spirals . . . the whole process revolves about a central point or some arrangement round a centre. . . . As manifestations of unconscious processes the dreams [images] rotate or circumambulate round the centre, drawing closer to it as the amplifications increase in distinctness and in scope.
>
> (Jung, 1952/1993, CW 12, p. 28)

Once we accept that we will spiral around material many times in our lives (and many times through generations), we are relieved of "resolving" our problems and released from having to be heroic in this work. Jung explained that no temple is built in a day—it takes many years to discover and understand our inner work, the purpose of our life, and to serpentine towards consciousness, working on one pillar at a time.[4]

Mandalas

Jung also referred to the center point of a mandala, an ancient symbol viewed in Jungian psychology as an organizing focal point of the psyche. The mandala, which means "circle" in Sanskrit, is both a spiritual and ritual symbol in Eastern religions, suggesting an image of the universe, or of the cosmos that holds all life. The original mandala images referred to the heavens, with four corners as gates or doors that marked the cardinal directions and paths to the ancient city that were placed at the center of the mandala. These were ancient patterns with profound meaning.

The mandala is well researched by art therapists, and is often used in art projects because it ignites this ancient place within the psyche and provides a contemplative and compensatory calming vessel to hold chaotic unconscious material (Cox, 2016; Finch, 1991/2010; Kellogg, 1978/2002; Perry, 1953; Potash, 2014; Potash and Garlock, 2016). It is reported that the Jungian analyst Joseph Henderson encouraged his patient, the artist Jackson Pollock, to work with mandalas so as to help contain his inner chaos, but he was not agreeable to this suggestion. While the mandala is useful, it can also feel contrived or constraining for artists who need larger space or have different intentions that follow along the lines of the relationship between the ego and the Self.

Jung began working on mandalas during World War I (1914–1918). Each morning he sketched a "small circular drawing, a mandala, which seemed to correspond to my inner situation at the time. With the help of these drawings, I could observe my psychic transformations from day to day" (Jung, 1961, p. 195). Eventually he came to understand this process for himself. To Jung, mandalas were

> cryptograms concerning the state of the self which were presented to me anew each day. In them I saw the self—that is, my whole being—actively at work. To be sure, at first I could only dimly understand them; but they seemed to me highly significant, and I guarded them like precious pearls. I had the distinct feeling that they were something central, and in time I acquired through them a living conception of the self. The self, I thought, was like the monad which I am, and which is my world. The mandala represents this monad, and corresponds to the microcosmic nature of the psyche. . . . I had to let myself be carried along by the current, without a notion of where it would lead me. . . . It became increasingly plain to me that the mandala is the center. It is the exponent to all paths. It is the path to the center, to individuation. During those years, between 1918 and 1920, I began to understand that the goal of psychic development is the self. There is no linear evolution; there is only a circumambulation of the self.
>
> (Jung, 1961, p. 196)

Jung was naturally connected to the healing capacity of images and determined, from his experience, the circle as the ordering structure of the psyche, which was one of his definitions of the Self.

An example of this is when Elizabeth, a mother of young children, painted her mandala (Figure 2.1) and it provided her with a sense of containment and meditation. "In the poetic space I find some distance." This was a counterpoint to her demanding responsibilities as a parent. Using a large canvas to work with intersecting colored circles, Elizabeth accidently discovered the *mandorla*, the ancient center almond shape that is associated with the sacred light found in the darkness. Elizabeth sometimes sat with the painting to listen to the magic of the unconscious. She touched into the mysterious intimacy and sustaining light of the image that also lived deep within her. When she wasn't painting, she could think about the painting. It grew in her imagination. The large mandala was an anchor for Elizabeth because of how it connected her to a sense of spaciousness and wholeness that compensated for her busy life.

Figure 2.1 Elizabeth's Mandala

As images speak to us, our curiosity draws us close and we move towards the center, a position of separation and difference, yet profound intimacy within ourselves. In addition, the center suggests the core of the image where archetypal patterns may become visible to the conscious mind.

Circumambulation is a function of the Self that takes us around the outside. In Figure 2.2, Eric created a spiraling path that leads us into the center of the circle. Eric explained that as he passes through various stages he moves towards a center of knowing that is paradoxically also the place of "emptiness" or stillness. The path leads us through the various stages of development towards the unconscious. Figure 2.3, which was another spontaneous mandala, shows us there is both a circumference and a circular path that leads us inwards to our interior self. As we search for our center point through the movement of life, we also discover new states of consciousness. This is why Sue named her mandala "Parachute," because held in the cloth of her life were both her emotional darkness and the "bright colors" in life that she was able to enjoy after a period of depression.

Jung's Structure of the Psyche

According to Frey-Rohn, Freud did not focus on defining a structure of the psyche until 1923, whereas Jung began formulating his ideas early in his career on the totality of conscious and unconscious processes. Jung already

Figure 2.2 Spiral Mandala

Figure 2.3 Parachute Mandala

used terms like "unity" and "totality" or "wholeness" in 1913, and he understood that the reaction of the whole psyche was a developmental process which was made up of all aspects of the human personality (Frey-Rohn, 1990, p. 111). In this section we will consider the parts of Jung's view of the psyche that make up the whole psyche—first focusing on each term or concept to provide a brief introduction, and then in subsequent chapters we will deepen and integrate these terms in relationship to the psyche as a whole with clinical vignettes and images.

As we begin to establish a shared common language, Jung's terms and concepts are not meant to be mechanistic or formulaic. If we hold them too firmly as concrete entities, they become saturated, empty words that sound like jargon. We lose our imagination and the words lose meaning. Instead, Jung's model of the psyche has a dynamic, energic configuration in which we wrestle to understand not just the concept itself, but also the relationship between the concepts. Jung relied on the image to illustrate the inner world of the psyche. I have chosen to use spontaneous images, made by patients and students who were engaged in their psychological process, to denote the principles and concepts because what Jung discovered was autonomous and authentic. Some have argued that he was too focused on the concept and not enough on the life of the image. But if we look at *The Red Book* (2009a) we can see that he was clearly interested in the life of the image and the power of the symbols. His desire to establish a theoretical foundation arose from his personal life.

The Psyche as Circle

Jung's view of the psyche is often depicted as a circle, or a mandala, such as the figure below (Figure 2.4). This circle is divided in half with the top half representing *consciousness* and the bottom half representing the *unconscious* (including the personal and the collective). The conscious part of the psyche is small while the unconscious is large and expansive. Art therapy, as a psychological approach, emerged from a psychoanalytic

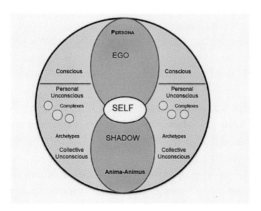

Figure 2.4 Psyche as Mandala

orientation precisely because it naturally makes the unconscious visible, recognizes and documents the unconscious as real, and captures it as an image that transforms the psyche.

Consciousness is made up of what we are conscious of in our day-to-day life or what is known to us in space and time. Another way of thinking about it is that the conscious sphere of the psyche "reacts and adapts itself to the present, because it is that part of the psyche which is concerned chiefly with events of the moment" (Jung, 1927/1972, CW 8, p. 152).

On the other hand, the *unconscious* aspect of the psyche is everything that we know but are not accessing in that moment; it also contains all we have not known and even may never know. It is all that we sense, desire, plan, and imagine for our future, but have no consciousness of until these become known to us. Jung warned us that the unconscious is paradoxical: it is expansive and innovative yet conservative—there is a creative factor and a destructive force (Jung, 1930/1985, CW 16, p. 34). The tension between the conscious and the unconscious is a major principle in Jungian art therapy that fuels the dynamic nature of the psyche, stirs instinctual energy, and can result in a psychological renewal and transcendence.

Consciousness

Within the conscious sphere of the psyche, two primary concepts are used in analytical psychology: the *ego* and the *persona*.

Ego

Jung described the *ego* as the seat of consciousness within the personality that determines reality and adaptation and has a high degree of continuity and identity (Jung, 1921/1990, CW 6, p. 425). The ego orients the psyche to its concern with identity, a range of personal memories, and thoughts and feelings about the past, present, and future. The ego also discriminates and navigates both our subjective (inner subject) as well as our objective (outer object) worlds, but the ego is only privy to conscious aspects of the psyche, so while the ego is actively engaged with its agenda, there is also a need for it to be fluid enough to accept new information not previously considered from inner and outer sources (adaptation and individuation).

For example, as we read and learn about Jungian theory our ego takes in new information, so we soften our perceptions in order to receive it. The ego is like a sifter, forming attachments to what it believes is most important so as to maintain a level of reality and stability for the whole psyche. At the same time, as the sifter and stable center of the psyche, it is confronted by images that surface from the unconscious that may seem irrational. Jung's idea of the ego was initially consistent with most psychoanalytic views; however, part of what evolved out of his separation from

Freud was his ongoing development of the ego's role in the psyche when confronted by unconscious material. According to the extensive investigations on Jung's development of the ego by Evers-Fahey (2017), Jung's psychology fulfills the accepted criteria for an Ego Psychology if it were not "overshadowed by his fascination with the archetypes and the Self" (p. 185). From her investigations, she established that his ego concept was actually organized around what she determined as "Jung's four different attitudes" (p. 185) that incorporated several theoretical ideas:

1. **Subjective Ego** is the part of our personality concerned with our identity, and living as an authentic self with continuity and an individual narrative. The dream ego is included here.
2. **Structural Ego** is the unconscious aspect of the ego that essentially defends, adapts, and collaborates with the Self to regulate the individuation process.
3. **Developmental Ego** assumes that as the individual grows and changes the ego mirrors this process over time and through various stages. Post-Jungians have tied this development to the relationship with the Self.
4. **Cosmogonic Ego** is a position that "is unique to Jung . . . the ego is an instrument in the incarnation of the unconscious in the world through the ego–Self mutual dynamic process" (Evers-Fahey, p. 195).

Contrary to popular thought, Jungian psychology clearly values ego consciousness (rational) while equally holding the alternative or contrasting views from the unconscious (irrational) as prized material. Jung thought we were healthiest if both the conscious and the unconscious aspects of the psyche could collaborate. Jung's investigations into alchemy further revealed that the opposing forces created the energic dynamic within the psyche that ignites an encounter with the unconscious. This can feel like a shock, or a wake-up call, to an overly narrow or rigid ego.

The student who created Figure 2.5 in class following discussions on the ego and the unconscious explained: "This is slanted—it illustrates how disoriented my ego feels when faced with something new pushing up from the unconscious." When the ego is dimly aware of life outside its existence, any type of intrusion may feel like a massive disturbance. When a confident and adaptive ego responds to surprises, uncertainty, or difficulties that arise as a manageable force, the ego is less reactive. A solid ego can hold its seat of consciousness and adaptation. In other words, the ego becomes better equipped to engage with the unconscious. Jungian art therapists sometimes work to support and solidify the ego, while other times the focus is to

Figure 2.5   Ego Confronted by Unconscious

compensate for an inflexible ego by working directly with unconscious content.

Persona

The *persona* is how others see us and provides an interface between the inner and outer worlds. How the psyche "meets" the world is part of how we are known, received, or rejected by the world; the persona serves as the connection or interface between our interior subjective world and the outside objective world that Jung often called the *collective*. The persona needs to be connected to the ego so that it is adaptable and able to perform and relate in socially acceptable ways, depending upon the situation, the type of environment, and the culture in which the ego is living. As the definition implies, the persona is a mask that we wear in our world and this mask can change depending upon the situation. For Jungian art therapists, mask making is a way to get in touch with the persona and its relationship to various situations, and this is most striking when masks are used in role play.

Figure 2.6 is a mask of Pippi Longstocking made by a 10-year-old girl. It offered her an image for courageously navigating the expectations of the

Figure 2.6   Pippi Longstocking

collective. Pippi was an image for an adventurous spirit in the world even though sometimes the girl felt nervous or introverted. If the persona was connected to her ego then she could gain confidence, and connecting to the mask image empowered the young girl to express her confident Pippi-self when needed.

When teaching Jung's theories, I encourage students to imagine how they might depict Jung's map of the psyche. Figure 2.7 was created by a student who explained, "The right could be the conscious world with the persona and ego facing outwards. On the left is the shadow and the personal and collective unconscious. The green circles represent complexes and the blue form with five limbs on either side expresses the ego at the center and how the psychic energy moves." The mandala came spontaneously and as she spoke her personal understanding of Jung's map of the psyche came alive.

In a clinical setting, our initial interaction is with the persona of our patients. Image making can quickly reveal what is underneath this presentation, allow us to relate to the personality behind the mask so as to carve out the creative space that incorporates unconscious content and images. For the whole person, complete with *complexes* and the *personal shadow*, to become known, Jung was interested in what emerged between the analyst and the analysand, which included the images and symbols. A natural curious circling of the shared material cultivates a particular field of energy and visual space within Jungian art therapy. This space was taken up by Donald Winnicott (1971) to mean a "potential space" or

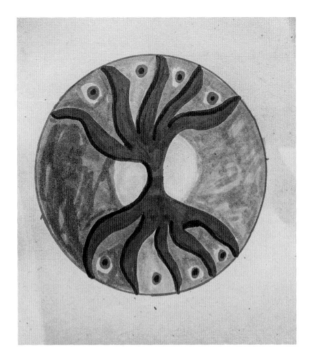

Figure 2.7   A Map of the Psyche

"transitional space" that forms and exists between the mother and the baby. He formulated that the therapeutic space varied in its "potential" expression depending upon the original relationship between the two (mother/baby). In Jungian work this space is called "the third."

Unconscious

The unconscious for Jung was a source of opportunity. It "includes not only repressed contents, but all psychic material that lies below the threshold of consciousness. . . . The unconscious also contains all the material that has not yet reached the threshold of consciousness. These are the seeds of future conscious contents" (Jung, 1928/1966, CW 7, pp. 127–28). Jung divided the unconscious into two components: the *personal unconscious* and the *collective unconscious*. In other words, there exists a dynamic interplay between Jung's concepts, with each having personal qualities as well as connections to the collective unconscious. The personal unconscious contains the unconscious material such as *complexes* and the *personal shadow*. Jung said the "'personal unconscious' must always be dealt with first, that is, made conscious, otherwise the gateway to the collective unconscious cannot be opened" (Jung, 1936/1993, CW 12, p. 62). This point is often overlooked when we idealize the collective unconscious and bypass the personal unconscious.

Jung discovered and named the *collective unconscious*. Sometimes he referred to it as the *objective psyche*, to mean the realm in the psyche that contains the common or universal structures that connect us to extended family, community, and humanity through unconscious cultural content, as well as ancestral and archaic material, all of which resides *furthest away* from the judgment of ego consciousness. With its autonomous nature, meaning our ego has little or no control over it, the collective unconscious offers compensation to the conscious psyche and its one-sided attitude. Whenever we refer to the conscious psyche, we consider at the same time the compensatory role of the unconscious that brings wholeness to the psyche. In other words, what is missing in consciousness will be supplied by the unconscious. In 1946 Jung wrote in a letter to a psychotherapist that he felt the collective unconscious surrounded us. He compared the collective unconscious to an atmosphere in which we live, rather than something that lives inside us. Jung defined it as unknown and that it did not behave psychologically (1973, p. 433). In other words his notion was that it was furthest away from ego consciousness.

What Jung meant by this may be explained by using an image of an aspen tree—while it appears to be standing as an individual tree above ground, its root system intersects and reaches out across the landscape with other aspen trees and their roots, creating clumps of trees that are interconnected via an intricate root system called rhizomes. The root system represents the collective unconscious and how human experience is connected on many different levels. Jacobi (1942/1973) also illustrated the differentiated levels within the unconscious with the image of islands connected beneath the ocean of the unconscious with common land in the seabed (p. 34). Phrases such as "cultural unconscious," "racial unconscious," "religious unconscious," "family unconscious," or "somatic unconscious" are now common Jungian phrases that explicate our understanding of the collective human experiences.

Jung determined that human beings are interconnected through communities, cultures, humanity, animals, and the essential energy of life. While we may think we are not impacted by events that occur in another town, state, or country, there is evidence that our thoughts and human reactions are indeed resonating throughout the root system of human*being-ness*. While Jung noted that the collective unconscious did not behave psychologically, Jacobi (1942/1973) clarified the impersonal nature of the unconscious as somewhat impervious to the critical and ordering activity of the ego and consciousness (p. 35). Based on Jung's research, clinical observations, and his own personal work, he could find no other explanation for inexplicable events, spontaneous images, or thoughts other than the concept of the collective unconscious. When we cultivate our individual connection to humanity, we unearth the well of creativity within the collective unconscious. Certainly this was true for Jung. His research in the area of psychology, alchemy, myth, art, science, and cultures gradually invigorated him and reaffirmed his ideas of the collective unconscious.

While painting Figure 2.8 Gail was discussing her role as a parent. She spoke of personal emotions, but these deepened into patterns found in her family lineage, styles of communication, and cultural heritage. Circling back to the personal, she considered her place in the collective as a divorced mother. Gail's image illustrates the complicated interconnections between the personal and collective unconscious.

Gail's image-making process was to first draw shapes and then to use a wet brush to fill in the forms and make connections between the shapes, sometimes bleeding the boundaries and sometimes reinforcing them. She fluidly moved between marker and brush, dry and wet, warm and cool colors, as she negotiated internal conflicts. The image contains a focal point, a blue center amidst the layers of unconscious material that gathered energy around the blue, which may illustrate an organizing force occurring in her psyche. Because the image sits on the right side of the page, there is a natural suggestion of passage of time and psychic material moving towards consciousness (Abt, 2005).

Figure 2.8 Personal and Collective Unconscious

Shadow

The term *shadow* is now common nomenclature; we are easily familiar with shadow, which represents what the ego has disavowed, repressed, or disregarded as unworthy. Shadow content is easily cast in images. When we take our morning walk our shadow may stretch out in front of us or at midday it may tightly follow us home. Sometimes we know the shadow is there, while other times it may not be easily seen as we project it onto another person. Another way to think about the shadow is that it represents all of our unlived life from when we were born—this could be what we perceive as either negative or positive aspects of ourselves. In some cultures, the shadow is viewed as the "bad part" of the person that is feared, while in Western culture it is viewed as what we project onto others and are unwilling to own as ours. Jung distinguished between a personal shadow and a collective shadow.

The *personal shadow* contains our rejected parts that we believe are inferior even if they are positive qualities. We discover our shadow personality within the other, or the shadow contains the feelings that are constellated *within us* when we encounter a person that we may not like. A common way to understand shadow is to think about a difficult individual in our lives. If we explore our reactions regarding what we don't like about this person, these qualities are usually disavowed aspects of ourselves. In dreams, figures of the same sex, a different race or culture, or a sinister figure that intrudes all alert us to personal shadow material that can be investigated further. Jung considered the shadow a complex when we have powerful emotional reactions.

Early therapy begins with what Jung referred to as a stage of *assimilation of personal shadow material* (see Appendix), which pertains to reclaiming disavowed contents that may be projected or denied (dissimulation). Finally, Jung clarified and expanded his clinical view of projection through his concept of the personal shadow.

The *collective shadow* refers to disavowed archetypal or collective content within the collective unconscious. In the individual this may be an expression of the unconscious "herd mentality," or a collective projection, which points to undifferentiated aspects of powerful feelings, thoughts, and behaviors towards a group or within a society. Collective shadow is projected onto another race, country, culture, or religion. Jung was adamant that when we work on our personal shadow we are less susceptible to the collective shadow (although with no guarantees).

These shadow projections are captured in Jungian art therapy by way of images: "Make an ugly image" or "Use materials you dislike the most" are ways to stir affect in the psyche. A woman who had an unresolved traumatic childbirth experience might be gripped by emotions, but will find temporary relief when

> she gives birth to her fears and intense imagery, creating a new form outside of herself. The very process is transforming and healing. By seeing her feelings [shadow/complexes] before her as symbolic images . . . she diffuses the energy she has invested in her fears and begins to experience . . . a reorganization of her perceptions.
>
> (Swan-Foster, 1989, p. 291)

Discussion of the elements within a picture allow the analysand to assimilate shadow material that had been temporarily rejected. Clarifications of personal material and better understanding of her relationship with the collective become possible. A reorganization of our perceptions is a multilayered process that arises with the help of making images, working with materials we dislike, or grappling with a literal shadow within a picture (see Dana in Chapter 4, Figures 4.2 and 4.3).

Complex

Jung's development of the *complex* came from his WAE research carried out at the Burghölzli prior to meeting Freud. He was interested in patterns created by clusters of complexes that might reveal an unconscious narrative. Ultimately, this led to his ideas on the collective unconscious, but initially Jung was concerned with complex indicators and its relationship to the image: "What . . . is a 'feeling-toned complex'? It is the *image* [original emphasis] of a certain psychic situation which is strongly accentuated emotionally and is, moreover, incompatible with the habitual attitude of consciousness" (Jung, 1934/1972, CW 8, p. 96).

Without our complexes we would not be alive. Some complexes cause a lot of pain and suffering while others are considered positive, such as feelings of love or gratitude. Complexes are expressed through affect, the body, and images; they are found in artwork and in dreams. These autonomous "splinter psyches" (Jung, 1934/1972, CW 8, p. 97) penetrate deep into the psyche and are facilitators of tremendous change. Jung's work on the complex is recognized for its exceptional relevancy when working with trauma, particularly early relational trauma (Kalsched, 1996; West, 2016).

Jungian art therapy provides a method to map and visually see our personal complexes because the image directly harnesses the expression of instinct and affect into a concrete representation and extracts it from the grips of the visceral and somatic realm of the body to place it in a concrete form. Jung's colleague Sabina Spielrein clarified that: "The complex is thus robbed of its personal quality. . . . This tendency towards dissolution or

Figure 2.9 Complex

transformation of every individual complex is the mainspring of poetry, painting, and every form of art" (as cited in Jung, 1912/1967, CW 5, p. 141). When we are gripped by a complex, our body is taken over by dramatic reactions. Figure 2.9 above illustrates a complex related to the loss of a close relationship. The student felt "thrown to the ground" with the betrayal and anger that she had to stomach. Using art materials allowed her to translate the affect and emotion into images so that she could begin to find her words and articulate her grief.

Archetype

Archetypes cannot be seen directly, but are known to us through instincts, or drives, patterns, images, and symbols. *Merriam-Webster* cites the origin of the word *archetype* as being from the Latin word *archetypum*, which suggests the original pattern or mold from which all similar representations are made (Archetype, n.d.). This initial point, which is invisible to us, lays an inherent structure for a pattern to fulfill itself. Like a dry riverbed, the archetype remains inactive or unknown until it fills with water, which suggests the psychic process is now enlivened with energy.

Archetypes are universal potentials and patterns of imagination, images, behaviors, thoughts, and feelings that cannot be "fully integrated, nor lived out in human form" (Samuels, Shorter, & Plaut, 1986/1993, p. 27). Jungian art therapy has the potential to bring an awareness of "the archetypal dimension in a person's life"; through archetypal images the numinous cross-cultural and mythological components inherent within the human psyche may become known, but not without the personal (p. 27). Although archetypes can at times *feel* personal, that is because they are at the core of a complex and carry somatic elements. However, they are structurally located in the collective unconscious and are considered impersonal from an orthodox viewpoint.

For Jungian art therapy, archetypal images are "generated by a certain archetype" (Schaverien, 1992, p. 21) and specific images may surface from individuals in a similar condition. For instance, pregnant women were found to draw themselves with transparencies or in nature (Swan-Foster, Foster, & Dorsey, 2003) suggesting the simultaneity of their experience. We might surmise the mother archetype generates an archetypal image, such as the tree, to express her somatic experience of living out an archetypal pattern (Figure 2.10). Because of its archetypal significance, Jung devoted a whole essay to pictures of trees in "The Philosophical Tree" (1945/1983, CW 13, pp. 253–349).

Numinous archetypal images may express the ineffable and wordless moments. Figure 2.11 was painted spontaneously by Louisa, who realized what was created was the memory of being in a cave looking out at a beautiful Mediterranean sky when she took a pilgrimage to Greece. She saw the image as a reminder of her own isolation and desire for inner psychological work.

Figure 2.10   Pregnant Woman and Tree

Anima/Animus

The *anima* (soul) is the inner image of a woman in a man and the *animus* (spirit) is the inner image of a man in a woman. Traditionally, they represent soul/spirit images, but structurally speaking, they are the "not-I" part of our psyche or the *other* within us, suggesting a psychical aspect that is the furthest away from consciousness (or the ego) that pushes for psychological wholeness. Working with the anima/animus is integral to or often

Figure 2.11   Cave

follows work with the shadow as a differentiation process of early psycho-therapy unfolds. These principles "operate in relation to the dominant *psychic principle* [original emphasis] of a man or a woman and not simply . . . as the contra-sexual psychological counterpart of maleness or female-ness" (Samuels et al., 1986/1993, p. 23). Keeping this in mind, we gather information about the dominant psychic principles to understand what operates in relation to it. Although the original idea was that a man had an anima and a woman had an animus, a contemporary view considers that both anima/animus exist within the psyche and either the anima or animus matches the dominant psychic principle, which is also the shadow.

The following mandala (Figure 2.12) was made in class by a student following a lecture on anima/animus. The image also describes the idea of *syzygy* (Jung, 1954/1990), which is the yoking of two opposite principles. In this case it is the masculine and feminine.

As intermediary images, the anima/animus move autonomously between the ego and the unconscious as a *psychopomp* that bridges the worlds. Their contents are integrated and used by consciousness, yet they also carry energy that expands the personality. Consequently, they are both com-plexes and archetypes. The psychological work of attending to such a gift is illustrated by Eleanor's dream: *"I see a man who is a plumber—he shows me to a manhole, lifts off the cover, and together we see vibrant green and purple irises coming into bloom. We admire the flowers."* This dream expresses both soul and spirit; the feminine dream ego and the animus represent a rela-tional pair of opposites, much like yin/yang or passive/active. The animus

Figure 2.12   Anima/Animus Mandala

is active and reveals something from the unconscious: irises within a circle. Also, the animus offers a complementary image for the dreamer who had just registered for a new academic program the day before. The dream suggests gifts of wisdom (the Greek goddess Iris is a messenger). It is also noteworthy that the animus is in service to the feminine. The dream animus was a useful image for Eleanor when exploring her own animus energy and preparing to access the *logos* side of her personality.

From an orthodox perspective, the anima has moods and impulses and the animus has beliefs and inspirations. The animus/anima take *possession* of us and we might act in ways that push people away, such as becoming overly needy, moody, critical, controlling, judgmental, or rigid. When the anima/animus are working *in right relationship* to consciousness, they serve the ego as guides and bearers of gifts from the unconscious. They are not "out front" disrupting relationships, but are the furnace behind the ego supporting relatedness.

As a *psychopomp*, the animus/anima also bring the ego into connection with the soul through "gifts" from the unconscious. This is their mediating function within the psyche. The anima/animus function like complexes because they express qualities of the personal father and personal mother *imagos*. Additionally, the anima/animus can be archetypes when they link us to greater patterns in the collective unconscious through archetypal images of immortal figures such as Aphrodite and Hera or Zeus and Poseidon, mother and father archetypal images.

The notions of the anima/animus are one of Jung's most controversial and, as a result, sometimes most difficult concepts to work with, especially as LGBTQ issues become more conscious in the collective. This principle should not be concretized as gender but seen as expressions of both the energic and symbolic paradigm. They are useful change-agents that carry and express the multiplicity and symbolic diversity within the psyche and they come and go as they please. Most important is that the anima and animus (soul and spirit) are intimately connected to the creative and imaginative rhythms within the psyche.

The Self: The Numinous Psyche

As both the center and the circumference of the psyche, the *Self* is a psychological principle that represents the reality of the invisible archetypal world. The Self, in relationship to the ego, pushes for consciousness and individuation. In Jungian art therapy, the Self is consistent and ever-present even if it is not explicitly discussed. It is one of the most pioneering contributions to psychological theory and practice. The Self is not God, but is a god image that opens the door to transcendence and depth. In collaboration with the ego, the Self mediates aspects associated with the symbol and synchronicity as well as the therapeutic relationship where two people receive meaningful moments and gifts through the love of connection, understanding, and creative expressions (Evers-Fahey, 2017).

Eleanor's dream image of the irises illustrates the presence of the Self: she felt the image to be vibrant or numinous. The manhole is an *a priori* image of the circle that Jung related to the Self, thus, it is present in both an ineffable feeling tone of the dream, and in the visual archetypal pattern of the circle. For a woman, the animus is thought to carry psychic energy from the Self for a feeling of wholeness or integration within the psyche (syzygy). Knowing these details about the dream did not limit the imagination, but encouraged a deeper relationship in her painting and dream world.

In Jungian art therapy, the Self is visible in various ways, but especially through specific symbols, shapes, numbers, and colors, all of which carry archetypal associations used within the analytic work (Abt, 2005). For instance, the circle is often associated with the archetypal pattern of the Self because of the innate ordering and unifying properties as discussed above with the mandala. The Self is also present when the whole gestalt of an image is so perfectly unified that it conveys an aspect of the utterly inexpressible human experience. Artist and art therapist Michael Franklin (1999) describes how the phenomenon of the creative process is

> much wiser than I could ever hope to be. It leads and I follow. I make decisions, putting into action a wide range of choices, hopefully pursuing the "authentic." Even when I think I am in control, I am not. I am not the doer, only a participant who is listening to the rhythms of the Self.
>
> (p. 10)

An example of the presence of the Self in an image can be seen in Figure 2.13. Ellen made a clay image of the window she remembered looking out of as a toddler standing in her crib. The framed view of nature signified freedom and expansiveness coming in from outside. She remembers the scent of the morning summer breeze that touched her skin. The expression of nature and her somatic memory suggests the presence of the Self. Ellen first painted the window image. Then she created a representation in clay, which reinforced the early memory

Figure 2.13 Clay Window

within her psyche of the enduring image. In our work together, this image of the window is metaphorically called upon as a reminder of a resilient life force because the image was compensatory and generated a sense of expansion and wellbeing.

Psychoid

Simply stated, Jung used the term *psychoid* to describe the interface between psyche and body. It is known to us through synchronicity or transference/countertransference events, such as shared dreams, or mysterious, unexplainable events within the therapeutic dyad, like continually misplacing notes of a particular patient. These are rare moments that we listen to because they express the profound depth of the psyche located in the central nervous system. Jung saw the central nervous system's reflex-processes as an adjective, not a noun, "that expresses the autonomous vitality of a *second psychic system that co-exists with consciousness*" (Jung, 1947/1972, pp. 176–177). Essentially, the psychoid realm has its own source of knowledge and we may gain an inkling of knowing through the world of *soma* and images associated with somatic experiences.

Jung's interest in the psyche/soma interface remains for the most part unacknowledged and yet he was one of the original explorers of this intersection of energy systems based on his early training with Bleuler. He understood that the psychical aspect is incomprehensible to the ego, and contains unknown and even *unknowable* material within our autonomic and sympathetic nervous systems, and ancestral material passed along through our DNA. This is all considered psychoid material.

Ellen's window (Figure 2.13) is an explicit description of the psychoid because of its psyche/soma interface. She remembered a soft sunlight and the scent of early morning carried by a sensation of a light breeze as she stood in her crib. These are faint visceral and instinctual markers of body memory that express a profoundly healing moment stored deep within the psyche and within her autonomic nervous system. And, the sustaining image has offered consistency and reliability through difficult times. Consequently, the image nourished an inner trust of innate healing that was held within Ellen's somatic memory.

Psychic Energy

Psychic energy is Jung's name for Freud's libidinal energy; however, Jung's term expanded and modified the concept. An important feature of psychic energy is its involvement with animating the psyche and the above concepts so that they are alive, not just abstract or overly concrete terms. Jung found that psychic energy is integral for the symbolic aspect of the psyche to become known and that it imbues the personality with experiences that influence change and transformation. It is an important topic for Jungian art therapy and a more detailed discussion can be found in Chapter 4.

Individuation

Jung was interested in the creative psyche—at times he referred to the "creative instinct" or the "religious instinct" and the "instinct of individuation." Jung's formulation of individuation included life stages and a developmental process by which the psyche moves towards consciousness. The general *teleological* movement of psyche's development towards wholeness or totality is noted in all biological life. With this brief introduction to Jung's concepts, we will keep in mind that analytical psychology is not a mechanistic, predictable recipe to use in art therapy, but a dynamic imaginal psychology that relies on the lived experience arising from the depths of the individual (personal unconscious) as much as from the bedrock of human knowledge (collective unconscious).

Endnotes

1. Contemporary psychology verbiage may use *preconscious* or *subconscious* when referring to personal material that is repressed. However, Jung used the terms *unconscious* or *personal and collective unconscious*. Furthermore, Jung hypothesized that repression had *both* conscious and unconscious processes while Freud thought that repression was a conscious, ego-driven process.

2. Jung referred to repression as having both conscious and unconscious processes, which explains why Jungian art therapists may not automatically view some clinical images or material as repression in a pathological sense but as a natural movement of progressive and regressive psychic energy, or a process of affect regulation, that is integral to the development of psyche and individuation.

3. The ego–Self axis was first formulated by the Jungian analyst Eric Neumann and then expanded upon by Edward Edinger. While debated by some, the notion provides a visual explanation of the relationship between the personal and the collective.

4. The word *pillar* reminds me of an important dream that illuminated how our work with the unconscious is a slow deliberate process. Max Zeller was a Jungian analyst who survived time in a concentration camp, eventually escaping Europe to London; then, with his family, he moved to Los Angeles, where he was one of the founding members of the Jung Institute. After the war, Zeller returned to further study in Zurich in 1949. He had questions about why we do this work and at

one point shared the following dream with Jung: *A temple of vast dimensions was in the process of being built. As far as I could see—ahead, behind, right and left—there were incredible numbers of people building on gigantic pillars. I, too, was building on a pillar. The whole building process was in its very first beginnings, but the foundation was already there, the rest of the building was starting to go up, and I and many others were working on it* (Zeller, 1975/2015, p. 2).

CHAPTER 3

Jungian Art Psychotherapy

Creating Bridges to the Past

Jung's Contributions: Analytical Psychology as a Framework for Jungian Art Therapy

Jung created his theory with the *image* as the central focus. It is a word found throughout his *Collected Works*. The notion of the image greatly influenced his clinical work; it was included in his complex theory and linked to the role of the archetype. This chapter will consider Jung's inner work around his separation from Freud and his use of the image as a means of exploring the unconscious. His investigations with *The Red Book* (2009a) illustrate the early clinical history of analytical psychology at the Burghölzli and its eventual influence on art therapy. It's this work and his separation from Freud that impacted the key figures who influenced Jungian art therapy in America and founded Jungian art therapy in the United Kingdom.

Jung moved between two worlds in many different ways, but what Evers-Fahey (2017) defined as two paradigms (energic and symbolic) gives us insight into his theoretical model. Within his own cultural style, Jung was innovative with his intellectual stretching and pulling of scientific ideas. He valued associations, symbols, and interpretations, but he also valued rigorous observations, which he learned from his years at the Burghölzli. We may overlook that our generational experiences of history and culture are important biases that influence our perspectives. Certainly,

Jung's biases were sometimes glaring and revealed his own personal and collective shadow, but he had the courage, drive, and fortitude to make conscious the vast complexity of the individual psyche that is woven out of the deep intricacies of culture, history, and the collective unconscious.

Jung did not want a psychology named after himself, although now his name designates a particular theoretical orientation. "Which Jung are you referring to?" is an important question, because as a body of work Jung's ideas evolved as his own individuation impacted his theoretical focus. In *Approaches to Art Therapy*, Edwards (1987) pointed out that in psycho-analytic history, the Freud/Jung split took on archetypal dimensions; the differences often remain a wedge within some areas of our field, and are endlessly prolonged by the attitudes of mentors and colleagues through transference relationships (p. 97). In fact, as Shamdasani (2003) pointed out, the words *Jung* and *Freud* are like signs that designate the two poles of a theoretical argument. Yet we know it's all too easy to constellate a power shadow through professional *otherness*. What Jung knew well was that there was no singular psychological approach that could fit all psyches. The complexity of his work has led to various philosophical and theoretical differences within the Jungian field amongst individuals that fosters a dynamic exchange and opportunity for new consciousness within analytical psychology. The essentials of Jung's theoretical model remain, however, particularly his ideas on the image and symbol, shadow, archetypes, and the collective unconscious, which express some of Jung's most well-known contributions.

Theoretical and philosophical biases, splits, and separations are common in all professional fields. Within the field of psychology and art therapy, there have been philosophical disagreements regarding theory, method, and application. If the differences are held with curious discussions, solutions, and mutual respect, then the friction serves to stimulate and enrich the field and we are all better for it.

It is also important to keep in mind that those of us who work with the unconscious have more in common with each other than with other psychological disciplines, so it is invigorating when room is made for collegial intermingling. In a polarized world, it is vital that we, as Jungians, hold the space for diversity of thought that allows for professional individuation and the possible reseeding of fallow ground. Not all splits and separations are psychologically negative, as Jung explained:

> [T]he inherent tendency of the psyche to split means on the one hand dissociation into multiple structural units, but on the other hand the possibility of change and differentiation. It allows certain parts of the psychic structure to be singled out so that, by concentration of

the will, they can be trained and brought to their maximum develop-ment. In this way certain capacities, especially those that promise to be socially useful, can be fostered to the neglect of others.

(Jung, 1937/1972, CW 8, p. 122)

Based on his early clinical work with multiplicity, psychosis, and dissocia-tion, Jung identified a natural and innate process of psychological splitting that occurs within the psyche and benefits the creative process and indi-viduation. This ultimately leads to new innovations, as Jungian analyst Rich Ryan elaborated:

> We must break things apart to discern this from that, good from bad, what we like from what we don't. New knowledge comes from friction and holding the tension of the opposites. . . . Life itself comes from friction. Cells divide. Clearly there are some forms of splitting that are under some form of conscious control and some that are more unconscious and out of control. We can assign healthy or non healthy labels, yet even destructive and unconscious splits have led to new creations, analytical psychology being one of them. Some of the Freud/Jung split was conscious, some of it was clearly not.
>
> (Ryan, 2008a)

Understanding the framework of analytical psychology is relevant in the development of art therapy. Like Jung separating from Freud, there is a partial unconscious split in the field, but there is also a conscious differ-ence between them, making individuation inevitable. To understand these roots, let's turn to the origins of analytical psychology—its history, theory, and application to art therapy.

Origins of Analytical Psychology: 1900–1912

Jung's decision to study medicine was not simple—there were threads from his childhood and family life that eventually brought his destiny into focus. From *MDR* (1961) we gather that his early emotional conflicts, his deep reliance on nature, his interest in literature and culture, his exposure to family séances and paranormal activities, his mother's dissociation and depression, and his father's religious role as a minister were all vital factors that piqued his curiosity in psychiatry. Jung's discovery of a purposeful unconscious had roots in three primary sources: his own personal develop-ment and dreams, his exposure to psychic phenomena, and Friedrich Nietzsche's writing (Hauke, 2006).

By the early 1900s, Jung had abandoned his interest in archeology, trained in medicine, and taken a position at the Burghölzli psychiatric hospital in Switzerland, which at that time was a renowned center of research and psychiatry in Europe. The famous Burghölzli was linked to the University of Zurich—established as a humane center for the research and treatment of the mentally ill—and combined the French school of "dynamic psychiatry" with a biological orientation. This innovative approach gave it status in Europe, as it became known for its extremely difficult patients, innovative psychiatrists, and pioneering research.

As a scientific investigator, Jung was eager to learn, observe, and research his ideas. He established himself as a respected researcher and clinician under the supervision of Eugen Bleuler, who had made several psychiatric accomplishments, including differentiating bipolar disorder from schizophrenia; coining the terms schizoid, autism, and ambivalence; and developing a model for working with alcoholism (Ellenberger, 1970, p. 286). In contrast, Freud analyzed young hysterical[1] Viennese bourgeois women. Jung was steeped in treating psychotic patients under Bleuler's guidance and direction (Hauke, 2006). It was Bleuler who brought in psychoanalysis, concluding that not all mental illness was organic. This was a profound departure from the dogma of the day. As both men came from the countryside, their appreciation for the subtleties of language and regional dialects afforded them the patience and empathy to consider seemingly baffling behaviors and verbalizations as meaningful and purposive in nature (Hauke, 2006).

While at the hospital, Jung took a short break to work in Paris under Pierre Janet, who explored ideas on dissociation and "fixed ideas" or rigid psychological thoughts. Upon his return to the Burghölzli in 1903, Jung plunged into the Word Association Experiment (WAE), invented by Sir Francis Galton and furthered by Ziehan (Ellenberger, 1970). This experiment measured patients' reaction times to specific words—these reaction times revealed "indicators," emotional and somatic disruptions, or affect expressions, that distorted rational cognition and provided evidence of unconscious content; the disturbances were called complexes. This research was the beginning of Jung's formal dive into the irrational psyche.

Initially Jung used the test as a diagnostic tool, but it also revealed the nature of mental processing, the movement of psychic energy, and the compensatory role of the unconscious. Janet's hypothesis of "fixed ideas" fit nicely with Jung's complex theory, which could be scientifically documented. In fact, Jung's research was structured and rigorous, quantitative and qualitative—much like research today. Around the same time, Freud discovered that his patients' associations could lead them to a core experience, the memory of which had been repressed and kept from the conscious mind; however, his work lacked the more robust (quantitative) evidence offered by the WAE (Papadopolous, 2006).

By 1905 Jung's psychiatry career was blossoming: he was appointed clinical director at the Burghölzli, which meant that in the hospital hierarchy, he came just after Bleuler. Jung was also appointed head of the outpatient department where hypnosis was being replaced by other psychotherapies, and he was a respected professor at the University of Zurich, where he taught on psychiatry, hysteria, and psychotherapy (Ellenberger, 1970, p. 668). By 1906 Jung and Bleuler published their much-acclaimed results of the WAE, and because of their work Burghölzli became the center of the psychoanalytic movement (Shamdasani, 2012, p. xii).

When Bleuler and Jung's research was published, it received accolades from psychopathologists in America who were attempting to formalize their diagnostic tools. Janet had been interested in the results as well, although later questioned the research methodology, a possible reason that Jung dropped the research (Shamdasani, 2003, pp. 48–49). Nevertheless, Jung's research, built on those investigators before him, paved a pioneering path into the field of psychiatry with empirical results that revealed intergenerational themes we may now refer to as intergenerational trauma patterns found in various diagnostic conditions. Evidenced by his positions within the hospital, his pioneering research, and his considerations around psychological principles, Jung was firmly established as a vibrant psychiatrist and psychoanalyst in his own right *prior* to meeting Freud in 1906 (Hauke, 2006).

Bleuler recommended that Jung read Freud's book *The Interpretation of Dreams*, which encouraged him to send his research to Freud as an expression of enthusiasm about furthering the cause of psychoanalysis. Jung hoped the WAE research would validate and expand Freud's ideas, which he found fascinating and accurate, particularly Freud's work on the unconscious. Shamdasani (2012) asserted that it was Jung who actually bolstered Freud's reputation in Germany:

> Within the German psychiatric community, Freud, as a neurologist in private practice, did not have a strong reputation. However, when his views were defended by respectable psychiatrists who had been conducting scientific research at a major mental hospital, as were Bleuler and Jung, they had to be taken seriously.
>
> (p. xi)

In February of 1907 the two men finally met and talked for thirteen hours straight.

By early 1909 Jung left Bleuler and the hospital to further focus on the world of psychoanalysis. However, he told Freud that his decision "did not leave me unscathed. Once again I underestimated my father complex"

(Jung, 1973, pp. 19–21). This difficult but important step in Jung's professional individuation led to new roles, challenges, and responsibilities. Jung was now married to and starting a family with Emma Rauschenbach, the daughter of a wealthy industrialist, and

> devoted himself to his growing private practice, and played an eminent role in the psychoanalytic movement from 1909 to 1913. He continued to teach psychoanalysis at the university and was the first president of the International Psychoanalytic Association and the managing editor of the *Jahrbuch*, the first psychoanalytic periodical.
>
> (Ellenberger, 1970, p. 669)

In private practice, Jung's research interests turned to folklore, myth, and religion.

As the first president of the Psychoanalytic Association, Jung appeared to be the heir apparent to Freud. Jung prided himself on his ideas, research and forethought, and for bringing the Zurich school, "then a leader in international psychiatry, into contact with Freud's psychoanalytic movement" (Zabriskie, 2015, p. 38). He saw himself as a scientist supporting psychoanalysis by adding his empirical knowledge and psychological perspective. Jung worked with Freud and others to promote, defend, and further the ideas of psychoanalysis. In many ways, there was not just one psychoanalytic theory and "Jung *never* [original emphasis] broke with Freud in some of the most important respects, which are highlighted in these [Fordham] lectures" (Wertz, 2015, p. 15). Freud and Jung had more in common through psychoanalysis than they had differences, simply because of the integration of rationality (energic) and observation (symbolic). In fact, Wertz explained that:

> Psychoanalysis expands the scientific enterprise by drawing on new forms of data collection and data, and, like the other sciences, it draws upon the full range of creativity of the scientist, whose ideas are never dogmatically held and change within an iterative process of expanding observation and comparative analysis.
>
> (2015, pp. 31–32)

A pivotal moment for psychoanalysis came in September 1909. Jung, Freud, and Sándor Ferenczi travelled on the ocean liner *George Washington* to lecture at the Clark University Vicennial Conference on Psychology and Pedagogy, or what is now referred to as the Clark Conference (Sedgwick, 2012). This ship brought the three men and psychoanalysis to America for the historic gathering of the fathers of many disciplines, including William James, who only lived another year.[2] At age 53, this was Freud's only trip to America.

During the voyage, the three men shared dreams, but when Freud refused to entertain Jung's response to an association of an image in his dream because he did not want to "risk his authority," Jung concluded that Freud was over-identified with his role as the "father" of psychoanalysis (Jung, 1961). Jung also recognized his idealization of Freud at that moment. It was a pivotal insight in which Jung realized that his purpose was to support the *movement* of psychoanalysis, not the *father* of psychoanalysis. Freud did not welcome Jung's withdrawal of his idealizing father projection, nor did he favor the idea that Jung would step into his own pursuits.

In 1912, Jung returned from his Fordham lectures in New York and informed Freud that he had "made room for those of my views which deviate in places from the hitherto existing conceptions, particularly in regard to the libido theory" (Jung cited in Wertz, 2015, p. 17). Despite the pending separation from the European psychoanalytic community, Jung's scientific input towards psychoanalysis was influencing the American avant-garde in Greenwich Village as well as the formal psychological communities in both America and Britain.

Prominent psychologists, who were impressed with the dramatic diagnostic results published by Jung and Bleuler, had invited Jung for his second trip to the United States, where he fulfilled a rigorous and impressive teaching schedule that included the New York Psychiatric Institute and Fordham University. Wertz (2015) explained that there was also tremendous enthusiasm for his pioneering thoughts that any signs of stagnation and retreat were:

> the first groping attempts to find new ways of adapting. His retreat to the infantile level does not mean only regression and stagnation, but also the possibility of discovering a new life-plan. Regression is thus in very truth the basic donation for the act of creation.
>
> (Jung, 1913/1970, CW4, p. 180)

In the same year, the *New York Times* published an interview with Jung believed to be written by Charlotte Teller (Sherry, 2015). As the first article that acknowledged psychoanalysis, it was clear that Jung was the one who was sought after, not Freud (Shamdasani, 2012).

Jung's Separation from Freud

The differences between the two men eventually became too contentious. Jung was not alone in his disagreements with Freud's singular focus on his sexual drive theory; several psychoanalysts had brought this to Freud's attention and were also ostracized for not supporting this theory. But Jung's pivotal publication sealed his separation from Freud; *Symbols of Transformation* was first published as journal articles in two parts from 1911 to 1912. In this book Jung expanded on Freud's libido theory and adopted the term *psychic energy* as the fuel that expresses the psychic functioning and promotes the healing nature of the unconscious through the image and symbol.

This was a pivotal shift in the history of psychoanalysis. Jung's psychic energy was more inclusive than Freud's libido theory; however, Wertz (2015) pointed out that the dominant traditions of the times defined psychology solely on experimental science and data rather than the observational science that Jung and Freud were actively pursuing through working with the unconscious. Wertz (2015) also made the connection that the trend against psychoanalysis and the unconscious continues today, dictated by quantitative evidence-based treatment requirements.

Following the separation, in 1912 Jung's attitude towards Freud remained professional, but was also committed to the expansion of psychoanalysis: "It has been wrongly suggested that my attitude signifies a 'split' in the psychoanalytic movement. . . . Such schisms can only exist in matters of faith. But psychoanalysis is concerned with knowledge and its ever-changing formulations" (Jung, 1913/1970, CW 4, p. 86). Jung's reflections remind us that as modern Jungian art therapists working within medical systems and managed care organizations we may be required to follow treatment protocols that disregard an artful observation, yet our ability to maintain respect for the individual's unconscious content is still essential.

Although Jung believed psychoanalysis was developing in a variety of theoretical ways based on the observations of the unconscious, Shamdasani (2012) thought it a mistake

> to consider Jung's theoretical differences with Freudian theory as leading to his break with Freud. Rather, the collapse of their personal relationship and the political alliance they had formed led to a situation where, in the public domain, theoretical differences were presented as rationalized justifications.
>
> (p. xx)

In other words, from the start there were differences between these two men that could no longer be ignored even though they were both dedicated to the observation of the unconscious. What resulted was an orchestrated series of attacks by Freud and other colleagues that followed the separation. Karl Abraham and Ernest Jones wrote disparaging reviews of Jung's Fordham lectures (Shamdasani, 2012, p. xx), which threatened his standing in the psychoanalytic community. Shortly after this, the new inner circle exchanged rings with Freud as a seal of re-unification without Jung. When Freud read Jung's lectures, he wrote to Ferenczi. His letter included words such as "stupidity" and "mistakes" but he also admitted that even Jung's most disagreeing statements were "congruent with psycho-analysis . . . even excellent" and concluded with "On the whole . . . I have very much overestimated the danger from a distance" (Wertz, 2015, p. 18). While the two had more in common with each other through psycho-analysis than the academic traditions, the professional damage had already occurred.

In January of 1913, Freud wrote his famous letter to Jung about ending their personal relationship. Jung had resigned as President of the Psychoanalytic Club and stepped away from his professorship at the University of Zurich. Following in Adler's wake, Herbert Silberer, who had explored the symbolic meaning of myth and was the first to translate alchemy through a psychoanalytic lens, was also ostracized for his desire to expand Freud's libido theory. The psychoanalytic waters were turbulent. Jung's departure from Freud, in the rough political waters of psychoanalysis, gave him the freedom to investigate his own interests, but it was undoubt-edly a disorienting and distressing time of turning inwards, even with the continued support of and collaboration with others in Zurich. It is also worth remembering that World War I was right around the corner.

When we stop to reflect upon this separation, the sheer complexity comes into focus. Ellenberger (1970) reminds us that from the beginning of their friendship there were actually fundamental misunderstandings between Freud and Jung (p. 669). Sedgwick (2012) wondered if Jung was ever a psychoanalyst but was simply attempting to please Freud. We must remember that Jung was openly critical of Freud's single-mindedness, and yet he never withheld his respect for Freud's pioneering ideas. Jung's courageous decision to turn away from the accolades and discipleship that he would have gained from being in Freud's inner circle brought about a deep personal analysis that laid the foundation for the rest of his life's work.

Jung's Creative Descent and the Liber Novus: The Red Book, 1913–1930

Up to this point, Jung's public life had been extraverted, successful, and powerfully heroic (Shamdasani, 2009) and so after the separation from Freud, he committed himself to the inner work and personal research where he thought he might find answers and nourishment. After several repeating visions, Jung decided he would devote himself to listen to whatever arose from the unconscious. The images he encountered shocked him, but nevertheless Jung persevered during the five months between October 1913 and March 1914 to record the overpowering material that insisted on becoming conscious (Schweizer, 2017). This became a kind of disciplined practice taken up in his daily life through writing, seeing patients, creative work, play, and time in nature. Jung's individuation process during this time is highlighted in *The Red Book* (2009a), which illuminates personal psychic travels or what some refer to as his "creative descent" (Ellenberger, 1970).

Although Jung's rigorous process, or what he referred to as a *confrontation with the unconscious* (Jung, 1961), technically took place between 1913 and 1918, the overall process lasted until 1930 (Schweizer, 2017). In this time, he had hypothesized and fleshed out a more in-depth understanding of the psyche's structure. Jung had also more fully claimed his own style of analysis based on the imagination of the individual psyche and the inherent search for wholeness.

In an exploratory work of striking diversity and complexity, Jung first recorded the imaginations and then began digesting the material in his black books, which were eventually transcribed and copied into a large portfolio where images were added. We know now that *The Red Book* is the result of an in-depth creative process that combined the structure of active imagination, image-making, associations, and analysis or interpretations.

This ritualized exploration of studying himself through his own personal analysis provided Jung with sturdy ground as he travelled back and forth from what he called "the spirit of the depths." Jung admitted later in life that any concerns about his own sanity "should have been allayed by the amount of success he was having at the same time in the outer world, especially in America" (Hannah, 1976, p. 109). His sculpted works still remain in his gardens, such as the small erect head of a snake and a figure of a bearded manikin with three pairs of arms that duplicated the wooden figure from his childhood. We know from the painted walls in his private room at Bollingen that Jung was dedicated to the creative expressions from the unconscious. The publication revealed Jung's deliberate and talented aesthetic skill as a painter, calligrapher, and eventual stone carver. Clearly, his unfolding process expressed the persistent dedication and curiosity to the image that is required in the field of art therapy.

Through his faithful dedication to the heavy lifting of documenting the multiple layers of his psyche and the emerging symbols rooted in his own experiences, Jung also demonstrated that immersing ourselves in the suffering and engaging with emotions and altered states of consciousness was an integral part of becoming conscious. Using play, art, dreams, and active imagination were pathways for Jung to relax his ego and find meaning during difficult times. These early approaches became the foundation for analytical treatments or Jungian approaches to the psyche. We continue to benefit from Jung's courageous spirit, or perhaps he did not have a choice.

Hannah (1976) reported that Jung needed experience to know something and he felt physically sick and irritable if he could not work with these transpersonal forces. He would often be filled with a plethora of ideas that needed constant attention and expression. In order to be on this path, Jung had to be disciplined as he explored the edges of consciousness and the edges of his own sanity as he had created and known it to be.

During this "creative descent" Jung also wrote his pivotal and foundational essay "The Transcendent Function" ([1916]/1957/1972). In 1916, thinking that it was too complicated, he put the essay in a drawer; it was eventually published in 1957. The essay is an exploration of psychic energy, the birth of the symbol and new consciousness based on what Jung had discovered from observations on his life-long interest in *the opposites*. (See Chapter 4.)

As art therapists, we have been unconsciously relying on Jung's personal and theoretical explorations with images as the center of our work, but how much of what is known about these early theoretical formulations often remains absent from our education? The publication of *The Red Book* (2009), nearly 50 years after Jung's death in 1961, was a momentous event for the field of art therapy as an intimate illustration of the historical formulations of a deep personal process that was undertaken by one of the early founders of psychoanalysis. Clearly, Jung was far greater an influence in the lineage and formation of art therapy than we have been led to believe.

He was one of the first psychoanalysts who openly used the making of images to actively process his inner psychical experiences as well as encouraging his patients and those in the Zurich Psychological Club to do the same. The personification of images from the unconscious became one of the central components of his psychology. Jung noted that everything he did after *The Red Book* harkened back to that period of personal research and observation. What followed for Jung were essays that deepened and supported his clinical and theoretical model of psychology, including alchemy, which provided the visual imagination for the working therapeutic relationship. Since there are several excellent historical accounts of Jung's life already published, we will now consider a brief history of art therapy.

A Personal Journey into Art Therapy

As art therapists, we come to Jungian work for personal reasons. Despite my enthusiasm, analytical psychology was not part of my supervision or hospital internship seminars, so I was caught between two worlds. The art therapist and Jungian analyst Ethne Gray—who taught the course on Jungian psychology and alchemy at Lesley University in Cambridge, Massachusetts—insisted that we know Jung's role in the history of art therapy and his clinical contributions through alchemy. She recommended *The Artist in Each of Us* (Cane, 1951/1983) and *The Inner World of Childhood* (Wickes, 1927/1966) and reminded us that Florence Cane and Frances Wickes both worked with children using art, imagination, and analytical psychology. Gray also pointed us towards Edith Wallace and Michael Edwards, who were early Jungian analysts and art therapists. She asked us if we knew about Withymead—and if we didn't, we should. She was warm, forthright, and knowledgeable.

However, as a student, I was caught without clear direction in the original traumatic archetypal split that had occurred between Jung and Freud (Edwards, 1987). Although not conscious of it at the time, I absorbed the intergenerational messages that post-Freudian methodologies were clinically more robust and preferred while Jungian methods were secondary and lacked empirical relevance. The message was something like: Jungian work was fun and creative while Freudian work was serious and clinically respected. Jung's influence on art therapy is perhaps more recognized today, yet its theory still remains only slightly clearer and rarely is it explained within academic programs. Contrary to these biases, analytical psychology is not simply an intellectual investigation to define unconscious archetypal symbols, nor is it merely concerned with the process of art making. Jungian art therapy is a *synthetic* integration of both these principles plus the observation of somatic energy and emotion that surfaces in the art-making process and the therapy. Jung's work is about *experiencing* the unconscious. Art therapists often live closer to the unconscious than most, yet they may give up on understanding Jung's theories. *The Red Book* has given art therapists the opportunity to re-vision their history based on Jung's exploratory process of active imagination and making images; one of the best ways to understand Jung's theory is to follow our personal experiences within the context of his model documented in *The Red Book*.

For purposes of this historical review, I have chosen three art therapists who have the deepest roots in the Jungian world, and therefore had tremendous influence on the early foundations of Jungian art therapy. In the United States, Margaret Naumburg and Florence Cane were in Jungian analysis early in their career. Their American individualism perhaps rejected the confines of Jung's Swiss Jungian lineage to pursue their individuation as American educators and art therapists. Another example during the same time period was Irene Champernowne, a British Jungian analyst and art therapist. Her art therapy path developed through using her Swiss Jungian lineage.[3]

Jung's Influence on Art Therapy: American and British

American Art Therapy

Margaret Naumburg and Florence Cane were sisters who both analyzed with the Jungian analyst Beatrice Hinkle between 1914 and 1917. It is interesting to note that Dr. Hinkle originally trained as a doctor in Stanford, California, but relocated to New York City because of her interest in Freud and psychoanalysis. She studied with Freud in Vienna around 1909; however, she found Jung's ideas on the feminine psyche far more acceptable and innovative for both men and women. Making a theoretical shift, she studied with Jung in Zurich and eventually began working on the translation of Jung's essay into English under the title "Psychology of the Unconscious," which was published in 1916. Sherry (2015) emphasized that this made her "*the* key figure in promoting Jung's new approach to psychology in America" (p. 70). Edwards (1987) noted that Hinkle's analysis with Jung took place at a time when relationships between Jungians and Freudians were at their most vitriolic (p. 95). The fact that Naumburg and Cane were analyzing with Hinkle during an immensely significant time in psychoanalytic history within American culture bolsters the idea that Jungian psychology is a significant part of art therapy's forming history and lineage. They were clearly influenced by his ideas, but Sherry (2015) also suggested this influence goes both ways: "Might we not imagine Hinkle as the Beatrice to Jung's Dante, the woman who helped point him down the path to the interior journey he was about to begin?" (p. 71).

Naumburg is considered the founder of American art therapy, eventually establishing the first training for students in Philadelphia, and Cane was an art teacher who developed an art therapy method that had unmistakable ties to Jung's theories. The sisters lived in New York City amidst tremendous shifts in consciousness at the time. As part of the Greenwich crowd, their fertile social life included philosophers, artists, musicians, and educators. The suffragettes were active alongside those discussing race issues and fighting for workers' rights. It was a historic time when innovative and creative influences gave American culture a notable vibrancy. This was the period when Jung made his solo return trip to New York and visited Fordham University. At the same time, Frances Wickes, a psychology graduate of Columbia, began her work with children using analytical psychology while making trips to Zurich to study with Jung. Consequently, this was "[a] moment in American cultural history that is usually seen through a Freudian lens had, in fact, a remarkably Jungian character" (Sherry, 2015, p. 71).

What is not well known is that while Naumburg's husband, Waldo Frank, worked on his novel *Dark Mother*, Naumburg guided him through a self-analysis that drew on Jungian ideas, such as shadow and archetypes, and while they "accepted and highly respected the wisdom of Freud and Jung, they both favored Jung in describing the depth of the unconscious" (Karier, 1986, p. 303). Jung's theoretical ideas appeared in Naumburg's and Cane's theoretical notions and publications. Psychoanalysis and Jungian philosophy in particular were both clearly instrumental in their creative thoughts and ideas, which included a cosmic view of reality and connection with the collective unconscious. With this in mind, it is likely that Naumburg and Cane were well aware of Jung's early visits, lectures, and seminars in New York City. Moreover, we can easily conclude that Jung's ideas were at the foundation of American art therapy with much greater force than we may currently acknowledge. The following will further explain.

Margaret Naumburg: The Mother of Art Therapy

Naumburg was a powerful visionary with a forceful personality. Early on she was an activist and when she relinquished this passion, shifting her focus from collective issues to the individual (Karier, 1986), she carried the banner for art therapy within educational and clinical settings that began in New York City. Naumburg is now commonly referred to as the "mother of art therapy" (Junge, 2010, p. 5). She was undoubtedly an innovative and integrative thinker who drew from her many mentors, advocating for the individual, and for the creative process to be included within hospitals at the same time that psychology was being integrated into medical environments. Naumburg named her approach *dynamically oriented art therapy*.

Understanding more about Naumburg's history may explain some of her theoretical decisions. Naumburg became disillusioned with her career as a social activist and focused on the individual through her approaches to education and eventually the formation of art therapy (Karier, 1986, p. 300). First, studying education at Columbia University, Naumburg was exposed to the ideas of John Dewey, who advocated for art as *experience*. He believed it was a fundamental requirement in a democratic education. According to Dewey's model, creativity, exploration, and self-motivated learning were most successful without competition or grades. Although Naumburg was initially interested, she eventually found criticism in what she believed was Dewey's support of a herd mentality (Karier, 1986, p. 300). Naumburg had also studied with Maria Montessori in Italy but found her approach too rigid. In 1914, she opened the Children's School in Manhattan, which then became the well-known Walden School that was the first of its kind. It drew leading thinkers of the time.[4] Consistent with Jung's training analysis, she encouraged her teachers to get to know themselves psychologically by entering psychoanalysis so as to better support the *spiritual health* of the children (Karier, 1986). Cane was hired to teach art and so the ideal for these

> Jungian-teacher-therapists was the integrated person who had worked through the problem of opposites in harmony with a universe where time ultimately disappeared and all psychic existence was unified. The teacher as a therapist was to be a guide, interpreting the unconscious through a Jungian prism that showed character as dualistically divided but searching for an integrated soul . . . the "chief problem of education" was the identification of personality types and the construction of an educational environment to aid the child in fulfilling the potentiality of that type . . . the freedom Naumburg advocated was not license but the freedom essential for Jungian sublimation to function and to allow for the emergence of an integrated personality.
>
> (Karier, 1986, pp. 298–297)

Known for spontaneous painting and scribble drawings, Naumburg eventually took this process into the New York State Psychiatric Institute, where she conducted three years of art therapy research. Although she was influenced by Freudian theory, Edwards (1987) pointed out that Naumburg did not fully agree with all of Freud's ideas nor did she appear sympathetic to all of Jung's theoretical notions. Despite Jung's lectures and theoretical contributions of the time, Naumburg referred to Nolan D. C. Lewis of the 1920s as the first psychiatrist to employ analysis of the art productions of patients either singly or in series (Naumburg, 1950, p. 13). Later, Naumburg also referred to H. G. Baynes's case material of schizophrenic art in his book *Mythology of the Soul* (1940). By this time the Withymead community in Britain was established and Jung's essay on "The Aims of Psychotherapy" (1931/1985), where he discussed painting as essential for psychotherapy, had been published several times. Naumburg did credit Jung for his symbolic work and his idea of the collective unconscious, but she lumped Jung together with all of psychoanalysis, suggesting her lack of differentiation and clarity regarding his pioneering ideas on psychic energy, the symbol, and the use of art in psychotherapy. Given the dominant Freudian atmosphere in the 1950s, perhaps she thought that if art therapy were to live and breathe, it could not have theoretical ties to psychoanalysis, let alone Jung's model of the psyche.

Naumburg's Academic Accomplishments

When Naumburg published her first book, *Schizophrenic Art* (1950), she showed a preference for Freudian thought and terminology, even though Jung's work focused on psychosis at the Burghölzli and his research was widely published and readily available. In her second book, *Dynamically Oriented Art Therapy: Its Principles and Practice* (1966/1987), Naumburg softened towards Jung's philosophical and clinical approach, suggesting that she never fully disregarded the early influence of her Jungian analysis with Hinkle and came to appreciate Jung's inclusion of the transpersonal and collective unconscious (Karier, 1986). Edwards (1987) also concurred that Jung's ideas seemed "to have been absorbed into her own theories of art therapy, which she steadfastly contrasts with more reductive approaches" (p. 95).

Naumburg made great strides with diagnostic clues of children's pictures and the artwork made by individuals with schizophrenia—this was a step towards using drawings for diagnostic purposes. At one point she referred to the Thematic Apperception Test (TAT) but omitted the psychological orientation of its creators, Christiana Morgan and Henry Murray, who were at the Harvard Psychological Clinic and had spent several years in Zurich gaining extensive knowledge of Jung's theories and methods through their analysis. Although Naumburg had advanced art as a diagnostic tool, she also expressed discontent with how psychoanalysis interpreted and defined the meaning of individual symbols and visual content rather than giving preference to the natural healing process innate within art making such as spontaneous images. "Such conflicting interpretations point to the need of giving further attention to encouraging patients to make more interpretations of their own symbolic material" (Naumburg, 1950, pp. 33–34). In support of spontaneous painting, Naumburg was interested in the artist developing her own visual vocabulary about her symbolic creations when spontaneous painting is used as a primary approach to therapy.

Naumburg's declarations on how to work with patient art work echoed Jung's already published recommendations: that patients are encouraged to provide their own associations and interpretations, and analysands are encouraged to use spontaneous painting to personify the unconscious. Without a doubt, Jung also preferred the analysand's perspective of the dream (or painting) because it represented what they were closest to in their unconscious. Moreover, Jung saw the purpose of analysis as a process that educated individuals to eventually find their own inner analyst; thus, he advocated the essential freedom associated with individuation.

By 1950 it was also well established that Jung's emphasis was on dreams, spontaneous painting, work with myths and symbols, and the inclusion of active imagination to personify unconscious figures. By the time Naumburg published her first book, Jung had published the majority of his clinical and theoretical work and would have only 11 more years to live.

It seems that Naumburg straddled Jung's and Freud's theories, perhaps a natural result of her own Jungian and Freudian analyses, and her own dilemma between working with the rational (ego) and the irrational (unconscious). Wanting to find her individual path, she traveled along the *edges* of analytical psychology, drawing on Jung's most popular concepts while leaving his actual clinical ideas in the shadows. Clearly, Naumburg was greatly influenced by Jung's work, but had she recognized him for key theoretical ideas that were the basis for her work, American art therapy may have taken some different paths. It's encouraging that Jung's key ideas are more explicitly visible in Cane's work.

Florence Cane

Naumburg's older sister, Florence Cane, was a teacher at the Walden School. She is less known as an art therapist, but her role is noted within art therapy programs for her aim to liberate creativity and individual expression through movement and emotions. In *The Artist in Each of Us*, Cane (1951/1983) outlined her teaching method, which focused on the functions of thought, feeling, and movement by way of rhythm and breath and she expanded on spontaneous painting and scribble drawing. On the first page of her book she sounded like an advocate for Jungian art therapy when she said:

> Nature and art have this in common—a form comes into existence by the union of two opposites. In nature, male and female create a new life. In art, two opposite states of being within the artist are needed to create form.
>
> (p. 21)

Cane also integrated Jung's ideas on the psyche/soma connection, typology, the opposites, and his notion of psychic energy. Specifically, Cane's teaching contained some of Jung's theory on complexes as well as his pivotal two kinds of thinking (directed and non-directed) (Jung, 1912/1967, CW 5), which will be discussed in Chapter 4. Cane (1951/1983) emphasized the importance of using both kinds of thinking in a creative process: "The active and receptive states must alternate to produce and complete a work" (p. 21). She encouraged a child to solve a problem, not through action, but by covering the eyes with the hands to introvert and see what the unconscious might offer. Not only do we hear clear echoes of Jung's reliance on the unconscious in Cane's method, but she also valued Jung's notion of the reflective instinct.

Undoubtedly Cane absorbed crucial Jungian principles in her analysis with Hinkle because specific ideas found in Jung's *Symbols of Transformation* (which Hinkle was in the process of translating) were later promoted to facilitate the innate development of her art students. Cane's approach included the use of sound and rhythm that arises from the body. This echoed Jung's departure from the singular mechanical reductive approach to also include the spontaneous and symbolic in her message:

> The simplest form of rhythm and the one first manifested in the creative process is repetition. It is present in the lowest form of life. Its earliest expression is the expansion and contraction of breathing. All the intricacies of form and design grow out of it.
>
> (Cane, 1951/1983, p. 24)

It is interesting to note that Jung had previously used the early rhythmic sucking of the infant as symbolic of a generative creative process while Cane used the early rhythm of breath that awakens the force from the unconscious.

Cane's (1951/1983) educational approach was to rely on the unconscious and the synthesis of the opposites: she aimed to both educate and strengthen the child, and to soften defenses (complexes) so the purposive nature of the unconscious could be expressed through the art. For instance, in teaching color, she offered limited choices so as not to overwhelm the mind. She encouraged the child to turn inwards so the answer could arise from the unconscious (p. 22). She also encouraged using reflective skills and deep listening when choosing colors in order to "draw the creative force to her" (p. 111). Cane integrated a psychological approach to her education when she considered four essential factors regarding skill and development:

1. body (movement and quantity)
2. psyche (contrasts and quality)
3. mind (organization and intensity)
4. spirit (emanation)

Each of these factors built upon key elements of Jung's theoretical material, including typology, reaffirming that his ideas on psyche/soma were beneficial to the development of her educational methods. Cane also observed specific formal qualities such as line quality, balance, quality of feeling, richness of color, imagination, and space for each factor (p. 178). Not only was she sensitive to the emotional content in pictures, but she valued the spirit of the child and "some outside source of wisdom" (p. 22). She noted: "If [the child] is functioning well and simultaneously on the first three factors, it is very likely that the fourth will follow, because when the whole child functions, the spirit awakens" (p. 179), suggesting a respect for Jung's notion of the Self and the collective unconscious.

Many consider Cane as the mother of all art therapists (Rubin, as cited in Junge, 2010, p. 31), which implies that the expansion of art therapy in America actually drew significant confidence from selected fundamentals within Jung's innovative approach to working with the unconscious. Sadly, his theoretical model was basically overlooked. The result is that those who are interested in analytical psychology may scramble to find the gateway into Jungian art therapy which includes differentiating Jung's model from a psychodynamic model with its roots in Freudian psychology.

British Jungian Art Therapy and Withymead

While Jung's influence remained in the shadows of American art therapy, the United Kingdom had an open foundation for art therapy that included Jung's ideas alongside Freudian notions of creativity (Hogan, 2001). Initially, in the early 1940s the term "art therapy" was used by Adrian Hill, a professional artist who utilized art as therapy for himself while recovering from tuberculosis (Hogan, 2001; Junge, 2010). Several others such as Edward Adamson and Rita Simon (both artists) were individually hired to bring art as therapy into medical settings. Alternatively, during the same time, Susan Bach brought Jung's ideas to the hospital with a painting group; she eventually expanded on a series of paintings in the same way that Jung looked at a series of dreams, and studied how mental illness was reflected in motifs, patterns, and colors (Hogan, 2001, p. 81). Bach's extensive work is controversial for art therapists who resist interpretation made without the input of the artist, but her early intuitions developed into extensive research. In addition, she had remarkable prognostic skills, using spontaneous drawings from medically sick children that reflected knowledge from the somatic unconscious.

A non-medical approach was created by Irene Champernowne through the Withymead art therapy community after World War II. Jungian analyst Anthony Stevens (1986) shared his personal story of joining the community as a young man and many of the included accounts come from his book. Not unlike Naumburg's Walden School, Champernowne's Withymead community was a fulcrum for the creative process, with studio space that allowed for collaborative and interactive opportunities, not all of which were smooth sailing, but which were informative and far-reaching.

Champernowne's Early Days

In the 1930s Champernowne, then Broomhall, was a young unmarried English woman who became involved with Alfred Adler's open clinics, which she found to be a welcoming community for learning and companionship while she lived in Europe. During this time, she began reading

Jung's books. By 1936 the presence and actions of the Nazi regime became more unsettling and Champernowne decided to return home. However, just as she was about to leave, she was introduced to the Jungian analyst H. G. Baynes (whom Naumberg referred to in her first book) and decided to enter analysis with him. Champernowne recounted that she learned "the essentials of art therapy" from Baynes and how to

> enter into the drama of the painting with the patient, how to drop right into the individual's own myth. He [Baynes] taught me how people can create their myth by dreaming, painting and modeling. He used to tell me about how Jung had done this himself, for he knew all about *The Red Book*.
> (Champernowne as cited in Stevens, 1986, p. 24)

Champernowne's interest in Jungian thought led her to write a letter to Jung in 1936 in which she said: "I was not satisfied with Freudian psychology, nor with Adlerian, although I had learned a great deal from both. Yet neither had a corpus of theory or a *Weltanschauung* that I could really go along with" (as cited in Stevens, 1986, p. 23). She asked if she could come meet the famous analyst and received "an immediate reply telling her to come to Ascona, where Jung was attending the annual Eranos meeting. Irene set off at once, leaving Munich never to return" (Stevens, 1986, p. 23).

When Champernowne arrived in Ascona, Switzerland, Jung was sitting under a palm tree in the garden villa. She was overwhelmed and admits that at age 30 she was naïve and idealistic, and told Jung she felt as though she was "in the Garden of Eden with the God Almighty" (Stevens, 1986, p. 23). In the face of such idealization, Jung responded in such a way as to ground her through metaphor and put her to work. In addition to telling her to finish her psychological studies, Jung said that she was welcome to return to study in Zurich with him and gather material for her PhD.

Champernowne now found purpose as she taught and completed her undergraduate degree in psychology. By 1937 she was making regular trips to Zurich to analyze with Jung. Champernowne recounted that one of her most vivid memories in her analytic sessions with Jung was his attitude towards the psychological work. Those who knew him accepted that Jung's investment in people might be misunderstood or felt as demoralizing:

> I was deeply impressed by the way he was so utterly *present* with you . . . While you were there you were . . . the only important thing in this world. I used to feel that his research was being continued through *my* life, through what I brought to the session, and I believe that this

was his intention . . . he was there for his own reasons, that the psychology of the whole situation was part of the scientific material on which he was working with total commitment. I had never met anyone who was so completely *there*. He was no outside observer because he was experiencing all the time. That so impressed me . . . He affirmed one's life. And yet, if you were in any way weak or stupid he could be sharp and relentless.

(Champernowne as cited in Stevens, 1986, p. 25)

By 1938 Champernowne left Zurich with her psychological basket fully loaded; the dedication to her inner work would serve her well.

Upon returning to London, she married Gilbert Champernowne, completed her PhD, worked as an analyst, and hosted events for the London Analytical Psychology Club. As World War II intensified, Champernowne and her husband left London for the West Country, hoping to escape the regular London bombings. They found a house that could accommodate painting and pottery studios. Even though she wasn't thinking of starting an art therapy residential center, it was clear from Baynes' and Jung's influence that "she was determined . . . art therapy should form an integral part of her work and that her patients must be provided with all the necessary facilities to paint and use clay" (Stevens, 1986, pp. 27–28). Champernowne and her husband found a fourteen-bedroom house in Exeter that eventually became Withymead. The house required months of renovations while she built her practice.

On May 3, 1942, Exeter was flattened, with no accessible water, gas, or telephone. Withymead, still unfinished, miraculously was unscathed by the bombings and became a refuge for the victims (Stevens, 1986, p. 29). The community that followed was more than just a community for the expressive arts—it is an example of how Jungian art therapy facilitates the natural healing process within the psyche and how art interpretations are non-invasive and perhaps reserved for later. Artists interested in Jung and art became active participants at Withymead, where the art was considered a lived experience and overly rigid interpretations were thought to drain the regenerative breath out of the image (Hogan, 2001). For instance, the art therapist and Jungian analyst Michael Edwards lived with his wife and child at Withymead, where he began his career and gained a rich foundation for living his life. The threads of art and imagination would be carried forward by both Michael Edwards (1987) and Edith Wallace (1987). With Champernowne's investment in community and the expressive arts, Withymead was known as one of the more innovative pioneers of art therapy in Great Britain, developing early notions on transference/countertransference, trusting in innate holistic healing of the psyche, and honoring the spiritual meaning and transformative moments that appeared through works of art (Hogan, 2001; Stevens, 1986).

In contrast to the individualism within the United States, particularly following World War II, and the disdain for Jung that permeated psychoanalysis and psychology in America, the development of Jungian art therapy in Great Britain had unfolded and evolved. Perhaps the dire need to find resiliency, maintain connections, and rebuild communities made it vital for the psychological community to consciously embrace nonverbal approaches that also honored and acknowledged the role of the collective unconscious. Certainly, there seemed to be a psychological compensatory response to the massive destruction that Europe and the United Kingdom had endured—the creative process found with Withymead offered the necessary innate healing for the amount of endured suffering and intergenerational trauma.

Endnotes

1. *Hysteria* was a diagnostic term given by men and used exclusively for women to describe unstable or volatile emotions that could not be contained. It is currently thought that women who were given this diagnosis were actually trapped in the suffering of active trauma or post-traumatic stress. They were having trauma reactions that resulted from sexual, physical, and/or emotional abuse. Indeed, many of Jung's "psychotic" patients were also women whose trauma was undiagnosed.
2. Sedgwick pointed out that in 1911, the same ship that brought the men to America would be the ship that alerted the *Titanic* about the iceberg, offering us a foreshadowing for the turn of events and the break in relationships within the psychoanalytic movement.
3. I am well aware that I have selected brief historical accounts to highlight and validate Jung's influence in art therapy. An expanded history of art therapy has been published elsewhere.
4. The Children's School continued until 1988, merged with another school, and then eventually closed in 1991.

CHAPTER 4

Psychic Energy
The Psyche's Life Force

Two Kinds of Thinking and Psychic Energy

Jung's *Symbols of Transformation* opens with an essay on two types of thinking: directed and non-directed. Directed thinking is an objective and logical phenomenon while non-directed thinking is concerned with subjective aspects such as emotion, creativity, and imagination. Jung used the concept of two types of thinking that began with William James's thoughts on differentiating logical thinking from associative thinking, or the *tender-minded* and the *tough-minded*.

Jung's directed thinking was linear and empirically based, working itself out more or less in verbal form, such as if we want to express it, teach it, or convince someone of it. It is directed towards the outside world, and adapted to reality, so that the images inside our minds follow one another in the same strictly causal sequence as the events taking place outside it. We can also call this "thinking with directed attention" (Jung, 1912/1967b, CW 5, p. 11).

Jung's non-directed thinking is inwardly focused and concerned with emotion, reverie, and imagination. As the psyche produces images, verbal thinking needs to cease for a lowering of consciousness, or a softening of ego consciousness, to occur. When we are engaged in non-directed thinking it often evokes vision, fantasy, spontaneity, and innovation. Jung explained that non-directed thinking is effortless and adaptive.

In Jungian art therapy, when we reference working with both sides of the brain, we are actually using Jung's synthetic method, which is discussed in more depth in Chapter 5.[1] In this method we circle around content from the unconscious without the need to immediately grasp its meaning and depth. Just as we open the front door to start a new day, we have thoughts and expectations about where we are going, but we also recognize the possibilities of the unknown.

Psychic Energy

In 1912, when Jung's thoughts on the two types of thinking were published in *Wundlugen und Symbole der Libido*, or *Symbols of Transformation*, his views on libidinal energy and the value of symbols were magnified. Jung no longer saw an energic paradigm simply based on scientific rules. He also noted a symbolic paradigm as purposeful with its antecedents in philosophy, phenomenology, and religion—but not simply materialism (Evers-Fahey, 2017). Jung amplified this expanded view by investigating the fantasies of Miss Frank Miller. These fantasies contained unfolding images and symbols that Jung viewed as living expressions of the psyche and reflected the inherent suggestibility of the psyche, yet he emphasized that these visions contained a purpose and were just as much facts as the mathematical reaction times of the WAE.

This dramatic shift in perception is not so shocking today, but in Jung's day it was a tremendous departure from the scientific view that was just beginning to validate the field of psychology. Furthermore, it was "incompatible with the energic paradigm. . . . Fundamentally, the symbolic paradigm is based on principles of relationship and relatedness rather than the fundamental laws of science" (Evers-Fahey, 2017, p. 41). When our ego becomes overly invested, we can lose our way of relating. As mentioned in the Introduction, Evers-Fahey (2017) offered a useful investigation into the ego's relationship to the unconscious that clarifies Jung's theory by highlighting two paradigms: the *energic paradigm*, which is based on scientific assumptions and rules, and the *symbolic paradigm*, which is purposeful and mythopoetic with roots in philosophy, phenomenology, and spirituality. These two viewpoints are useful to remember when using Jung's theoretical model or reading his essays because we hear him move between the two paradigms. While I think this is partially why his theory is considered complicated or overlooked, this differentiation clarifies the purpose behind his two types of thinking, and that is the role of tension and friction. Without friction, there is no energy. In Jungian art therapy we often use art materials or images to explain or express the inherent tension that exists within the psyche. Suggestions to "draw your inner weather," or to use two sides of the paper for opposing feelings or thoughts, are examples of how we encourage the friction to become conscious.

Without a doubt, Freud's ideas on the unconscious and libidinal energy were groundbreaking. Jung acknowledged the relevance of Freud's biologically oriented sexual drive theory as sufficient for Freud's purposes, but from Jung's assessment and from his clinical experiences at the Burghölzli, the idea that every symptom is reduced to infantile sexual instinct was too simplistic. For Jung, libido referred to biological forces of energy, but *psychic energy* was a psychological term that better described the intensity of the psychic force and, for our purposes, the creative force within the larger realm of *life-energy* (Jacobi, 1942/1973). Psychic energy embraces a symbolic view of a human instinctual world and the ego's relationship to the unconscious. While Freud eventually broadened his ideas on libido theory, many of Jung's original ideas on psychic energy remained hidden in the shadow of psychology. For instance, Jung's model described the psyche as a partially closed, dynamic, continuous, complex, and diverse system—principles that have been incorporated into contemporary psychology but without direct references made to analytical psychology.

Although it is fundamental to Jung's psychological methods and his ideas on the working of the psyche, complexes, and symbol development, psychic energy is not easily understood, yet it is key for image and symbol formation and Jungian art therapy. Psychic energy is the force that moves emotion in the psyche and fills the forms with lines, shapes, and color. It is also responsible for symptoms, or complexes, which Jung said are the psyche's attempt to heal itself. These were innovative thoughts in the history of psychoanalysis and psychology, yet even those of us working within Jung's model may overlook his most basic notion of the unconscious having its own direction fueled by psychic energy, which facilitates not just healing, but individuation through symbolic means.

Jung understood that the energic paradigm alone, which was relied upon in psychology and psychoanalysis, did not adequately reflect what he was uncovering about the psyche—which was that the imaginal was an integral aspect of psyche—so that actually both the energic and the symbolic were necessary dynamic components of the psyche.[2]

By 1928, Jung had returned to the difficult topic of energy with his essay, "On Psychic Energy," where he explicitly unwrapped the fundamental, empirical principles of energy and metaphysical considerations for psychology. This prepared the soil for his life-long interest in alchemy, which he thought was the best symbolic visual language for the dynamic psyche. Although alchemy is an esoteric system related to mysticism, alchemical processes and substances accurately and visually illustrated the symbolic dual nature of energy within the psychotherapeutic relationship as well as its influence on individuation. Essentially, alchemy integrated imagination into the energic paradigm through the mythopoetic and symbolic.

In Jungian art therapy, alchemical motifs sometimes spontaneously emerge through images and art products by individuals who know nothing about alchemy (for example, snake eating its tail, salamander in a fire, tree growing out of the body, or *genius loci* images). Jung understood that the arrival of archetypal images awakens the awareness of the mystical aspect of the psyche and the autonomous quality of the collective unconscious that presses on us. In these moments, the ego may feel demoted to a place of surrender and awe.

Tension of Opposites

Two kinds of thinking were the foundation for Jung's interest in the interplay of the internal tension of opposites, an idea that was consistent throughout his writing. When we look more closely at the core of Jung's approach to the unconscious, we see his reliance on this dynamic interplay. Jung referred to those who influenced his thinking, notably Hegel's philosophical idea of the dialectical model of thesis and antithesis. Jung also incorporated the psychological idea of *enantiodromia*, which was proposed by the Greek philosopher Heraclitus, who also referred to being "torn asunder into pairs of opposites" to describe how things can flip into their opposites. When we are grappling with these poles, we are typically wracked with emotion.

Contrary to a contemporary response that his reliance on the opposites only further perpetuated a binary psychology, Jung actually understood that *reconciling the opposites* was key to transforming the psyche. It helps to first recognize that since the unconscious is unknown, it is initially viewed as an undifferentiated *masa confusia* or chaotic mess to the ego. Jung believed that through a process of clarification, differentiation, and amplification, the conscious and unconscious became a pair of opposites that collaborated towards creating wholeness within an individual (Evers-Fahey, 2017). Second, Jung was interested in the full process in which psychic energy *chooses* a structure or form, particularly within a system that is symbolic and purposeful, yet energic and dynamic in nature. Does the ego choose, or does the Self direct the decision? This very question creates a quandary—a natural tension of opposites that Jung defined as an irritation that could occur internally or between two people. Consequently, Jung suggested the

> problem of opposites . . . should be made the basis for a critical psychology. A critique of this sort would be of . . . value not only in

the narrower field of psychology, but also in the wider field of the cultural sciences.

(1937/1972, CW 8, p. 125)

Analytical psychology relies on the premise that energy demands two opposing forces to create friction, which in turn creates heat or psychic energy (thermodynamic theory). The interaction between the opposites, according to the thermodynamic principle, creates a fire that results from two sticks being rubbed together. In his essay "Freud and Jung: Contrasts" (Jung, 1929/1970, CW 4), Jung addressed the results of one-sidedness. Jung's premise was that the opposite side is naturally constellated to cause friction that will spark a transformation of consciousness:

> I hold that psychic energy involves the play of opposites in much the same way as physical energy involves a difference of potential, that is to say the existence of opposites such as warm and cold, high and low . . . I have summed up the various psychic drives or forces . . . under the concept of energy.
>
> (p. 337)

For instance, in his essay "The Transformation of Libido" (1912/1967a, CW 5), Jung further explored the meaning behind the rhythmic movement of two sticks against each other that create fire. Far too simplistic to reduce this process to the sexual instinct (although he doesn't deny the possibility), Jung considered how rhythm provides energy for what he defined as additional instinctual needs: hunger, reflection, activity, or creativity. In the case of discovering fire, the expression of adaptation and the need for survival was connected to the hunger instinct, which is expressed or *psychized* through the rhythmic sucking of the infant. A similar *psychized* process occurs with all the instincts, including the creative instinct, which is expressed through such paths as art making and its inherent movement and breath. "The psychized instinct forfeits its uniqueness to a certain extent . . . losing its most essential characteristic—compulsiveness" (Jung, 1937/1972, CW 8, pp. 115–116). Without technology to prove his theories, he relied on archetypal images of opposites from nature to support his expanded notion of instincts and the symbolic paradigm—sun/moon, dark/light, inner/outer, hard/soft, masculine/feminine.

Jung continued to expand his discussion of the opposites to include subjective/objective, introvert/extravert, rational/irrational, feminine/masculine, and conscious/unconscious. His ideas on typology (1921/1990, CW 6) included introvert/extravert, thinking/feeling (rational functions), and intuition/sensation (irrational functions) as a psychic system organized around the opposites placed within a mandala.[3] How we access and express energy is based on the ego's dominant orientation. The tension of opposites (conscious and unconscious) is the foundation for the constructive work of the transcendent function as a conscious process where amplification and differentiation are used to ignite the required tension for change. From this tension, new images and symbols arise, carrying a healing capacity that regulates the energy, and seeks to reunify the psyche. Jung unmistakably observed the purpose of the opposites as partially an innate self-regulation if there is consciousness, but his notions were the initial construction for regulation and resiliency that are considered essential when treating relational trauma (West, 2016). Jung declared that: "Multiplicity and inner division are opposed by an integrative unity whose power is as great as that of the instincts. Together they form a pair of opposites necessary for self-regulation, often spoken of as nature and spirit" (Jung, 1928/1972, CW 8, p. 51).

Validating Jung's ideas when referring to her painting process, the artist and psychoanalyst Marion Milner (1950/2010) considered the repetitive rhythm found within painting to be a profound instinctual urge that represented a renewal and nourishment of life or, in the extreme case of alienation, it signified death. Finding a form for this rhythm was either imposed or inherent (pp. 115–117). If we bring consciousness to the tension created by opposites and rhythm, we discover an inherent multiplicity and inner division within the totality of the psyche. Most naturally, a Jungian art therapist works with this movement of energy, or affect regulation, by noticing how the tension between the conscious and unconscious are expressed. Without enough tension, there is not enough energy to shift to a new individual perspective. This is illustrated in Jungian art therapy when we have a vague or ineffable poetic feeling or thought that becomes concrete through a making process. Working with one image over time, we find the most suitable or correct container to hold the expression for the described phenomenon. Without enough tension, there is not enough energy to shift the "poetic idea" into consciousness, or to find a new individual perspective, but still, even in the repetitive experimentation and exploration, the psyche is impacted.

Jungian Art Therapy: Dana's Story

Dana worked on several versions of a tree image that illustrated a *genius loci*, or sacred place. The tree was a personal healing symbol that arose to compensate for memories of childhood trauma. Dana began with a small pencil sketch and several close-up paintings; she then used watercolor to paint a specific nature scene that captured a soft, poetic feeling that counteracted self-loathing thoughts. In these final images she struggled to have the paint accurately reflect the light and shadows. She wanted the image to express the illumination and sacred quality of the rock that she found protected by the sentinel-like trees. This was a powerful process for Dana, to translate an experience in nature into a sketched image, and then work with watercolors for the first time. She encountered the internal opposites and the complexes associated with skill and control, in order to successfully express what mattered to her. Conscious throughout of her engaged process, Dana's paintings reveal the emotional integration and assimilation of shadow material that ultimately renews the psyche.

Jung knew the psyche was a self-regulating system with an innate capacity for healing. Dana's images below illustrate the natural oscillation between unity and division, as the unconscious works to provide compensation for balance and wholeness. Jung reminds us that the importance of opposites and repetition is that it causes friction, which gives the psyche enough energy to investigate the differences within these opposites. This includes an investigation into the relationship between making and meaning, as described by the Cuban-born artist Enrique Martinez Celaya (2010). "Meaning flickers between what is facilitated and embodied by the making as well as by the experience that seems to hover outside or beyond the making" (p. 60).

Figure 4.1 Aspen Grove #1

Figure 4.2 Aspen Grove #2

Body and the Opposites

Pregnancy is a distinct archetypal image of the tension of opposites that is held within a biological and sensory process. There are others, such as aging, chronic illness, or physical disabilities, that constellate opposites related to the body. The pregnant woman encounters an obvious tension between her psychological states and her body, the conscious and the unconscious, or between her body and the fetus (Swan-Foster, 2012). Jungian analyst and dance therapist Joan Chodorow (1995) explained that:

> We are organized via pairs of opposites, physically and psychologically. No human action can be accomplished without the operation of two sets of muscles, one contracting, one extending. As three-dimensional beings, each body axis contains a pair of opposites: up–down, left–right, backward–forward. One-sided psychological attitudes manifest themselves and can be explored at the body level. To sense consciously the simplest body movement is to experience an interrelationship of the opposites.
>
> (p. 397)

In other words, by becoming conscious about our bodies we are engaged with the internal opposites. The anthropologist Bruce Lincoln (1981/1991) referred to "the play of opposites" (p. 97) as a specific type of feminine initiation for a pregnant woman, where she is caught in a discrete initiation because it lacks a locus of apparent action, but has a dialectical complexity. She is engaged with the synthesis of what she is enduring: the changes in her body and her hidden psychological adjustments are opposites that bring a momentous change in consciousness.

In Jung's model, the body (soma) and the mind (psyche) are intricately intertwined. When the autonomous feeling tone complex is activated we automatically know it in our body. For strong complexes, we can feel the irritation of their energy like an electrical charge. A Jungian art therapist becomes aware of the patterns of energy associated with a patient's image-making process, and the movement or discharge of the psychic energy is seen and felt in the affect expressed in the room as well as through the choice of materials and the making process.

Movement of Psychic Energy

Jung often drew parallels or used analogies from science when developing his ideas. Using thermodynamic ideas, he made the assumption that the psyche never loses its energy but instead transfers it from one place to another, from one instinct to another, in search of balance. He assumed the psyche naturally seeks both balance and opposition. In relation to the ego, psychic energy moves inwards and outwards, as in introversion and extraversion. Paralleling the autonomic system within the body, psychic energy can flow, or may become blocked, with the associated symptoms or pathology (Jacobi, 1942/1973, p. 53) that benefit from a Jungian art therapy approach.

Levels of intensity constellated by an image may be related to intergenerational or somatic memory or early relational trauma as well as emotions and thoughts created by basic instincts. The following sections describe the progressive and regressive energy associated with gradient, equivalence, constancy, and intensity, and introduces how energy is observed in the practice of Jungian art therapy.

Progressive and Regressive Energy

Energy moves along a gradient, which describes the degree of a slope, either a descent or ascent. Psychologically, Jung imagined psychic energy as water that moves in a pathway of two different directions: progressive and regressive. Progressive energy moves in accordance to the wishes of the ego; it feels comfortable when there is an outward or upward movement that finds expression through meaningful structures and images. With a regression, the energy moves away from what the ego wishes. Regressive energy is a psychological descent into the unconscious, which illustrates a time of refueling, or emotional states such as sadness, depression, or some other emotional discomfort. Jung did not view this regression of psychic energy as necessarily worrisome, but as a natural ebb-and-flow process that would eventually gather enough energy in the unconscious to spark a compensatory response. The energy is renewed and progresses towards a return to consciousness once again. This explains why "problems" repeat and resurface and we circulate around them. Jung often called the regression of psychic energy "enforced introversion." Upon its return to consciousness, it brings with it "gifts" from the underworld; knowledge and insight about the suffering, the grief, or the depression. Working with the unconscious in this way is a kind of initiatory process for the ego to endure so as to gain its suppleness.

Psychic energy that flows along a gradient is visible through affect, and is purposeful even with "desperate exertions . . . despite the fact that the object chosen or the form desired impresses everybody with its reasonableness, the transformation still refuses to take place, and all that happens is a new repression" (Jung, 1928/1972, CW 8, p. 53). In other words, simply because there is energy does not mean that it supports psychic development and individuation. Jung perhaps drew this conclusion based on his own investment in the psychoanalytic movement with Freud. He had energy that expressed itself and appeared heroic, but there was a personal sacrifice for Jung—his own psychology was left without energy. This is probably why he thought directed thinking drained the psyche.

Progressive psychic energy does not necessarily mean there will be an immediate change in consciousness either. Nor does the right amount of energy create the right form (image or symbol) for psychic change or a shift in consciousness. As Jung explained: "Form gives energy its quality . . . mere form without energy is equally neutral. For the creation of a real value, therefore, both energy and valuable form are needed" (1943/1966, CW 7, p. 47). For Jungian art therapy, this point explains why not every art exercise will bring about a psychological transformation. One can impose a form (intervention) or the form can arise naturally through a consciously engaged creative process—the latter carries far more potential for meaning. Yet even so, depending on the energic quality, the impact can be fleeting. Sometimes it takes many attempts to find a form that satisfies the expression of the psyche, as illustrated by Dana's watercolor process, which began with pencil drawings (Figures 4.1 and 4.2). While she focused on the structure of the painting and faced some frustrations and limitations, the meaning began to emerge from both the making and the painting itself.

Adaptation and Individuation

Since the premise is that psychic energy is always changing and does so with purpose, we benefit when we become consciously attuned to these shifts and patterns. Today we may consider this as becoming psychological aware, but Jung wanted to understand the underlying dynamics of becoming conscious. If there is a gradient movement towards consciousness (progressive) or a gradient movement away from consciousness (regressive), the psyche makes an adjustment in attitude, which Jung called "adaptation" and "individuation." When the energy is progressive, it suggests that we are responding to conditions or demands within our environment with a flexible conscious ego (adaptation); when the energy is regressive, we are responding to an inner condition with a conscious ego (individuation). These two directions create a dynamic interplay and provocative friction between the conscious and unconscious psyche. The two directions also suggest the potential for collaboration between the ego and the Self found through the expression of the picture. The metaphor of unstoppable flowing water (Figure 4.3) is an example of progressive or regressive energy. The image depicts the flow of river water in a lush environment.

When the water is backed up and collects in an eddy, the regressed psychic energy is stored in the unconscious until it finds a new channel and can begin to flow again.

Jungian Art Therapy: Gail's Story

This natural flow of regressed psychic energy is illustrated in Gail's painting from her dream (Figure 4.4) where she sat between two loved people in her life who had died. The dream image expressed a necessary regression to a

Figure 4.3 The Flow of Psychic Energy

Figure 4.4 Dream

"pond" of affect that reconnected her to her deep emotions of love during a time when she was struggling with sadness and anger associated with the end of her marriage. The unconscious offered a touching image of protected space that reminded her of authentic love and support. From the regression of energy that gathered in the pond, the "depression" was also a reminder of renewal during difficult days.

Progressive energy is known through a reengagement with life, an increased amount of energy, a new interest, a desire, or purpose. Each time this ebb and flow occurs, there is a recalibration and purposive balancing effect within the psyche. While not directly acknowledged, this progressive and regressive energy is also conveyed through the two kinds of thinking—directed and non-directed—discussed earlier in this chapter, although directive thinking can also be an "over-drive" that tries to counteract the regression of energy. Ultimately it is thought that the unconscious will win out. In Jungian art therapy, we may see the conflict or search for the unconscious regression that is pulling on an individual to retreat from the world and surrender to an enforced introversion. A common example of this regression is often noted during midlife when change is afoot and the psyche is pushing on the ego consciousness to shift its attitude.

Principles of Constancy and Equivalence

Similar to the rules of thermodynamics, Jung considered specific principles for psychic energy. The *principle of constancy* says that energy remains constant and is neither increased or diminished in excitation, while the *principle of equivalence* refers to movement and states that "for a given quantity of energy expended or consumed in bringing about a certain condition, an equal quantity of the same or another form of energy will appear elsewhere" (Busse as cited in Jung, 1928/1972, CW 8, p. 18). Jung believed the equivalence principle was "of great heuristic value in the treatment of neuroses . . . when a conscious value, say a transference, decreases or actually disappears, you immediately look for the substitute formation, expecting to see an equivalent value spring up somewhere else" (Jung, 1928/1972, CW 8, p. 19). Energy may disappear and reappear again in some other image or form (unconscious/conscious) since it cannot be created or destroyed. This idea is fundamental to Jung's notions with the symbolic paradigm, especially when working with traumatic states such as dissociation. As the psychotherapist, we consciously consider how best to mediate dissociated states of consciousness as we track the movement and expression of psychic energy expressed through memories, emotions, and images.

For instance, the law of constancy or entropy occurs when we manage overwhelming feelings—someone suddenly turns cold or "frozen" and while we feel the shift it's difficult to track the energy. The notion of constancy is not necessarily neurotic or pathological if one is conscious about the occurrence because then there is the greater desire to regulate, to hold the tension of the opposites, rather than becoming one-sided. Holding the balance is a difficult task to accomplish while we discern and differentiate the opposites. Being unable to hold the tension may result in familiar or old habits or more destructive actions like self-harm and abusive behaviors. Here we might acknowledge a transference of energy to another form of expression (law of equivalency).

Jungian Art Therapy: Meg's Story

The principle of constancy is explained in the following example. Meg drew a picture of how her anxiety felt in her body, but struggled to express the energy as lines, shapes, and colors. She did not invest in the picture-making process, but abandoned it to talk about another topic. I wondered if we should return to the art or follow her present anxiety through words. In that moment, I became aware of the opposites at play within myself; the path forward was uncertain. Perhaps the topic was temporarily too great for Meg and she needed a momentary break, or she may have been deliberately rejecting the opportunity to delve deeper. There was constancy with Meg's suppression of affect, but I also wondered if she was conscious of her process and was depending on me to take notice within the therapeutic relationship. I presented her with the the two-sidedness of the moment.

It is possible that Meg lacked faith in or was embarrassed by her lack of art skills; it is also possible that the image she began to draw suddenly increased her somatic reactions beyond a certain level of arousal that was no longer comfortable for her. Over several sessions we circled around Meg's images in her dreams and art products as she clarified her experience of being in therapy. Eventually there was enough psychic energy to make the significant shift in her attitude towards the unconscious content and our therapeutic relationship. She was more emotionally forthright about her fear and resistance, but also expressed interest in making changes, which opened her to imagine what that would require from her.

These principles are relevant for art therapists—when someone uses art materials, they are transferring their psychic energy into an image, or a form, as an expression of thoughts or emotions (complexes) through a creative experience that requires the capacity for self-reflection. The visual expression has specific lines, shapes, and colors that carry and document the analysand's psychic energy. There is a particular placement on the page or intensity of pressure and color. There may be repetitions that spawn renewal or death—we never quite know. It is the gradual progression of concentrated energy that leads to an "embodied" image (Schaverien, 1992). Committing to work on an image until it is finished requires *constancy of energy*—a particular energy that contains affect, yet the patient remains focused and engaged with problem solving through the affective and reflective process. This is the same energy that leads to the method of what Cwik (2011) named "associative dreaming," a symbol formation process that evolves within a relational psychotherapy session when engaged with an image, picture, or modeling. Over-heightened tension, or hyper-arousal, can disrupt this constancy; but if the ego's attitude is supple, the psyche can withstand the process of differentiation long enough to persevere and gain insight.

The principle of *equivalence* may occur with a powerful somatic emotion and we translate it into a picture. When drawing a line on an empty white piece of paper, the line defines and divides the space, creates a boundary, and ushers in a *reaction* of energy with the next mark of color, line, or shape so that the somatic feeling may continue to find its visibility through "lines, shapes, or colors." A new form is created. The image may compensate the ego's attitude or be complementary, to affirm an attitude that has never had support. The making process and the image both tell the truth. Additional relational engagement with the image, through the law of constancy, is required until the psychic energy finds its best current expression. This is what Jung says about symbols—that they find their best current form and when they are no longer useful they fall back into the unconscious until a new improved symbol is found by the unconscious.

Another way of tracking psychic energy is the following. After some excitement in a clinical situation, a withdrawal of energy may follow.

The analysand might become quiet, settle back in her chair, and look into the distance. There is a stillness. There is a natural compensation between expression and withdrawal (progression and regression of energy). Perhaps the energy has shifted between instincts—from action to reflection. There is a lowering of consciousness, which might bring insight or further constancy of energy. This is the moment where we may see action and reflection come together to form the creative instinct, where the mechanism of the symbol has the possibility to transform the energy within the psyche.

Depending on the content, as the art therapist, we may feel a quieting, an emptiness, or a pull to react; whichever way, we are affected by the relational field. Tracking the energy (our own and the patient's) requires us to locate and follow our own energy as well as our own images and complexes. If we downshift our excitability, we become more constant. The analysand's withdrawal of energy can be a relief, but also anxiety producing—for both the analyst and the analysand—because we may suddenly believe that we have to *do* something in the face of not knowing *what* to do. But that is our own anxiety. On the other hand, we could suddenly feel relieved, then we might be searching for constancy to distance and settle our own nervous system. There is a middle place where we pause; this opening is an invitation for our imagination—but it's a momentary space to endure together as much as to discover together. If we are not defensive, but remain conscious, then both of us are able to draw on our capacity to reflect using reverie to imagine and speak *from* the images (Cwik, 2011). However, if all the energy has been

> swallowed up by the unconscious, with no new value appearing in its stead . . . it is advisable to cling firmly to the principle of equivalence, for careful observation of the patient will soon reveal signs of unconscious activity, for instance an intensification of certain symptoms, or a new symptom, or peculiar dreams, or strange, fleeting fragments of fantasy, etc.
>
> (Jung, 1928/1972, CW 8, pp. 19–20)

The loss of energy can be paralleled to a state of mourning because psyche/soma experiences it as a loss of potential, a loss of the image or symbol, that falls back into the unconscious. The "fleeting fragments of fantasy" may surface with the analyst or analysand—a new movement of energy may arrive in time through connection and insight. Other times, there is nothing. Yet, paradoxically, nothing is also something. An empty page is empty, but it also expresses something in Jungian art therapy. We might see several days of an empty page. Is the individual defending against the making of a picture? Or is there a complex to which we might gently attend? Or is it essential to wait for the right moment? Maintaining faith in this natural ebb and flow of energy from the unconscious is found in both the expression as much as the lack of expression. In Jungian art therapy, both are valuable images from the unconscious.

Intensity

Jung noticed the intensity of energy can transfer from one structure to another, taking with it both its similarities and differences. This intensity is related to the image and the constellation of a complex as well as the creative activity of the psyche as it transforms the chaos of the unconscious contents into images that appear in dreams, fantasies, visions, and a variety of creative art (Jacobi, 1942/1973, p. 59). If the first structure, or complex (an autonomous feeling-toned image or idea expressed as a symptom or image), was focused on the sexual instinct, it follows that when there is a release of psychic energy, or enough intensity, it can shift to another complex or image—so a feeling of grief can be translated and transferred to a picture or sculpture that expresses what could not be verbalized. Art therapists see this movement of psychic energy visually within art therapy on a regular basis and have assigned clinical relevance to the changes, but it is not typically recognized as the movement of psychic energy. From a Jungian perspective, we would be wrong to assume that if the first symptom was sexual, such as a sexual dream, then the substitute would also be sexual. Jung tells us this would be a false assumption; it illustrates how we become psychologically stuck with *reductive* thinking. In fact, the shift in energy must move from one symptom to a *new substitute* and Jung named this energic shift in psychic life *psychization*.

Investigating the initial image may lead to unconscious emotions associated with loneliness, longing, or a need for creative expression. An intense attachment to a symptom or idea or image can only be shifted if the released psychic energy is replaced by another image or interest that also has enough energy, which is why a release of libido from the symptom does not takes place without substitution (Jung, 1928/1972, CW 8, p. 21). Jung pointed out that if we follow Freud's single substance of the sexual component, then the energy never has another structure to attach to and it becomes a "'sublimation' of the basic substance and a masked expression of the same old thing" (Jung, 1928/1972, CW 8, p. 22). This is also known as a repetition compulsion. A useful remedy for this is amplification through continued symbolic thinking and imagination so that the new symbol can shift the psyche.

Jungian Art Therapy: Jill's Story

Jill, a 30-year-old mother of a toddler, was given a new leadership position at work. She described her anxiety as often "swallowing me up," while other days she felt confident. She had excitement and fear about this new position, so her psychic energy was progressing and regressing—she was negotiating the internal tension and friction.

One day, Jill took her child to the zoo. She made eye contact with a large lion and felt captured by the connection—the powerful energy of the lion was both terrifying and exhilarating. "It felt like forever. He felt so close—just looking right into me. We locked eyes . . . I was both afraid but incredibly moved."

In a later session she said, "I wasn't going to mention this, but since I made contact with that lion at the zoo, I have felt less anxious about taking this position at work—do you think that's weird? We've been back to the zoo since and he's either preoccupied or sleeping. That day, he seemed to respond to a question I had about myself—it reminds me of Harry Potter with the snake." She laughed.

Later, she was in a waiting room and opened a magazine to a page with a lion looking right at her. Using the magazine image, she made a response to her encounters (Figure 4.5).

Jill circled the Lion with gold to signify her special encounter. She thought the blue "balanced out" the power of the lion while also letting him be the center of attention. Working with this animal transference experience was a stretch for Jill. Unconsciously we are all susceptible to reducing the image to a wish fulfillment or sexual regression. But Jill's projection and strong somatic memory was evidence for her that something transcendent happened—she had been touched. Secretly, she decided the encounters were purposeful and symbolic. Jill then admitted she had used the image of the lion to calm her and give her strength. The image was a compensation for her anxiety, but it also was a confirmation of her own authority and steadiness. We won't know if the eye contact with the lion shifted a neural pathway, but it did provide an imaginal resource that changed her thinking, a result of the principle of equivalence, or psychic energy shifting from fear to leadership. In other words, the symbol of a powerful lion carried her somatic experiences into a new expressive form that she could make use of in her own development.

Jung was one of the first psychologists interested in how the movement of psychic energy made itself visible through images and the body's reactions. Like Jill's story, psychic energy is often first felt through somatic reactions (complexes) that express equivalence and intensity. The visual image can then be constellated and the memories, thoughts, and emotions are differentiated (Jung, 1921/1990, CW 6, pp. 455–456). As we wrestle

Figure 4.5 Lion

with the dynamic forces within the psyche, the psychic energy begins to fall into a narrative structure, which allows the inner madness to dissipate. This is the purpose of a complex, and the healing effects of the archetype.

Transference/Countertransference

Jung pioneered the idea that therapists needed their own psychotherapy. He based this recommendation on the transference/countertransference issues related to energy within the therapeutic couple:

> The emotions of patients are always slightly contagious, and they are very contagious when the contents which the patient projects into the analyst are identical with the analyst's own unconscious contents. Then they both fall into the same dark hole of unconsciousness, and get into the condition of participation . . . the phenomenon which Freud has described as countertransference. It consists of mutual projecting into each other and being fastened together by mutual unconsciousness.
>
> (Jung, 1936/1968/1989, CW 18, p. 140)

Participation is characteristic of an undifferentiated merging between the subject and the object and comes from *participation mystique*, an anthropological term published by Lévy Bruhl in 1912. Jung expanded Freud's ideas of erotic transference to include other forms of projections, including on animals (1936/1968/1989, CW 18, p. 141) and used the notion of the shadow as a way to unwrap our projections.

Jung's ideas also shifted psychoanalysis from a one-person psychology (in which the analyst works with the analysand's projections and unconscious material assuming there is no influence from the analyst—it is simply about the analysand) to the relational model of a two-person psychology (in which the analyst and analysand work together on transference/countertransference, projections, and unconscious material within the relationship of the analysis or therapy). Eventually Jung clarified how the unconscious plays a purposeful role in the analytic process: the images are made visible and known and their healing capacity is shared by the two therapeutic partners (Jung, 1946/1985, CW 16).

The current relational psychotherapy model as we know it today has some of its roots in Jung's ideas. Figure 4.6 illustrates the patterns of interconnected conscious and unconscious psychotherapeutic relationships. It is based on Jung's diagram and ideas from his essay "Psychology of the Transference," where he investigated notions of transference/countertransference and used alchemical images to explain his ideas (1946/1985, CW 16, p. 221). This figure illustrates how the energy can move within a Jungian art therapy session with the intermediary space holding the shared images. As shown, energy moves in all directions and the therapist or analyst is not exempt from the experience in the room. Instead their therapeutic participation is actually an essential ingredient for the psychological work to occur.

Transference/countertransference is a broad topic for Jungian art therapy and extends far beyond the scope of this book. Schaverien was one of the first to expand upon Jung's ideas of projection, specifically considering the notion of the picture as a shared image of the therapeutic relationship (1992; 1995). She used the metaphor of the scapegoat to amplify the transference process of working with the shadow and unconscious material. The scapegoat is a complicated archetypal symbol, but essentially it explains how the disease or suffering is transferred to an object, animal, or person who relieves the suffering for the community or individual. Through a transference process, the unwanted "material" is disposed of through the art-making, contained by something separate from the person who had been "dis-eased" by shadow material (Schaverien, 1992).

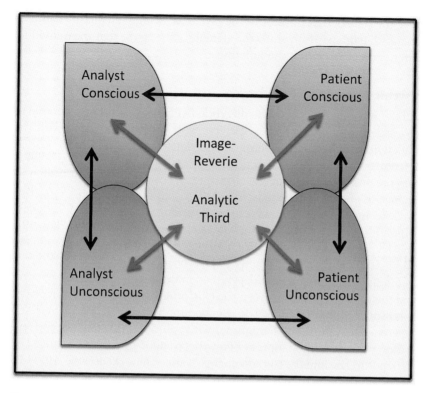

Figure 4.6   Movement of Energy

Jung underwent this type of transference process with the creation of his manikin that was stored in the attic when he was a boy (Jung, 1961). There is tremendous relief that comes from putting the internal suffering into a form outside the body; however, the ego does not have the power to make this shift meaningful, particularly if the interventions are absent or too forceful or reductive. The energy will not take hold or last for any significant time simply because of our rationality (Jung, 1943/1966, CW 7). If this occurs organically, Schaverien (1992) explained that psychologically, the analysand can reject or banish unwanted material within the picture that the therapist then holds as

> part of the alliance. The therapist takes care of the picture, the pain, and so, symbolically, the patient. A distinct separation from the suffering begins as soon as the image is visually articulated . . . available to be looked at or continued later.
>
> (p. 48)

Like the symbol that transforms the psyche, a meaningful picture contains energy that dramatically shifts the attitude of the ego so that the individual can tolerate and endure the suffering.

Psychic Energy and Teleology

A brief word on the purposeful direction of energy that is often referred to as *teleological movement* of psychic energy. It is often associated with the underlying archetypal pattern of individuation. Evers-Fahey's (2017) reference to the symbolic paradigm suggests that there is a constructive purpose and direction, but the *telos* of energy is not simply a mechanical change in energy and attitude that the ego can force through a reductive process. Jung explained that: "Psychic energy is a very fastidious thing which insists on fulfillment of its own conditions. However much energy may be present, we cannot make it serviceable until we have succeeded in finding the right gradient" (Jung, 1943/1966, CW 7, p. 52).

Finding the right gradient depends upon the compensation by opposites and the natural rhythm between the two, otherwise no forward movement is possible. Milner (1950/2010) searched for a meaning of sameness and difference that propelled her forward with painting: "this tendency to repetition was an essential aspect of growth, provided that it was balanced by its opposite, the impulse towards change, variety, new experience" (p. 113).

For Jungian art therapists, psychic energy is not serviceable until the *telos* of the story, emerging from the unconscious, becomes known through the use of images and materials that facilitate the unfolding of tension and differentiation. Even then, the enigmatic access to the unconscious through the expression of the telos of the psyche, expressed by psychic energy, is not easily made visible. At times, if we stick with it, the energy flows into the right image or the best form for that moment and we are gifted with a mysterious representation of something unexpected and perhaps far larger than us. This is a moment when change is possible, an idea emphasized by the Boston Process of Change Study Group.[4] What then ultimately becomes most important is not the visual object or the making process, but our attitude towards the whole enterprise that will ultimately impact the development of our consciousness.

Endnotes

1. Today some may refer to these two types of thinking using the model of the left and right hemispheres of the brain, which was formulated by Allan Schore. Directed thinking may correlate with the left-brain functioning which is expressed through more ego-oriented aspects of logic, strategy, and psychological defenses, while non-directed

thinking refers to right-brain activities such as images, creativity, unconscious emotions/affect, and other inherited material that is psychoidal. Jung conceptualized directed thinking as draining the psyche, so both types of thinking (directed/non-directed; left/right hemispheres) were exerted for change, psychological transformation, and creative expression.

2. In the same way, current research has found that working with both sides of the brain (somatic and bilateral therapies) is successful for healing trauma. In fact, contemporary psychotherapeutic approaches contain many overlaps with Jung's original ideas of using images and accessing psychic energy to work with complexes. These include but are not limited to: EMDR, Brainspotting, Sensory Motor Psychotherapy, Focusing, and FOAT®.

3. The four types—feeling, thinking (rational) and sensation, intuition (irrational)—are found throughout history, dating back to the four humors within Greek philosophy. Jung's work influenced and was the foundation for many contemporary personality tests.

4. The Boston Process of Change Study Group emphasized a "now" moment, as well as a certain level of necessary engagement, that was necessary for an unexpected creative change to occur within psycho-therapy. This opportunity may still exist even if it remains invisible or is overlooked while we fall into a particular impasse within the therapeutic relationship.

CHAPTER 5

Synthetic Method and Transcendent Function and Art Therapy

Jung's Synthetic Method

The synthetic method (sometimes referred to as the constructive method) is specific to Jungian psychology and is an essential technique in analytical psychology. Basic to this method are the two types of thinking mentioned in Chapter 4: directed and non-directed thinking. The synthetic method is used to work with dreams, but the Jungian art therapist may also apply this method to pictures and other art pieces. Freud's reductive method of association is complementary and occasionally used, but it differs in that it focused on reality and reduced an image to primitive instincts or a single meaning. By contrast, the synthetic method relies on gathering subjective and objective content that then undergoes a process of differentiation and amplification. Both personal and symbolic possibilities must be considered in order to facilitate a shift in the ego attitude.

The synthetic method is how Jung worked with opposites to facilitate the individuation process. Both the energic paradigm and the symbolic paradigm are integral to Jung's synthetic method with a "to and fro" that develops when collecting personal associations, and amplifications. In this method, we suspend our judgment and remain open to the unknown. Like gathering firewood, we gather associations to the image; both the conscious and the unconscious are engaged like two sticks of wood rubbing together. Metaphorically we are tending a fire within the psyche. Jung's synthetic method eventually made manifest an expansion of consciousness, whereas using only the reductive method forced a solution through ego-oriented ideals or heroic agendas, which, according to Jung, was not a long-lasting solution for psychological change.

Let's explore how the synthetic method works. Within a dream or picture there are co-existing subjective and objective elements: progressive and regressive energies. There are also images that are considered more archetypal (discussed in Chapter 8), that is, they are associated with the collective unconscious. When analyzing images or dreams, a Jungian art therapist would continue to return the analysand back to the *original image* for a new association until the energy associated with the image has been drained. It is vital to attend to both subjective and objective elements because the associations will most likely aid in the interpretation as Jung explained:

> But why do I encourage patients to express themselves at a certain stage of development by means of brush, pencil or pen? I wish to produce an effect. . . . It is true, I must add, that the mere execution of the pictures is not all that is required. It is necessary besides to have an intellectual and emotional understanding of them: they must be consciously integrated, made intelligible, and morally assimilated. We must subject them to a process of interpretation.
>
> (1931/1985, CW 16, p. 48)

By "interpretation" I understand Jung to mean a process of gaining perspective and accessing language that awakens the voice of the images, not a trampling or suffocation of the images. In all likelihood, the associations begin the discovery process that reveals the opposites that need differentiation and amplification. Tending to this creates the friction mentioned in Chapter 3 that ignites the transcendent function (discussed below). To facilitate this, the synthetic method uses directed and non-directed thinking and explores the subjective and objective points of view.

Subjective

The *subjective* view is the personal view and relates to the individual (the subject) and their personal associations to the image. Basically, subjective associations are concerned with an individual's life where the image may have been encountered before or where there is a pure affective response that may appear irrational or random. Subjective associations are also phenomenological descriptions (a story), or relate to other dreams or situations. For example, Randy said looking at his picture made him feel mad and reminded him of another drawing. This is not detailing the formal details in the picture, but the formal elements as a whole may constellate useful reactions and projections that require inquiry. Subjective associations echo the WAE, where a word is stated and a spontaneous response is given, which is why we return to the original image and why subjective associations may appear irrational (not rational), yet these elements shine light on the invaluable threads from the personal unconscious that lead to potential connections and insights. Subjective associations are also important because they anchor the image into the analysand's deep internal imaginal and symbolic life and open the gate to the language of the unconscious.

Objective

The *objective* associations are concerned with real external events in the person's life (work, family, recreational) that have influenced the analysand. The dream or image may depict a story related to the analysand's personal life, such as trouble with a neighbor or a family member or a recent celebration. The story is often easier to see in dreams than in art; however, the personal story associated with the image is important for uncovering the nature of the complexes. In art therapy, an analysand may associate a particular color with a person or an event. For example, Randy associated the color white with funerals and death because of his personal association with the image of white lilies at his mother's funeral, and the color black with a black belt in karate that he practiced to protect himself from his father. These are personal objective associations specific to the individual, which is why we should not make our own interpretations.

Amplifications

What makes Jung's synthetic method unique is the process of amplification that follows. The phenomenology of the image comes alive through the personal and collective unconscious. The amplification process selects an image and associations are collected. These associations are not just personal associations, but also may come from a movie, novel, or mythic references that reveal archetypal themes. For example, let's say a mirror appears in a particular dream or image produced by an analysand in a session. Mirrors might be associated with the myth of Narcissus, where Narcissus spends his time looking at his own reflection in the surface of a pool that acts like a mirror. Although the name Narcissus is synonymous with a personality disorder that has the features of self-involvement, self-centeredness, and an inability to see or empathize with others, we should resist jumping to conclusions that suffocate the image, because the mirror is also associated with Perseus in the slaying of Medusa. His shield was polished to form a mirror, which he used to reflect Medusa's image rather than looking directly at her face and being turned into stone. The myth of Perseus and Medusa may indicate a motif of protection, our inability to confront danger, or it may hint that the sword can solve the problem and we need a strategy. The sword represents differentiation, discrimination, and discernment. In this case, within the personal, subjective associations, the patient may need to become more discerning about a particular situation and there is a need for her to differentiate what is valued, tolerated, accepted, or even chosen as the right action, just as Perseus had to do. In other words, the analysand might need to adopt a more assertive attitude. Circumambulating the image expands our knowledge of it. At some point the amplification will add enough energy that the meaning and purpose are ignited.

Next Jung tells us that it would be important to translate the image into a concrete form. In Chapter 2, Ellen had a deep connection to the window image (Figure 2.13), but it wasn't until she painted it and modeled it in clay that she realized the profound impact it had throughout her life. This image also carried an important metaphor in our work—understanding when the emotional window is open or closed. At times amplifications may be more useful for the therapist's imagination but, if shared too spontaneously, they can easily miss the mark; these associations can too easily disturb the relational connection and interrupt the internal imaginal work of the patient. While the therapist's amplifications help elucidate the nature of the archetypal underpinning hinted at by the subjective and objective aspects of the narrative, there are many times when these are not helpful for the patient (unless they come from the individual) as they feel unrelated or too intellectual, and disrupt the flow of psychic energy. The therapist learns to know when it is best to reserve these archetypal associations for their own clinical formulations or understanding.

Art Therapy and the Synthetic Method

When the analysand translates an internal image into a visual image, she has made use of the synthetic method without realizing it. The method is used in Jungian art therapy in a similar way as to how it's used with dreams—there is an exploration of both the subjective and objective as well as directed and non-directed thinking that finds a reconciliation. When Jung urged his patients to paint, he was often met with "objection . . . I usually reply that . . . it is not a question of beauty but only the trouble one takes with the picture . . . To paint what we see before us is a different art from painting what we see within" (1929/1985, CW 16, p. 47). And, sometimes it's hard to "see within" until we begin to form an image.

Often trained artists have just as much difficulty freeing themselves to use art materials in their therapy as those who feel childish and incompetent.

They are subjugated by an ego that holds dominance over the psyche. Jung recognized that the ego could easily suffocate the unconscious images by giving them too much narcissistic value or criticism. His provocative statements regarding the images not being art may be taken too literally or out of context. I imagine he was encouraging us to embrace the riddles in life, the spontaneity of expression, and to maintain a respect for those images that the ego rejects or reformulates as acceptable, but lacking in soul. Jung's message is complicated but I suspect he was speaking for the individuation of the images themselves so as to avoid an over-identification and over-idealization of them. One way to escape the ego's dominance and over-identification is by making "ugly images" that lead us to attend to the psychological dialogue and image-making process.

Sometimes, when the picture is spontaneous, we gather associations after the image has established some separation from the maker. Other times the subjective/objective opposites are spontaneously discovered within the making through the use of specific materials (oil and water or tissue and glue). A tension of handling and negotiating the materials demands concentration for an image to take shape. During other times we might be in the grip of a pair of opposites and through making them visible we are able to drain the associated complexes of energy and find a new place in the image that is of interest. This is a shift in psychic energy. Once the opposites become concretely visible through paintings, drawings, or 3-D forms, further associations can be gathered over time and these may reference particular memories or moments that elucidate the complex. Whenever someone is "torn asunder," the tension is building within the psyche and there is both a conscious and unconscious desire to escape. But sometimes we must turn against nature, Jung tells us, and steady our mind and emotions. Such investigations constellate the transcendent function to generate a symbol that speaks some aspect of the truth.

Transcendent Function

The Role of the Transcendent Function

Jung developed the notion of the transcendent function—a process within the psyche that changes our attitude through our struggle to find a solution to a problem or symptom. Our clinical questions often focus on what the unconscious is trying to make conscious and what the purpose might be for the psyche as a whole. Jung found that the reductive method was less effective than his synthetic method because of the powerful role of the transcendent function and its relationship to the opposites and to symbol formation. According to Jung, the symptom arises from a tension of two opposites, and out of the opposites, a third thing emerges, which he named the transcendent image or symbol. This is why Jung was so adamant that the mechanism that transformed the psyche was the symbol.

While discussed in various poetic ways, the shift in the psyche had not been psychologically articulated until Jung named it:[1]

> The whole process is called the "transcendent function." It is a process and a method at the same time. The production of unconscious compensations is a spontaneous *process*; the conscious realization is a *method* [original emphasis]. The function is called "transcendent" because it facilitates the transition from one psychic condition to another by means of the mutual confrontation of opposites.
>
> (Jung, 1954/1975, CW 11, p. 489)

Finding the right solution requires patience and endurance. "The conscious mind is confronted with a new aspect of the psyche, which arouses a different problem or modifies an old one in an unexpected way" (Jung, 1954/1975, CW 11, p. 489); hence we may circle around the issue many times until the original problem finds resolution. This is not an ego-driven process, but one that arises from psychological work with unconscious material.

Constellation of the Transcendent Function

Faced with an external situation, the ego can either be impeded or energized by unpredictable autonomous energy from the unconscious. The ego, caught between the two, endures the tension as enough psychic energy gathers to facilitate change. The painful task for the analysand is to remain curious and conscious about both sides of a problem, with a willingness to be without answers and to suffer the unknown. Gradually there is enough psychic energy that

> the opposites [move] into a common channel. The standstill is overcome and life can flow on with renewed power towards new goals . . . the raw material shaped by thesis and antithesis, and in the shaping the opposites are united, is the living symbol.
>
> (Jung, 1921/1990, CW 6, p. 480)

While the process by which the images and symbols come to consciousness is straightforward, Jung recognized that the depths at which the transcendent function works also remain mysterious and ineffable. In the background is the influence of psychic energy and the Self with its psychological function to drive the psyche towards formation and wholeness.

Transcendent Function and Restoration of the Persona

Jung conceptualized that if the two sides are not held with some equality, if one side or the other is depleted or saturated of energy, then, much like a teeter-totter, there is an *imbalance* and a retreat to old familiar patterns of adaptation occurs. Jung referred to this as a *regressive restoration of the persona*. As a major collapse in consciousness the retreat to a familiar pattern prevents an investigation whether it be depression or inflation. An imbalance appears in various forms: if the energy is equalized, it results in a stasis within the psyche that appears as inertia and is expressed as depression. Imbalance of energy ranges from slight symptoms like neurosis to more severe dissociation and even an inclination to severe psychological splitting. When we can hold the balance, the depressive and dissociative symptoms become known as we become anchored by the images found through conscious investigation, curiosity, and analysis. Both sides of the psyche engage in a dynamic process rather than a one-sided resolution, and this "union of opposites . . . is the motivating force and the goal of the individuation process" (Jung, 1945/1983, CW 13, p. 307).

Florence Cane: Transcendent Function, Opposites

In *The Artist in Each of Us*, Florence Cane specifically based her art method on movement and rhythm to facilitate the energy of the transcendent function through the opposites. She encouraged spontaneity as well as skill. Cane illustrated how art therapists use energy, and in particular the "play of the opposites" that are so integral to analytical psychology. Undoubtedly drawing from her knowledge of Jung's theory, Cane wrote, "The idea of consciously—rhythmically—alternating the process of giving out and taking in is so simple that it seems obvious, but few people make use of it" (1951/1983, p. 22). Cane seemed to understand that Jung's model was compatible with art therapy and creative work. Rather than pushing in a one-sided way to make something happen, Cane explained that "if the student learns to proceed in rhythm, he will find a new energy, a fresh productivity; he will in short, be following the law of his nature" (p. 22). Cane used two photos of a child to demonstrate the active and reflective states and then continued to explain how the opposites

> balance each other . . . the relation between near and distant objects creates a tension which gives a sense of space; the play between dark and light builds form; the juxtaposition of warm and cold colours intensifies their values; the use of movement into and out of a picture establishes living form. Both the large tree trunk and the tiny leaf have their place in fine design. To be aware of the two simultaneously implies balance and understanding.
>
> (pp. 22–24)

Cane also remarked on how a young child's art is initially unconscious (less differentiated), but as their skill (ego) matures their art becomes more deliberate: "It is through this constant linking of skill and creative work that we strengthen the pupil's confidence and ability" (1951/1983, p. 44). Indeed, the creative process contains many intricate aspects, and it seems that Cane leaned on Jung's theoretical model in an educational sense. She understood that the imagination expresses the energy arising from the psyche/soma connection, which is also found within the rhythmic breathing that awakens the creative instinct. Indeed, rhythm is deeply instinctual and self-organizing for a young child and her ability to negotiate relationships because it aids in self-regulating and attunement functions that support social, emotional, and intellectual connection and adaptation to the collective as much as her individuation process. Also relevant is introversion and extroversion.

Given Cane's teachings, we can gather that much of what art therapists learn academically is rooted in Jung's theories of energy, two types of thinking, and the synthetic method. As demonstrated by Cane, Jungian art therapy is actively concerned with the opposites in various symbolic, somatic, and concrete ways when using materials and cultivating imagination and expression of skill. The making of images is a back-and-forth process, a working with the opposites, internal/external, subjective/objective, conscious/unconscious.

We may look for the development of an exterior image that illustrates the interior psychological landscape, but images also come from the interiority of our being. Struggling to listen, the images grow and flourish with meaning into symbols that transport the psyche to a new state of awareness as well as at times a revelatory place of unification and psychological peace. Affirming Jung's psychological theories and Cane's pedagogy, artists observe the quality of energy. Milner (1950/2010) independently examined this dynamic interplay and Celaya (2010) also accounted for this in his way:

I explore the relationship between the subjective and the objective in experience. With this conceptual tendency, making is a way to keep the work from becoming philosophy or poetry. Different that an intangible object of the mind, by means of making, consciousness and reflexivity are embodied in the experience of the artwork. Meaning, in this approach, is not only threatened by but depends on question of directness and staging, and perhaps, of authenticity and futility.

(p. 60)

Transcendent Function, Symbols, and Art Therapy

Jungian art therapy celebrates the symbols that are uncovered from the unconscious. Jung reminds us that "A symbol . . . lives only when it is the best and highest expression for something divined but not yet known to the observer. It . . . has a life-giving and life-enhancing effect" (1921/1990, CW 6, p. 476). Furthermore, the symbols are imbued with energy that relies upon the therapeutic relationship and the container for the psychological work.

Each Jungian art therapist facilitates the transcendent function with a personal style. My consulting room has a formal area yet it is flexible enough to create a more studio-oriented environment where individuals can work on the floor or the wall. At the very least, I always have paper and supplies available, as I believe there is an aesthetic quality of brushes and paints that visibly challenges the imagination with such notions as risk, failure, structure, courage, and possibility. At a particular moment in a session I might ask, "What do you imagine the unconscious is trying to tell us?" "What would that look like in lines, shapes, or colors?" Or, "Can you feel that in your body and put it on the paper?" Movement and breath can lead to a scribble that breaks through the fear and frees the mind. Some analysands use materials naturally throughout the session as they talk, while others need more time, encouragement, and education, with the explanation that they don't need to be an artist to use the materials. Sometimes we co-create images and this lessens the anxiety or builds the relational bridges within the work. Other analysands make images outside of sessions and bring them in for exploration. As art therapists, we know that any use of materials will bring about additional consciousness so I am hesitant about too quickly naming images as either productive or unproductive, progressive or regressive, as the purpose is not always immediately clear. This was made evident in an art therapy training group where whispers of movement or quiet words were sometimes tremendously rich with meaning and direction for the group process, and subsequent images (Swan-Foster et al., 2001).

I agree with Dougherty (2010), who explained that she does not use the word "art" but encourages marks rather than pictures after asking the analysand to "go inwards—to close their eyes and to deepen their breath" (p. 136). Dougherty joins the analysand by doing the same thing. She stays "attuned to the patient, I muse aloud about the conflict, sadness, confusion, or stuckness that seems to be pressing forward for attention" (p. 136). Then she encourages the individual to choose colors and make marks associated with their inner discoveries. Edwards (1987) pointed out that non-artists are often doubtful when confronted with visual materials, but he had his unique methods of stimulating the creative process; Wallace (1987) also had her approach of using tissue paper and glue to form spontaneous images that gradually took on their own shape and visual voice. In any of these examples, the patient is encouraged to bring attention to the interior space and to work with unconscious material, all of which fuel the transcendent function. Dougherty (2010) explained further that

> during the image-making process, the analytic couple is required to endure the liminality of regressive and prospective psychic energies activating infantile residue as well as archetypal potential, all seeking conscious expression through the common channel of the image. Obviously, when a patient makes an image in the presence of an analyst, it can be a meaning saturated experience for both.
>
> (p. 136)

Taking time with the image is invaluable; sometimes silence says more than words. And, interpretations are rarely acceptable in these first reflective moments, particularly if the patient may be experiencing infantile or regressed emotions from the process. Over time, as the ego finds stability, a reference to the images may include important connections or gentle questions or interpretations, but it's important not to interfere with the life of the image, to abort its unfolding process in favor of ego-oriented clarity and definitions. We hold in mind that the images are sacred, vulnerable to the eyes of the world, and deserve to be held with respect and protection. When they are ready to speak, they will do so.

The Transcendent Function in Action

Jungian Art Therapy: Julie's Story

The following vignette illustrates how Julie worked on relational trauma as she created her image (Figure 5.1). With the materials, she wrestled with the opposites by working steadily on a picture that frustrated her but eventually resolved itself. From the uncomfortable friction, enough psychic energy was produced so the transcendent function could spontaneously offer a shift in consciousness.

After talking about how hard and long she had worked on some specific traumatic material and what she wanted for the future (directed thinking), Julie asked for materials. She made a spontaneous drawing (non-directed) in silence, using large water pencils. When she was finished, she said there were four different sections of possibility, but named a fifth image at the bottom right corner as her "family trauma." "I don't like the colors or the combinations; it's too rigid—I didn't like it while I was doing it, but I kept going." Even these words describing the image spoke to how she had adapted during that time in her life—doing things she didn't like and continuing despite these emotions. Julie decided to use a wet brush to soften the boundaries of the pencil marks. That was unsuccessful—there was a sense of "the present moment of the past" (Ogden, 1994) in the room as she struggled to find a solution. Next she tried a white pencil over the colors and then brushed over it with water. Some softening occurred, but the pencil lines were there to stay just as her past had made its imprint.

With some frustration in her voice, Julie then asked for scissors. She thought she'd get rid of the fifth image completely. This was perhaps an unconscious desire to solve the irritation quickly, which could be a reaction to become one-sided and relieve herself of some tension. When she finished cutting it out, the part now remaining "didn't look right." There was a hole, but of the part she had cut out, she said: "This looks like an egg!" As she fashioned it more like an egg, she spoke about a positive event that had happened that week—this suggested she was beginning to imagine potential resiliency and resources beyond the past. She was taking things apart with the scissors. Psychologically she was differentiating, but at the same time she was making connections. Overall, Julie used a combination of directed and non-directed thinking rather than collapsing into a restoration of the persona.

On a fresh piece of paper, she painted the background purple and then glued down the now two different parts of the drawing to become one drawing again. Through the two different types of thinking and by wrestling with the opposites, it was clear that the transcendent function was

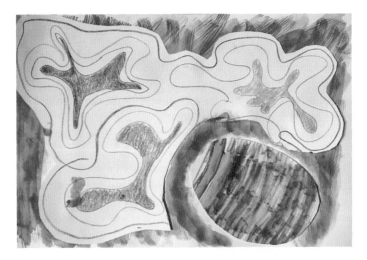

Figure 5.1 Julie's Egg

energized and working. She groaned and mumbled to herself as she struggled to find the right placement, intensify some of the colors, and add some detail. Now Julie was living the problem, not just in real life, but also through a symbolic *making* where she was unearthing meaning and purpose in exchange for her labors. Because she had stuck with the picture and endured the tension associated with her discomfort, she was now pleasantly surprised by what she saw in front of her in response to her regrets and suffering.

Julie was able to differentiate and clarify and then create a way to unify the opposites by making a new image, a new form, for the psychic energy to flow and fill with life force. We might also consider the final result an illustration of the "the third" or an "embodied image" (Schaverien, 1992). Julie felt a deep satisfaction because of what the picture held for her, and how her struggle in the process had revealed her ability to make changes. She thought some areas needed future work, and she smiled as she heard how her words had a double meaning, but the totality of the picture had visually offered some solutions. Describing an aspect of the Self, Julie said, "The purple background is the mystery that holds it all—the sacred or divine feminine." Then just before she finished, she returned to amplify the colors in the egg with even more color. She linked the smaller shapes by painting around each of them, acknowledging the connections. Julie was actively engaged in a process that Jung admitted is difficult to describe in which "[s]he is freed from a wretched state of mind by working at a symbolical picture . . . and [s]he will always turn to this means of release whenever things go badly . . . [s]he is no longer dependent on . . . dreams or . . . [the] doctor's knowledge" (1929/1985, CW 16, p. 49). Jung was well aware that lasting change came not from the therapist's interpretation, but from a moment of insight within the patient.

Jungian art therapy both requires and, at the same time, builds resiliency. The images can overwhelm us and other times they can strengthen us. Jung poetically reminded us that "by painting himself he gives shape to himself. For what he paints are active fantasies . . . he strives to catch his interior agent, only to discover in the end that it is eternally unknown and alien, the hidden foundation of psychic life" (1929/1985, CW 16, p. 49). Perhaps for Julie the color purple hints at a hidden foundation of her psychic life discovered through the elaboration and amplification of particular areas that she eventually reconnected into one picture. Integral to Julie's process was the separation and reconnection through the concrete repair of her image that nourished her confidence and resiliency—it counteracted the defeat and futility that often sits at the edges of a weary psyche that has endured abuse and trauma. As Julie underwent a process of making, taking apart, and remaking into a whole picture, she found meaning in the problem—and this afforded dramatic shifts in her psyche.

Julie's process illustrates how purpose of the synthetic method and the transcendent function

> produce an effect . . . [the analysand] begins to play an active part . . . he puts down on paper what he has passively seen, thereby turning it into a deliberate act. He not only talks about it, he is actually doing something about it.
>
> (Jung, 1929/1985, CW 16, p. 48)

Jungian art therapy builds on Jung's clinical discoveries surrounding the patient's ability to take action, wrestle with purpose and meaning. Jung had respect for the image when he remarked: "the concrete shaping of the image enforces a continuous study of it in all its parts, so that it can develop its effects to the full" (Jung, 1929/1985, CW 16, p. 49).

Jungian Art Therapy: Students' Stories

Several students have taken an "active part" in their process and have experienced Jung's theories in action. In class Karen admitted to feeling sleepy until she created a tissue collage—this fueled her vitality and she remarked how her energy had changed through grappling with the materials. She noticed the colors and emerging images stimulated her senses. There was also a discussion about chaotic discharge and primary process (Freudian), versus bringing to consciousness through the image making that first looked like primordial, elemental, or undifferentiated chaos within the psyche that could become known and further differentiated. Organization took shape as the student discovered basic structures and forms (archetypes) and acknowledged the emotions (complexes) associated with the gradual process of clarity and transformation found in the final image. In another class, focused on Jung and alchemy, we used a range of materials such as oil crayons, water colors, and salt to experiment with the *prima materia* stimulated by the substances (Figure 5.2). This spontaneous process encouraged a laboratory for exploration and reflection that used both directed and non-directed thinking and facilitated the imagination of the students. The images could then be used with

Figure 5.2 Prima Materia

Jung's method of active imagination, a method that is discussed in Chapter 10. Jung explained that "the hands know how to solve a riddle with which the intellect has wrestled in vain. By shaping it, one goes on dreaming the dream in greater detail in the waking state" (Jung, ([1916]/1957/1972, CW 8, pp. 86–87).

Jungian Art Therapy: Claire's Story

Claire, who had endured early relational trauma, used her hands to make small clay shapes she placed in a box. They represented the "bits and pieces" she talked about in sessions. The little shapes began to grow in weight over time, and that validated and gave "weight" to her story. The shapes were talismans, left behind in the office as scapegoats, objects for the unspeakable content (Schaverien, 1992). The heavy box reminded her each week that she had reason to maintain clear boundaries. Each shape held a story of grief, and documented a particular moment. Eventually this ritual ended. The energy had been drained, shifting to another place within the psyche—she began stitching and sewing, a very different creative expression. This shift in psychic energy reminds us of the law of equivalency from Chapter 4. At the end of treatment, Claire noticed the shapes had lost their energy, but she remembered the process as transformative and "planted" them in her garden. "They need to go back to the earth." She had spiraled around her history, but now Claire could live in the present and plan for herself.

Art and Individuation

The transcendent function also generates individuation, which is how Jung came to see it as an engine or a work horse within the psyche. Each time we engage with the unconscious we are faced with a new struggle, a fresh opportunity to "take our individuation under our feet" (Ruff, 1988). The images are an integral piece of both action and reflection. Jung thought that with too much value placed on art and its aesthetic quality, there was a risk for blockages of expression and insight. In the same way, a compulsive need for perfection interferes with the creative expression and defends against the unconscious and its tremendous depth of purpose and meaning. When we seek meaning, we are susceptible to overvaluing or idealizing the content, the interpretation, and the intellectual analysis. An example might be a painting that is skillfully realistic and aesthetically pleasing with not much meaning versus an art piece that holds conceptual ideas and intellectual formulations but lacks aesthetic appeal. Along with the tension there is compensation:

> After a certain point of psychic development has been reached, the products of the unconscious are greatly overvalued precisely because

they are boundlessly undervalued before. This undervaluation is one of the greatest obstacles in formulating the unconscious material.

(Jung, [1916]/1957/1972, CW 8, p. 85)

The undervaluing of the unconscious material is a difficult but persistent challenge we face as Jungian art therapists. We also confront it in ourselves as much as in our analysands. If we undervalue, then we can equally over-value. If we undervalue, we may neglect the role of the image, the voice of the unconscious. Jung sought balance within the psyche, seeking out what is not immediately visible, which may partially illuminate why Jung wrestled with the idea of "art" and refused to call his images from *The Red Book* "art" as an anima figure suggested. His rejection of her encouragement and perspective may disappoint some because he rejected his own dictum of respecting the wisdom of the unconscious. At the same time, Carl Jung the man became visible when he rejected her suggestion: even *he* was capable of defending against the unconscious. Or was he alert to something more elusive that we see in art therapy when we negotiate the flow of psychic energy? He valued both aesthetics and skill and he valued the sym-bolic and imaginative. Is there is a difference between therapeutic images and art created by artists whose goal is not psychological? For Jung, these questions mattered. He had a new message to promote, which was that art made through active imagination differs because it has a psychological intention to expand consciousness and further individuation. When we focus too much on our skill and technical aspects of the making, we are caught by the ego's expectations, and overlook the imperfect but inherent expressive need of the unconscious. Jung worked with these images by mostly omitting the personal clinical content and associations for publica-tion; thus, he has a reputation of viewing images from primarily an arche-typal perspective despite his salient reflections on the therapeutic process.

Jung's Two Approaches Towards Images: Creative Formulation and Meaning

When the art products from the unconscious become conscious, Jung thought there were two ways to work with the content until the analysand came to a certain psychological stage of development. One is through *creative formulation*, which works to hone and condense through analysis until there are refined motifs and aesthetic considerations, and the other is uncovering some understanding with a focus on *meaning*.

For example, in Chapter 2, Ellen was engaged in a psychological distilling process, and she refused to call her images and clay figures art (Figure 2.13). If she did so, she would have inhibited her making process. Instead, her image of the window had several iterations that had grown within her and alongside her, reminding us that both the image *and* the individual have separate but intersecting paths of individuation. By not defining her work as art, Ellen found her own process of "play" when she joined her painted images with her clay figures. Using her paintings as backdrops or nature settings, her clay figures were displayed in purposeful and meaningful ways to express the inexpressible.

It is natural to ask the question: is this art? It is less common to ask if this is the unconscious generating transformation. At times it may be both. But, just as Ellen showed me, by stepping away from the debate of "art" we can deeply value the creative process and the images themselves and yet not overvalue the results so that they are idealized and isolated, unable to express their true nature and be assimilated. According to Jung, without a dialectical relationship the symbols are prevented from providing their profound meaning. Having confidence in the synthetic method as a framework deepens the art therapy process from simply an ego-oriented personal treatment to one that acknowledges the underlying relational life force that nourishes the psyche with its purposeful need to become visible with its renewing capacity.

Facilitating the Transcendent Function

The transcendent function moves us from one attitude to another and liberates the personality. Below are a few considerations:

1. There needs to be unconscious content—from dreams, art, visions, or active imaginations—that is given conscious attention.
2. Don't trample and don't suffocate the images.
3. Recognize that images are content from the soul.
4. Name the image(s) within the presented material and acknowledge their specificity.
5. Use the synthetic method to amplify the subjective and objective associations to the original image(s).
6. Practice patience and slow the pace to match the dialectic process between the ego and the unconscious.
7. Consider this relationship between the ego and the unconscious—what does the ego want to avoid? What is the unconscious trying to make visible?
8. Investigate the tensions inherent within the image.
9. Spend time wondering about amplifications, archetypal themes, and connections to the cultural and collective unconscious, but without overemphasis and loss of the personal.
10. Remember the individuation process is driven by the Self; it is not an ego agenda.

11. Recognize the image also has its own right to the individuation process.
12. Do not overinterpret; stay close to the relationships between the image(s) and the affects expressed by the individual.

The synthetic method and the transcendent function are important structural approaches to working with unconscious material. When we understand how Jung used these methods, we are better able to remember that the unconscious has a powerful intent to facilitate individuation. Whether we consciously acknowledge it or not, our life unfolds, moving from one event to another. These internal or external events are landmarks on our journey that sometimes constellate symptoms and reactions. Jungian art therapy is a complementary process for Jung's primary interest in facilitating consciousness. One important element of his model was the use of imagination, which is discussed in the following chapter.

Endnote

1. Jung wrote the essay "The Transcendent Function" in 1916 while working on his own Red Book process and it was later published in 1957. The essay illustrates Jung's key theories regarding the psyche's creative process, the movement of psychic energy, the ego's relationship to the unconscious, and the creative and analytic processes that are applicable to art therapy. Most importantly, it outlines and emphasizes the autonomous aspect of the unconscious.

Part II
Attending
Engaging with the Unconscious

Attending marks the liminal phase of showing up for the tasks that the unconscious charges us to confront. This is not concerned with chronological or *Cronos* time, but rests in the liminal time of *Kairos*. Here we listen to the inner rhythms of our own nature. It is a period of stillness, darkness, and uncertainty as we navigate our complexes and work with archetypal energies. Waiting for the symbolic expression takes courage and patience. It also takes a good dose of imagination. Making time to record our dreams, draw, write in journals, or sculpt becomes an essential part of our day. We sacrifice our regular routines to carve out an imaginal space. The attending phase has qualities of being and becoming—it is a time of simultaneous stillness in the moment and a stretching into spaces unknown.

CHAPTER **6**

Imagination

Creating Imaginal Space

The Imagination

Imagination and the *imaginal* are well-used words in the field of Jungian art therapy. Imaginal is conceptualized as a living space within the psyche that holds these images and offers a noetic[1] path of relating to the unconscious (Corbin, 1969/1989). According to Corbin, the imaginal amplifies and aids in our discovery of this inner world that is not just imaginary, but is real. Imagination opens the mind and heart to include a living space for the symbolic to impact the soul (Corbin, 1969/1989; 1972). It follows that the imaginal realm is a state of musing and wondering that is experienced through our presence and perception of the moment; it is not a place of scrutiny, evaluation, or judgment.

Imagination is different from fantasy, even though fantasy was sometimes used by Jung and continues to be found in some psychoanalytic literature today. For our purposes, fantasy is defined as the circular, dissociative, nondirective, passive qualities in the psyche that are understood as unproductive or even destructive (Winnicott, 1971). Years prior, the alchemist Paracelsus had already determined that fantasy is an exercise of thought without foundation in nature; it is the "madman's cornerstone" (as cited in Corbin, 1969/1989, p. 179). In contrast, in Jungian art therapy imagination is the active and engaged process of *capturing* previously

115

unknown images from the unconscious that materialize in various forms and through various senses. Thus, we are consciously tracking and taking hold of these images from the imagination and giving them energy and life through lines, shapes, colors, form, and texture. Like a child reaching out to capture dandelion seeds blowing in the wind, we do the same with the images that come through dreams, visual images, and visions—sometimes with such ineffability that we barely sense what it is we are bringing to consciousness until it is finished, and sometimes not even then. With imagination, we engage with the un-worded aspect of the deepest parts of ourselves, those inaccessible places that remain in darkness until our courage and devotion grows strong enough. The process of producing images through creative action and bringing spirit into form and color is mysterious and magical (Corbin, 1969/1989).

James Hillman's wealth of poetic explorations into psychology and the imagination reinvigorated those of Jung's ideas that are integral for art therapists working with enigmatic images from the unconscious. He reminded us that the word "soul" is the central force of our existence: "If, as Jung says, 'image is psyche', then why not go on to say, 'images are souls', and our job with them is to meet them on that soul level" (Hillman, 1977, p. 81). The symbolic paradigm carries the soul through dark waters of the liminality of life and this imaginal world goes on whether we consciously track its unfolding or not. It is the soul that speaks our authentic truth, Jung and Hillman tell us, and with every image and whisper of spoken truth there is a bit of soul that is carried forth from within us.

From another direction, the vast topic of neuropsychology offers insights into the biological workings of imagination. More and more evidence points to how our mind can create reality at a neuronal level through imagination and make adjustments and shifts in our attitude. In *The Brain that Changes Itself* by Doidge (2007), there are several examples of how the use of the imagination stimulates changes in the brain. For instance, groups of normal subjects were divided into subgroups, with some given actual physical tasks and some imagining the same tasks. The results in several documented experiments showed time and again that those who used their imagination and practiced something only in their mind actually improved their muscle content and accomplished playing an instrument or increased their speed nearly as much as those who physically did the activity. While this research validates the fact that imagination can be neurologically transformative and is easily available to all of us, it does not guarantee that we will use it.

Imagination is also connected to play and has tremendous importance not only for the individual but for the development of culture, but that requires us to believe in its value, and to actively engage. Jung explained why we are indebted to the play of imagination:

> Every good idea and all creative work are the offspring of the imagination . . . The dynamic principle of fantasy is play, a characteristic also of the child and as such it appears inconsistent with the principle of serious work. But without this playing . . . no creative work has ever yet come to birth.
>
> (Jung 1921/1990, CW 6, p. 63)

With some women, a *pregnant imagination* can come about when they engage in the initiation process of pregnancy and are willing to play with the mystery of their condition; however, not all women are interested in this imaginal work despite the power of their condition (Swan-Foster, 2012). In contemporary Western culture, our habits and lifestyles do not generally incorporate the time or space for our imagination nor do those around us typically value such activities, so we are unmotivated, unpracticed, and lack confidence. Time in Jungian analysis or other forms of therapy offers a set time and space for imagination that is separate from daily life—it is the liminal ground where we are encouraged to locate our imagination. In Jungian art therapy there are distinct moments of motivation and courage that are required for a patient to reach for the art materials that await them. This requires a rejection of doubt and a willingness to be curious and make mistakes. Mostly, it's the strength to endure whatever comes to consciousness.

Cultivating a relationship with the *mundus imaginalis*, or the imaginative world, we uncover a biological and evolutionary need for creative reverie and "making special" (Dissanayake, 1988, p. 92). When we explore how art is a fundamental behavior tendency within cultures, we can see the role that it plays to honor special or extraordinary occasions by placing the object in a realm that is beyond the mundane daily life: "Making special implies intent and deliberateness . . . a specialness that without one's activity or regard would not exist" (Dissanayake, 1988, p. 95); it "recognizes [a] need to elaborate as well as shape, in certain circumstances to do more than is necessary, and to do this expressly to invoke an order different from the everyday" (Dissanayake, 1988, p. 96). With this in mind, Jungian art therapy uses art or dreams to amplify an emotional memory or experience and gives value to what the patient creates through "making special" the personal and universal psychological wisdom that is discovered through the reflective process, thus facilitating a new order to her daily life.

The process of making something sacred is another way of including the influence of the Self with its determined force to expand and stretch the ordinary condition of the ego. In addition, the Self offers the possibility for nourishment and healing, although this is not always guaranteed. When the Self is constellated in a patient, we enter a different "time zone." The psyche becomes organized around a center where consolidation and healing emerge. Our efforts are then focused on this purpose of constellating the Self while maintaining connection to the personal. When the ego enters into new territory the Self (transpersonal psyche) may join the creative process, and thereby encourages a collaboration and the spontaneous arrival of what is referred to as Self images and symbols. Jung valued this process of giving something vague and unknown more color and form so it becomes more knowable. If we listen deeply, we are in service to the life of these images.

For example, during pregnancy, a woman undergoes a physical expansion while psychologically she may feel the desire to stretch beyond her familiar territory. When she moves into a new imaginal landscape, her artwork expresses what was once unknown; the image expresses *mysterious tremendum*, or the numinous[2] that reaches beyond the personal emotional process. Similarly, our affect, felt by all our senses, brings us into contact with archetypal images that nourish us, like a bucket over a well or a cauldron over a fire. The images provide a spatial and visual experience of the imaginal—a psychological place where we courageously wait, stirring our thoughts, our feelings, and mixing our intuitions with real-life events until something new takes shape.

Jung used the German word *betrachten*, which means "making something pregnant by giving it your attention" (as cited in Chodorow, 1997, p. 7) so that consciousness is created by breathing life into an image or symbol. The image of pregnancy refers to the container of the uterus, or the alchemical *vas*, for imaginal incubation. Jung's notion of *betrachten* gave value to the imaginal process through engagement and amplification, which acknowledges the value of metaphor within the imagination. In Jungian art therapy, we make something extraordinary by turning our gaze inward to our emotions, thoughts, or dreams, and outward towards the materials and the images that are speaking through our hands onto the paper—both an inner and an outer process that constellates a natural tension of opposites. Using the metaphor of cooking, we value a process that opens and softens consciousness so the potential space of the imaginal can cook up possibilities into a flavorful and digestible form.

History of Imagination

Imagination and its relationship to the creative unconscious have a long and intricate history that travels far and wide beyond the scope of this book. However, a brief summary is worthwhile for those of us who are unfamiliar with the concept. The historic roots of imagination ebb and flow with a variation of hypnotism that dates back to Egyptian times. Imagination was of particular interest to philosophers and physicians during the Renaissance period and this laid the groundwork for later periods of imagination. An important source of the first dynamic psychiatry was an old concept of imagination—*imaginatio*—a term that described the power of the mind in a much broader way than we might consider today. *Imaginatio* was regularly used in the early days of psychology and included the idea of suggestions and autosuggestions (Ellenberger, 1970, pp. 111–112). At that time, imagination was considered a contagion that could lead to a range of diseases, emotional and mental disorders, stigmata, change of sex, and even death (p. 112), and yet imagination was also a way to cure these ailments. In other words, *imaginatio* was considered both a poison and a cure.

In 1875 William James used automatic writing as a scientific procedure in his psychology course at Harvard University. The fascination with these phenomena, prior to the naming of the unconscious by Freud, brought about not just a common interest, but a flood of curiosity about the medium who could "gaze" and access information, which might suggest some of the precursory elements of transference and countertransference.[3] Many researchers of these early days of psychology were deeply curious about the suggestibility and the dissociability of the mind. In the 1880s, "the 'Society for Psychical Research' came to the conclusion that these methods, much like that of automatic writing, were a means for detecting material in the minds of their patients" (Ellenberger, 1970, p. 121), further validating the role of the imagination and hypnotic language used by Charcot, Janet, and Flournoy (pre-eminent European psychologists).

Two important factors from the collective contributed to Jung's use of imagination: the occult and Romanticism.[4] Jung was born, raised, and educated in this *ethos* of occult fortune telling and hypnosis as his mother and female cousins held séances, and his early psychological research focused on occult phenomena. In addition, the tension between an individual's true nature and the demands of the industrial advances of the time and the demands of the collective were continuous themes in analytical psychology and in Jung's own personal explorations. For Jung, the imagination became both a method and a solution when confronted with unconscious material.

Imagination and Symbolic Thinking

Creating space and time where we are free to use our imagination shapes the possibility for symbolic thinking to arise. A softened state of consciousness emerges where the *imaginal* gives birth to associations and images, which eventually serve as symbols. The essence of symbolic think-ing is that we suspend our directed thinking and harsh conscious attitudes, soften the ego, and consider daily incidents and concrete events with a mindful imagination. Under these conditions, images and symbols eventu-ally emerge. We know, for example, that the snake is a rich chthonic[5] image with many references that extend across cultures. Through amplifi-cation, we can make the symbol larger and more visible by associating it to other mythic images of the snake, such as the story of Adam and Eve, Kundalini yoga, or Norse myths. We can also keep it close and specific to the personal until the psyche is ready for more transpersonal associations.

Symbolic Thinking: A Developmental Process

Imagination is thought to have its beginnings in pre-symbolic sensory experiences of infancy that relate to the ability to perceive, desire, and reject, but imagination is first observed and actively expressed in childhood, particularly in preschool, as a type of thought that is developed through the child's creative explorations. Winnicott (1971) explores how symbolic thinking evolves out of play, stimulating both excitement and precarious moments related to arousal and regulation. Symbolic thinking is the ability to think about things that are not rationally present in an imaginative, enigmatic, and magical way, and to give objects different roles or meaning for the momentary play process. Jung's essay "The Psychology of the Child Archetype" integrates both the real and imaginal child that symbolizes the creative and divine potentials within all of us:

> The "child" is born out of the womb of the unconscious, begotten out of the depths of human nature, or rather out of living Nature herself. It is a personification of vital forces quite outside the limited range of our conscious mind . . . a wholeness which embraces the very depths of Nature. It represents the strongest, the most ineluctable urge in every being, namely the urge to realize itself.
>
> (Jung, 1949/1990, CW 9i, p. 170)

A symbolic image is typically healing, first because of our attitude towards it—if we take it seriously. We might imagine the image to be like a battery that transforms psychic energy within the psyche and evokes the totality of the archetype. Images are the bridges that both express the motivation of our instincts and tie our emotions into our experiences. The dissociation can be cut through or undone and replaced by integration and a sense of wholeness. But first, our emotions are felt by way of accessing the images and the symbols, which thaw those areas of the psyche that had once remained frozen in the unconscious. Jung considered all unconscious material potentially symbolic because it had the capability to compensate for the ego's view of the world. Schaverien (1992) clarified that the picture is not just a projection from the inside to the outside (projection and introjection of shadow are part of the dynamic process), but the image grows more valuable than the symptom through the wrestling of emotions:

> It is the means through which the subjective and objective nature of the patient's experience is mediated . . . the picture is no mere handmaiden in the service of psychotherapy . . . it is a formative element in the establishment of a conscious attitude to the contents of the unconscious mind.
>
> (pp. 11–12)

While the language of the unconscious can be difficult to understand, it is a language we learn over time by playing with words, images, and dream content from our unconscious, and by drawing from symbolic references that aid in our orientation. Sometimes we may feel as if we are learning another language—and indeed we are because the unconscious speaks through each person in very personal ways, giving us the opportunity to more fully realize ourselves, our whole self, through the symbolizing activity. A "divine child" attitude towards the world around us through creativity, if developed during childhood, remains an ever-ready resource and capacity that can be drawn upon to find meaning and reconnect with our soul's purpose. Winnicott (1971) asked that every therapist

> allow for the patient's capacity to play, that is, to be creative in the analytic work. The patient's creativity can be only too easily stolen by a therapist who knows too much. It does not really matter, of course, how much the therapist knows.
>
> (p. 57)

What matters most in Jungian art therapy is that the therapist is an ally in the activity of creative discovery.

Productive Imagination

Like directed or productive thinking, Jung believed there was productive imagination. Post-Jungian and contemporary psychotherapy and psychoanalysis have produced a plethora of research from infant observation to early childhood developmental and attachment theories, and beyond, that verify how imagination, or *imaginatio*, has the capacity to heal broken connections and facilitate psyche/soma transformations. In fact, the imagination and the *mythopoetic*[6] nature of the unconscious is a tremendous healing factor when it comes to working with trauma; this has been recognized since the early days of psychiatry (Ellenberger, 1970, p. 150) and continues to endure time and through new theoretical applications.

Although he lacked the ability to verify his ideas, Jung was incredibly prescient when he prioritized the energy of imagination as a healing factor within the psyche, especially when he saw how symbolic thinking provided tangible resources through images that carried a meaningful life force. We now know that imagination is key in facilitating the energy within the brain to redirect neural pathways, repair traumatic memories, and heal ruptures within relationships. Moreover, imagination can at times soothe the overstimulated autonomic/sympathetic nervous system, and plenty of research verifies this fact. Some images compensate for an overactive mind through grounding or calming the psyche, or images stimulate a hypo-aroused state to take some action. Not only does imagination offer a bridge between the conscious and unconscious aspects of the psyche, but it is a living conduit between our existential aloneness and the connection with all that has purpose and meaning.

Hence, as Jungian art therapists we push and advocate for a dedicated trust in the noetic imaginal world as a source of purposive knowing that can be leaned into as a source of deeper understanding, renewal, and transcendence. Even when our imagination is overactive and flips into an opposite state of anxiety or dark imagination, the work of Jungian art therapy can introduce form to the discomfort by tethering the wild and destructive images to a proverbial rock or post and then bring them into our daily relational experience as Ellen did with her images, shown in Figures 6.1 and 6.2.

Without a connection to our imagination, we may feel adrift—lost not just to ourselves and others, but also to our soul. We may feel ill-prepared to engage with and speak about the deep meaning that is utterly alive in every moment and has a discrete knowing. Jung, in the early pages of *The Red Book*, described how many of us might feel during challenging times:

> My soul, where are you? Do you hear me? I speak, I call you—are you there? I have returned, I am here again. I have shaken the dust of all the lands from my feet, and I have come to you, I am with you. After long years of long wandering, I have come to you again.
>
> (Jung, 2009, p. 127)

His heartfelt words express how we can feel far from the shore, lost from our source of imaginal knowing, caught between conscious and unconscious forces.

Jungian Art Therapy: Ellen's Story

Ellen's long series of paintings entitled "Ridgeline" (Figures 6.1 and 6.2) describe her desperate moments of terror and abandonment, and loss of

Figure 6.1 Ridgeline #1

Figure 6.2 Ridgeline #2

ego consciousness. Her images were associated with feelings of being alone and overwhelmed, and when she got "caught" here Ellen knew she was vulnerable to the wildness of her psyche until we could tether her to something meaningful. The different formal qualities, (space, lines, colors) of the ridgeline pictures had slight variations that depicted the changing climate of her emotions.

Destructive Imagination

Sometimes we talk about being bored when we lack imagination. If we wait long enough, a spark may lead to something new. Creative people often have an over-active imagination that is expansive but can sometimes turn anxious and dark. When an overdriving *will* dominates everything in its tracks, then imagination is blocked and we are grabbed by a fantasy that won't let us free. We may feel locked down and cold. We might describe feeling depleted, dull, dim, or even dead. Metaphorically, the hearth is stone cold, or there is no water in the deep dark well.

Sometimes these dark places lead us to a new imagination, but that requires two types of thinking, alongside differentiating what is productive and what is destructive. In extreme cases, a destructive imagination leads us into traps and the ego is completely lost, so the path can be tricky. For instance, Ellen would sometimes get hooked by a particularly alluring aspect of her psyche that was inchoate. The fantasy could take her down a certain path where she ended up telling herself she was a bad person. This is the shadow side of imagination—it is an example of fantasy. When Ellen lost her spontaneity of thought, she was subjugated by a splinter psyche (complex); her ego was destabilized and she lost her ability to relate well to herself and others. In very difficult times, she could fall into feeling isolated, futile, and dread her future. The best parts of who she was and wanted to be were hijacked and she lost her way.

Some think that Jung's assessment regarding the powerful destructive forces that have played out in various cultural climates missed something vitally important. Therefore, Jung's *mythopoetic* explanation for these particular forces has not always fully satisfied those who follow Jung's model. For instance, Kalsched (2013) pointed out that because Jung attributed destructive and evil forces of archetypal proportions to the unconscious, he overlooked what we now know occurs within a developing psyche to protect against early relational trauma. A brilliant but destructive formation of defenses and splits within the psyche takes place so that we can survive perilous events in our lives. When there should be the natural development of aggression, it is instead suppressed and thwarted, and turned actively against the person within a complicated self-care system (Kalsched, 1996). Furthermore, Jung's explanation of the role of evil aggression as a natural process of destructive forces within the unconscious that require consciousness is now clinically unsatisfactory and limited today based on the accumulated evidence for defenses and complexes that develop during infancy and childhood (West, 2016).

Jungian art therapists cannot assume that the destructiveness of the psyche simply ebbs and flows as expressed through the creative process. This is too idealistic and we miss important factors that are deeply entrenched within the psyche for some people who experienced early relational trauma. According to Kalsched (2013), we must consider "the in-turned aggression of a *defensive process* [original emphasis] that inevitably threatens new life within the psyche after traumatic beginnings. In short . . . the post-traumatic psyche includes a *violent pathological (anti-life)* [original emphasis] force that becomes a resistance to healing" (p. 83). The anti-life aspect of the psyche lives in all of us—but if we had traumatic beginnings, this structure is groomed and poised to rule the adult in onerous and vitriolic ways, shutting out any possibility for course correction or self-reflection, let alone imagination and empathy. What is missing is what is searched for and hopefully found during in-depth psychological work within a relational model that repairs what had been ruptured.

Schaverien (1992) observed that the expression of rage through art therapy may be helpful for some, but it can also tilt the mind into self-harming actions. If we presume that images are living, then they can equally influence the imaginal process in destructive and dark ways. We need to be wary of "archetypal explanations" of a bad seed as an explanation for violent behavior or internalized negative thoughts. The making/destroying/remaking process within art therapy may be just this, but it may denote early relational trauma and reflect the psychological carnage both intra- and inter-psychically that is autonomous and compulsive. Jungian art therapy is an appropriate model when working with relational trauma because the materials are resilient and the forms provide a container for the unspeakable to be expressed. A story can be told. With slow in-depth clinical work focused on personal material, the capacity to endure the layers of grief grows within what is sometimes a stormy but resilient therapeutic relationship.

Speaking the unimaginable through images and metaphors loosens the knot of inaccessible trauma memory, when otherwise we can feel vulnerable or caught in a vacuous void with sensations of uncontrolled leaking or falling into raw *imaginal* spaces. These sensations are typically related to unresolved trauma that has not yet found words, but remains in the somatic memory, and is sensory-dominated and pre-symbolic or from the psychoid realm. The complexes that protect us from this deeply autonomous place also persecute us by limiting our emotional connections and turning off the tap on psychic energy and productive imagination. As will be discussed in the next chapter, complexes may arrive unbidden through painting or clay processes, especially when a potentially healing noetic imagination is faced with what may be a second terrifying opportunity of coming into being and living a full life.

What all this suggests is that while analytical psychology builds itself on cultivating the imagination and relying on the healing function of a symbol, it is not always a straightforward process when we are faced with issues associated with early relational trauma and violent pathological forces that block the relational aspect of the work and destabilize the ego. Jung's model prioritized the relationship within the therapeutic work and the incredible healing capacity that arises from shared images and symbols. The wounded healer is an image that is associated with Jung's approach. It imagines a process of mutual transformation, which allows the analytic couple to enter into the early childhood and relational traumas and find the path out together (Sedgwick, 1994). The work is not singular, but a joint enterprise. As Jung determined from his Burghölzli days, the thera-peutic relationship provides the essential emotional glue for psychic repair and healing.

Jungian Art Therapy: Carol's Story

Carol worked in a male-dominant environment and when she became more visibly pregnant for the first time, she felt increasingly abandoned by her work community. She felt conspicuous. However, Carol wanted to take notice of what was happening to her as she realized this might be her only pregnancy. In the past, she had identified with the masculine and sacrificed her feminine needs for her professional work. Carol's father was overbearing and her mother had died. Like a fairy tale, the mother or feminine was deficient in Carol's life. She often sought emotional support from her husband, but she was not confident that he could provide this while she was pregnant.

Carol was pregnant and wanted to explore the idea of femininity that had become visible to her through her changing body. She said, "I guess all these people (men) in my life have seen me as another guy, and I have no one to share my feelings with." Working from a more ego perspective towards the unconscious in order to understand her femininity was problematic from the start as there was no guarantee that she would accept and integrate this new attitude. I gave her materials and she began to decorate a box. She took great care and worked on the outside of her box with feathers and a shell that resembled a unicorn (Figure 6.3).

A box is an intricate symbol. It is associated with both birth and death; it is a "container" that holds new objects within fixed limits, and yet as a transitional space, it also holds the old and death. Framed with sides as boundaries, it implies the body as a container of soul, organs, life, energy and waste, as well as feelings, thoughts, and somatic experiences. A pregnant woman's womb might be symbolized as a box that contains the child. In slang language, the woman's "box" is sometimes used to refer to her vagina, a place that holds the potential for many things including joy and passion, as well as pain and suffering. A box with a cover would suggest different things than a box without a cover. The opening of a box induces

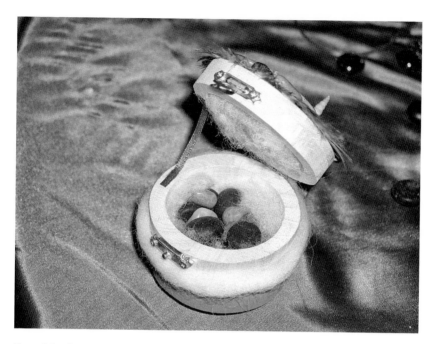

Figure 6.3 Carol's Box

emotions associated with anticipation, excitement, and perhaps fear or even dread. A common archetypal reference to a box is Pandora's box, referring to a container that holds both the terrible and joyful things in life. Another reference is the box of beauty that Psyche was instructed by Aphrodite to collect from Persephone, who lived in the underworld.

The metaphorical opening to Carol's box presented psychic representations: the shell suggested to Carol the unicorn, an expression of power such as when she found out she was pregnant and how miraculous it felt. And yet she also said, "It's such a 'girl thing' to feel," in a dismissive tone. She placed red stones inside the box to symbolize her femininity while the feathers reminded her of this transitory and mysterious relationship with her body. The feather and the unicorn also illustrated the opposing internal experience of the relationship between Carol's feelings of freedom and lightness versus the earthly internal quality of her feminine body, both of which were united by the box. Carol expressed these conflicts alongside words of pleasure, but her affect was flat.

Later, when Carol returned home with her baby boy (she had hoped for a girl), the box was one of the first things she saw as "a new person fully embodied by the energy of childbirth and meeting my new baby. I was on a high." In that heightened awareness may follow childbirth, she took the box outside and "smashed it and threw it away in the trash. I no longer had a need for it." She explained that destroying the box needed to be deliberate just as the making of it was deliberate. She stated, "I have my baby now and nothing is as beautiful." According to Carol, the box she made prior to childbirth could not compare; it had served its purpose.

As I listened to Carol tell me about how she had destroyed the box and casually threw it away, I noticed my countertransference reactions of shock, disbelief, and regret, even though she said it was deliberate. *Was I taking it personally?* I wondered. It was possible, but there was more to consider. While this destructive process sounded useful to her, and she had transferred her energy to her baby (which was positive), I was left with questions that we would never consider together as she was also terminating therapy to be transferred to a new office. If this was an case of a *restoration of the persona* then the following questions had their answers. Was she making an unconscious confession about her inability to integrate the depths of her feminine experience and respect the work of the unconscious? Perhaps she found it too difficult to face her shame and disappointment that she was unable to hold both sides of her process. She seemed captured by some powerful force. I realized that I had held a too-positive view for Carol; I had unrealistic hope that the overbearing and dominant complex could be drained by working creatively in Jungian art therapy. In fact, Carol's reaction may have been an unconscious confession about her destructive feelings towards what probably felt like excessive hope she could not bear. Carol thought her "deliberate" action was appropriate, and even necessary, when it was also possible that it was the insidious destructive act of an inflated aspect of her psyche that had just survived childbirth. Within this inflation was undoubtedly a self-care system that was destructive. In that inflation, she no longer needed the relationship, nor the reminder of her imagination; there was an *anti-life* force that spoke the pragmatic disregard for the gifts from the unconscious.

In contrast to Carol's unconscious destructive internalized aggression, the following example is of Lucinda, who had endured several life events that had changed, if not destroyed, parts of her life. Despite the hardships, she knew how to start over and actively worked to build and find ways to remain connected to her creative instinct and find meaning within the uncertainty. Illustrating the making/destroying/remaking pattern within the psyche, Lucinda's story draws from the imagination to work with the complexity of the unconscious forces.

Jungian Art Therapy: Lucinda's Story

Imagination relies on us to pay attention to what unfolds in the liminal *Kairos* time. The soul's rhythm and voice whispers more than a two-dimensional experience. We are captured by a deep emotion, a color, texture, or mood. For those who don't believe it, they have probably not been seized and carried by the imagination for fear of the journey, or of feeling silly or infantile. Below is an abbreviated account of how Lucinda's imagination and dream world caught her attention, and how she was able to draw support from its enigmatic expressions.

Lucinda, a 60-year-old woman, came to her session with the request that she use art materials. She worked quietly with water pencils, and while we were aware of the torrential rain outside, much of the session was silent. As is common when working deeply into an image, she found it challenging to talk with me while concentrating on the image that was emerging out of the red circular form on the page. Her use of water pencils brought forth a vibrant world of colors in the center of the page. When she did speak, she would stop, and focus on particular significant events from her daily life. The heart-wrenching losses that we knew had signposted her path to Jungian analysis were in the background; Lucinda had recently "returned" from a deep descent that had changed her life. She was confronting her emotions around what it meant to "belong" as she made her way into a new career while living as a single woman with grown children. At the end of her drawing Lucinda suddenly added a few strong black marks that contrasted the soft rhythmic unfolding of bright colors. The marks carried the energy of a deliberate statement—a punctuation of clarity and force.

We set the image at some distance. This space allowed a quiet moment of adjustment—a time when the relationship to the image shifted as the image took on its own separateness. With the piece between us we wondered about the imaginal world and reflected on the process, how she felt in her body, what she imagined. We appreciated the colors, the space, and the intensity. Knowing her religious background, I wondered if the black was a cross—it had been an image of her past that described the suffering, but Lucinda rightly said that, no, the black was more like a sword, cutting through the soothing maternal feeling of the image. "It felt sharp and strong."

Jung encouraged the analyst to follow the dreamer's interpretation, and Lucinda's perspective on her image was correct. She was closest to her unconscious and she needed my interest to follow her imagination. We considered the image of the sword, its qualities and feel and its capacity for discrimination, power, and knowledge. She noted that her marks were forceful, "cutting through" something. "There is some kind of conflict going on," she said. Rather than being immobilized by the suffering, it appeared that the unconscious was giving Lucinda the energy for action. We remembered the alchemical image at the start of her analysis—the blacksmith and the tempering of the heart (Swan-Foster, 2016). Now there was a sword. Lucinda made an association to the bull that had rushed into her kitchen in a dream; her daily active imagination was the only way to calm the bull and her somatic dysregulation. She noted the bull had been calmed; he no longer carried worrisome energy. Jung might say as a symbol, the bull had fallen into the unconscious so that a new, more appropriate form could be found for that psychic energy. Was it the sword? Perhaps there were elements that could have been interpreted, but it wasn't necessary. We held the faith that the "truth" was being told in its own timing.

And so we sat in the liminal, "betwixt and between" place with the image before us, with curiosity and wonder, open to potential. Lucinda had wrestled with plenty of complexes and had made sacrifices in her life that forced her to take her "individuation under her feet" (Ruff, 1988). "What is next?" she wondered. In my mind I wondered if this was a foreshadowing image of another confrontation with the unconscious, or if in the battle of slicing through negative thoughts or dissociations she would feel more integrated. For Lucinda, there was much to consider around a life that had died while a new life was forming. Was this image offering a symbolic sharper tool for her path forward? The unconscious was making a reference to changes in our therapeutic relationship, which is natural as analysands transform and step into living their lives.

Lucinda took her picture with her. I reminded her to continue working with it using active imagination, a method Jung encouraged to "make the image pregnant," to vivify the image with breath and imagination. In essence, we need to enliven the image with love as Hillman (1977) reminded us, "We might equally call the unfathomable depth in the image, love, or at least say we cannot get to the soul of the image without love for the image" (p. 81).

When Lucinda left my office she passed a downspout gushing with water and placed the picture under the water. The alchemical "washing" of her work brought further illumination once it dried (Figure 6.4). Later she said: "It revealed itself as a fairy tale land with castle, swords, mystery. I only got to the soul of the image by loving (devoting) myself to it!"

Then Lucinda had the following dream: A brief account follows:

> We were to do a ritual to restore the king to his position of faith. He looks to me to start it. I begin to sing. I find new words, new melody. A presence envelops us. The king says, "Oh yes, I remember you're making me homesick—singing makes us remember our purpose, our inheritance, and our calling."

Figure 6.4   Cosmic Conflict

For several sessions, Lucinda and I mulled on its energy, its images, and its impact on her imagination and her daily life. It lived inside her with its mood and energy; her complexes were stirred. Its elements and structure were psychologically useful, but if we made it concrete, too related to daily life, we suffocated its imaginal breath. There was a fine balance where Lucinda needed to live with her soul images in order to hear the music of her psyche. What she knew was her kingdom had lost its faith and she was being asked to collaborate with the king. In doing so, she found the music of her soul, perhaps a new language of the Self, that reconnected her to the mysterious process of renewal within her psyche. When Lucinda took the action to make a spontaneous image in her session (ego), this brought forth from her soul a fairy tale about the inner kingdom and its cosmic conflicts (unconscious material). The king had requested her participation, which she gave through song, love, and devotion. There was an inner story that was unfolding and becoming conscious. Shortly after this, Lucinda was thumbing through her journals and found a poem; she realized the "lost kingdom" had been present for a while. A portion of the poem is recounted:

> You dared not stay-away death's pain
> As it wrestled from my gripping hold
> My kingdom, my trophies, my reigning self
> My old world order and castle walls

Lucinda's psychological discoveries did not come from clinical interpretations or linear thoughts alone, but rather through a synthetic method of circumambulating the painful reservoir found within the images. A stitching together through our joint imaginations led her to be eventually awakened to the creative and challenging internal dynamics that were both personal and archetypal in nature. Together we delighted in the mystery of the symbolic unfolding of her images. Sometimes these ineffable moments occur unexpectedly and we learn to hold them lovingly and loosely like feathers in the wind. Lucinda had been called once more by the unconscious and she had responded with curiosity, love, and devotion. When we love our fate (*amor fati*) our attitude opens the door wide to welcome the imaginal realm of the soul and its most difficult stories. Lucinda reminds us that when we sit at the table of imagination, we may suffer the sorrow and the pain, but we also find deep satisfaction; each time we circle around and return to this place, we are fed a thousand times over, with the *numinous* food of wholeness.

Endnotes

1. *Noetic* is derived from the Greek word *noesis* that refers to a direct knowing or inner wisdom based on experience or subjective under-standing—through this direct wisdom we come into direct relationship with our soul.

2. In 1923 Rudolf Otto published the book *The Idea of the Holy* in which he wrote about the *mysterious tremendum* and the numinous aspect within human experience. He coined the term *numinous*.

3. Researchers had noticed that they became aware of the feelings of their patients, and Freud had developed the terms *transference* and *counter-transference* to describe this phenomenon. At this time many thought this phenomenon was used by psychics and mediums; and indeed, some of Jung's ideas have roots here. Today there is a whole area of clinical work focused on the topic of transference/countertransference.

4. This period, which occurred around the mid-1800s in Europe, was a reaction to the industrialization and the rational thinking of the Enlightenment period.

5. Jung often used the term *chthonic* in his description of symbols and images; it is a term describing or relating to forms or things from the underworld, the hidden, the dark, and unknown that we may not consciously understand. For example, in Greek mythology, Hades and Persephone are examples of chthonic gods from the underworld, and Hecate is an underworld psychopomp, able to travel to the depths and back. All are chthonic gods.

6. The term *mythopoetic* means related to myth and to myth making; it is often used in a modern psychological context around creating of understanding one's own personal myth.

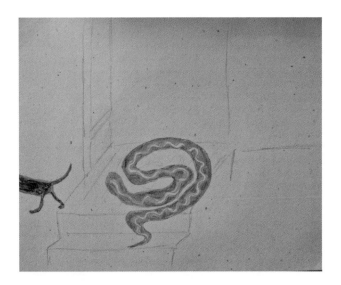

Figure 9.1   Snake and Cat Dream

Figure 9.2   Castle

Figure 9.3   Bridge #1

Figure 9.4   Bridge #2

Figure 9.5 Bridge #3

Figure 9.6 Bridge #4

Figure 9.7 Bridge #5

Figure 9.8 Snake Lady

Figure 9.9 Mandala

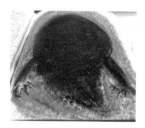

Figure 9.10 Mole

Figure 9.11 New Boy Animus

Figure 10.1   Tiger Tails

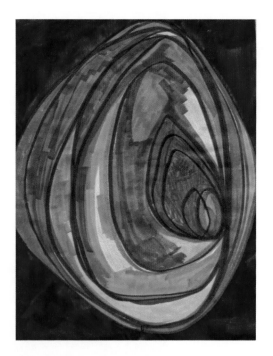

Figure 10.2   Layered Mandala

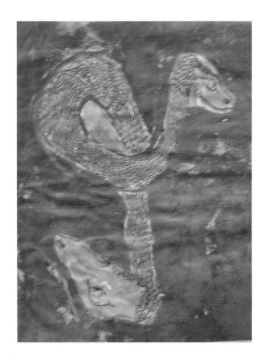

Figure 10.3 Snake

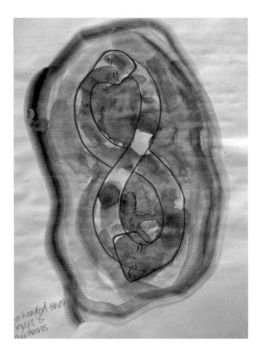

Figure 10.4 Snake Infinity

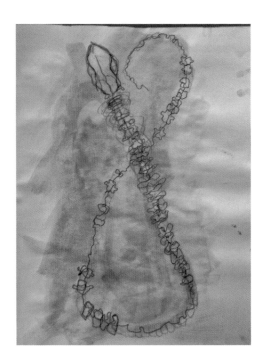

Figure 10.5 Snake Skeleton

Figure 10.6 Snake Eye

CHAPTER 7

Complex Theory

The Material for Transformation

Complexes are defined as a collection of autonomous associations, images, ideas, or memories that cluster around an archetypal core of meaning held together by specific emotional tones. Through images, the complexes make themselves visible. The Jungian analyst Patricia Vesey-McGrew (2010) drew from the myth of Sisyphus to illustrate the phenomenological relationship of working with our complexes. In the myth, the King of Corinth tempted fate with Zeus by thinking that he could outwit the god, but was banished to Hades, where he spent the rest of his days pushing a massive rock up a hill only to have it roll back down again—this image of a repeating pattern amplifies the autonomous complexes that are expressions of our personality and stem from our personal history.

The Basic Nature of a Complex

The complex has three distinct qualities for Jungian art therapy: it is visible through an image, it is autonomous, and it illustrates the multiplicity of the psyche. These three areas will be discussed in greater depth as we go along.

Image

A complex is made up of memories, somatic reactions, emotions or affect, and ideas, all of which are expressed through an image, which is something we apprehend or perceive. The complex can be made visible through anything from a picture to a dream, a vision, or a visual somatic reaction like blushing or heart palpitations.

Autonomous

Second, complexes are autonomous. Jung's emphasis on complexes was that they express the psychic energy associated with emotion and that they come over us, often unbidden, which makes the dominant nature of the complex autonomous and unconscious. We are often unaware when we are in a complex because it remains unconscious until someone points it out to us. Sometimes we may recognize an internal shift or mood. A complex is separate from the ego, and unless the ego is able to entertain its presence, the splinter psyche remains unknown. In contrast to other psychological models, Perry (1970) made an important distinction in his explanation of Jung's model of complexes, which is that Jung placed the emotions (complexes) as the autonomous function of the unconscious, not the ego, as is the case with other theoretical models. In other words, emotions arrive unbidden and they happen *to the ego from the unconscious* rather than emotions being the function of an ego zone that is concerned with adaptation (Perry, 1970, p. 1), which is a significant theoretical difference. Jung described the autonomous nature of the complex this way:

> It is the image of a certain psychic situation which is strongly accentu-ated emotionally and is, moreover, incompatible with the habitual attitude of consciousness. This image has a powerful inner coherence, it has its own wholeness and, in addition, a relatively high degree of autonomy, so that it is subject to the control of the conscious mind to only a limited extent, and therefore behaves like an animated foreign body in the sphere of consciousness. The complex can usually be sup-pressed with an effort of will, but not argued out of existence, and at the first suitable opportunity it reappears in all its original strength.
>
> (1934/1972, CW 8, p. 96)

This brings us to the third aspect of complexes, which is when we attempt to suppress them.

Multiplicity and Splitting

As we know, Jung saw the psyche as dissociative with an innate predisposi-tion towards multiplicity, so he recognized the natural tendency of the psyche to split. Splitting arises primarily because the conscious mind (ego) rejects the unconscious complex material. We all do this at different points in our life. The contents remain in the personal shadow. They are unconscious. The split-off contents are usually caused by a series of early experiences, a particular event, or the immediate conditions demand that the psyche compartmentalizes (for instance, a surgeon has to work on someone with a gunshot wound, or rescue workers have to work quickly in an emergency). These three aspects of the complex help us understand how Jung defined the presence of a complex as well as their overall influence on the psyche.

Without a doubt, complexes impact our sense of reality and interfere with the behaviors, illusions, and thoughts of the ego, and, because of their valence,[1] they bring about discomfort and suffering internally and within our relationships. Jung reminded us that when complexes interfere with the goals and intentions of the ego, what is "far more important theoretically, is that complexes *have us*" (Jung, 1934/1972, CW 8, p. 96). In the work of freeing itself from the overpowering energy of the complex, the ego is tempered like the metal of a sword and an assimilation of the complex may occur that makes the ego more supple. If dissociative splitting is extreme, the personality has pathological qualities because the psyche has no conscious center, no ego memory or identity, amidst the dissociation and multiplicity. Then the personality lacks the unity that is supplied by the conscious memory and identity of the ego as the center of consciousness.

The word *constellate* is a Jungian term describing the activation of a complex. As the energy around very specific content gains a charge, it readies for action in response to an external situation. The constellation of a complex is noted through *specific complex-indicators*, which are unique to that complex for that specific individual. The personal component of the complex is associated with personal memories, perceptions, and personal experience.

When we verify the stimuli that *constellate a complex*, the images may be translated into visual maps in Jungian art therapy. This process expresses, documents, and offers reflection regarding our complexes. We may temporarily subdue complexes, through meditation or relaxation techniques for instance, but there is no guarantee that we will gain control over them. Certainly, we aim to gain awareness and increase our consciousness, but because we are human, our consciousness may fail us. Jungian art therapy supports us to become less reactive or less constellated around a particular situation because the energy of the complex is externalized into a concrete form. If we block the natural flow of psychic energy, this may lead to detrimental effects that are expressed unconsciously, which is why Jung's model emphasizes a relational approach towards our complexes, despite the suffering, rather than trying to repress or deny their existence.

Jung determined that our individuation process is fueled by complexes; he often noted in his writing that we need complexes for our psychological growth and development as they push for consciousness. In a metaphorical sense, working with our complexes is like working with the gods— imbedded in our experience of them they reveal a particular purpose. Referring to overpowering emotions that usurp control over himself as "God," Jung said: "This is the name by which I designate all things which cross my willful path violently and recklessly, all things which upset my subjective views, plans, and intentions and change the course of my life for better or worse" (Jung, 1953/1975, p. 525). Besides detrimental effects, shutting off to the psychic energy means we limit access to a larger creative and transpersonal aspect of our psyche which includes the potential for spontaneity and vitality. Our psyche is like a potato sack—each complex has substance, weight, and potential energy; if we learn to "cook" with them, our personality is expanded by the impact they have upon us.

The Structure of the Complex

As the foundation of analytical psychology, complexes "are more like the construction workers who give visible and comprehensible shape to underlying archetypal blueprints. It is through the complexes that we manage to approach the unconscious without being overwhelmed and engulfed by it" (Shalit, 2002, p. 8). Sometimes our complexes are described by images or figures in our dreams such as construction workers, truck drivers, or plumbers who are literally making changes in our psyche.

Complexes are perceived as either positive or negative depending upon the attitude of the ego towards the unconscious content. For example, we all have images of our mother, or perhaps the absence of mother. However, Jung also reminds us that complexes can be stubbornly unavailable when we wish to constellate them. If we want to love someone, no matter how hard we try, it may not be possible to bring about the right complex, or emotional tone, to make that happen.

Originally it was believed that a complex formed out of a traumatic event, but we now know that they also form out of repetitive emotional interactions that build memories where early relational attunement between the subject and object was lacking, intermittent, or occasionally inconsistent. As we might expect, these complexes often have ties to infancy and early childhood (West, 2016). Later events then constellate specific complex indicators that help us better understand earlier events. When an emotional repair occurs while working on our complexes within a mutual process that is respectful and non-shaming, such as a relational psychotherapy, the charge of the complex may decrease enough that we gain reflection and can begin to assimilate some of the psychic energy that the ego had rejected or split off into the shadow.

Cluster of Complexes

One reason that complexes are difficult to discern is because they can have overlapping patterns, and rise to consciousness not as a single complex but as several complexes at once, forming around specific memories, ideas, or particular affects. The ego responds or reacts to a complex to preserve its view or agenda of consciousness, which is considered an ego complex, or a complex that is ego-aligned. The clustered complexes tend to gather around primary relationships and life events such as mother, father, sister, brother, power, anxiety, love, incest, addiction, and death. These autonomous clusters live a life beyond the ego's sphere of influence and can express themselves through strong reactions to particular family members or topics such as love or death.

Jung found that groupings had particular themes associated with the disturbance of the reactive complex, and that the themes were associated to a memory or event. For example, an abandonment complex coupled with a brother complex might refer to an experience of a brother leaving his younger sibling behind at the bottom of a snowy hill. The emotional experience carries a feeling-toned image that is useful for deeper investigations to facilitate Jungian art therapy. Over time the complex might manifest as "missing out" or "resenting or not trusting men." As a child, Rosemary's older brother left her behind in the deep snow. Her coquettish behavior became a way for her to remain connected to men in her life who had power and who she hoped would take care of her. Exploring these emotions through personal images, Rosemary discovered a cluster of complexes. Sometimes seeing the content of the memory can uncover the connections and the layers beneath the conscious psyche. Many Jungian analysts have theorized that through the genetics of the mother/father complexes, we inherit predispositions to specific complexes that we are not conscious of reenacting. The premise for this partially stems from the early WAE research with families at the Burghölzli where it was discovered that patterns were passed between mothers and daughters, for instance.[2]

When Jung theorized the *nuclear element* of a complex, he meant the unpredictability and autonomous patterned quality that he later referred to as the archetypal core. Although the archetype is more commonly referenced in popular culture, this does not mean that archetypal images are the only concern of analytical psychology. On the contrary, Jung thought that the first and usually preponderant attention in therapy is to depotentiate the "complexes particularly those contents derived from personal experience, infancy and childhood" (Perry, 1953, p. 133).

For instance, a mother complex is formed around the mother archetype as the nuclear element, and includes the projections and experiences of the personal mother. Perry expanded on Jung's ideas by explaining that complexes are bipolar (two poles); the entire psyche is structured not only in complexes, but they are arranged in bipolar systems of emotion that require the interplay of two complexes. He also noted that habitual emotions belong to habitual pairs of complexes (Perry, 1970, p. 9). In this pair arrangement, one pole is ego-aligned, or ego-syntonic, while the other pole is projected onto an external object and is unaligned from the ego, or is ego-dystonic. This bipolar nature can oscillate between the two sides or remain one-sided as an ego-aligned side of the complex without gaining any consciousness about the presence of constellated complexes. The analysand may continuously refuse to consider complexes as part of the psyche, but by maintaining a firm identity that disavows this part, the darker the unseen and unacknowledged fragments of the personality become (Vesey-McGrew, 2010, p. 17).

Complexes as Expression of Energy

For Jung, the emotional energy is bound into the image of a complex. Every emotionally charged situation or event has energy and contains the potential to form a complex—these can be everyday situations or major traumatic events. Complexes either cause a blockage of consciousness or they produce an expansion of consciousness, depending on the ego's attitude towards the constellating event.

Based on the formal idea that energy carries a charge, the emotional variations depend upon the magnitude of this charge; the charge can be slight (where we might feel a flush or somatic tingle) and we remain conscious, or the energy is powerful enough to push us along the emotional spectrum to dissociation. The extreme is that the complex is so autonomous that consciousness is destabilized.

In Jungian art therapy, when individuals draw or paint their emotions, the object of the charge in a complex is made visible and documents the condition within the psyche. The ego may protect against or deny the unconscious material or reflect on the charge so as to formulate it into an image that has meaning. Making an image can dissipate the charge. It is as if the act of using our hands to create an image related to the complex may drain the energy, like draining a battery, so that while in the midst of formulation, the ego regains consciousness and can access reflection—this is a time when both directed and non-directed thinking are used.

Imagination uncovers specific personal images that anchor and regulate psychic energy, or drain the complex, so the ego can resurface. For instance, Ellen might experience swirling when she feels overwhelmed. She uses her sketchbook to describe her dizziness and this anchors the swirling, a word that personalizes what she had come to understand as dissociation. When complexes become charged and constellated, the shadow content is revealed through unbidden slips of the tongue or annoying feelings, thoughts, or reactions. If we are willing to look at our failure, we may gain consciousness. In Jungian psychology, we may say "I am in a complex," but when we are in a complex we may also forget to use such resources as self-reflection or sketchbooks.

Complexes, Emotions, and Images

Hillman reiterated Jung's ideas on the complex when he said emotions are conceived under two aspects: *energetic force* (referring to psychic energy as discussed earlier) and the *image* (symbolic paradigm) (Hillman, 1960/1997, p. 61). These two aspects are seen in the following example.

Jungian Art Therapy: Tina's Story

Figure 7.1 was drawn by Tina, a 60-year-old woman who was going through a divorce. The day she discovered the details of her husband's affair, she was raw with emotion. I handed her the board with paper and she began with markers. The intense colors fit the intensity of her affect and offered both space and structure. First, the shapes and colors filled the page with fast and hard movements. She was also crying and her face was flushed. These were complex indicators. Her picture found form into which her raw emotion flowed. This was the transcendent function at work within the psyche—attempting to uncover all that was within her.

Figure 7.1   Tina's Anger

While Tina drew, the raw affect began to drain out of the complexes. Once she finished and we set the drawing at a short distance, she could reflect. Using her imagination with the help of art materials stirred other parts of her brain and mind. As part of her discernment process, Tina then returned to the image and added words to fit with the pointy parts. In time, when less aroused, the symbolic nature of the image began to formulate for Tina. From our earlier work together, we knew that when she started to uncover her symbolic thinking, she might not necessarily feel better, but what she discovered from her complexes was deeply satisfying.

Tina said, "This looks like a jaw with teeth. The roots are dark, but they are green, and there is redness—maybe an infection—ha, or maybe I am finally, at long-last, finding and feeling my aggression. This is progress." I wondered aloud about infection and inflammation—gums can become inflamed. She laughed and said, "I'm sure inflamed!" Now the image ignited some humor which allowed her to gain clarity and ownership of the visible inflamed state of aggression. The image and Tina's experience of being left also conjured up the Greek myth of Ariadne, who helped Theseus escape from the labyrinth after killing the minotaur, but was then abandoned by him on the island of Naxos after she fled with him. Tina's image may suggest an island in the sea of the unconscious. What became important for her was to explore the times she had been abandoned and then consider the bipolar aspect of how she might have played a role in abandoning either her husband or herself. Initially Tina could see only the ego-syntonic parts of the bipolar complex as she defended against her personal engagement and blamed her husband, but then she considered the possibility of an unconscious pattern that had been working inside her for many years. Perhaps her marriage failed partially because of her abandonment complex and how she was conflict-avoidant, often not speaking her true thoughts or feelings. In other words, she had resisted working with some of her complexes.

Complexes, Emotions, and the Body

Engaging with complexes is the psychological entrance into the mind/body connection, as we cannot have emotions without having somatic reactions. Although rarely known today, the psyche/soma interface was pivotal to Jung's psychology. Jung named this interface between mind and body the psychoid realm.[3] Because complexes are associated with physiological reactions, they are typically unpleasant and visible. The somatic reactions may come on suddenly. In his 1936 Tavistock Lecture, Jung (1936/1968/1989, CW 18) imagined the complex in a biological sense:

> It has its roots in the body and begins to pull at my nerves . . . A complex with its given tension or energy has the tendency to form a

little personality of itself. It has a sort of body, a certain amount of its own physiology. It can upset the stomach. It upsets the breathing, it disturbs the heart—in short, it behaves like a partial personality.

(pp. 71–72)

Jung's description probably sounds familiar to all of us, if we have any awareness of our body. Because complexes are felt throughout the autonomic nervous system, this is why body work is now often recommended alongside psychotherapy, as is some form of meditation practice. If someone is unable to settle, one image for depotentiating a complex is pulling the plug on a bathtub of water (representing psychic energy) and letting it drain out while we breathe and imagine our nervous system settling.

Jungian Art Therapy: Gia's Story

Gia was a successful 43-year-old woman who worked in the technology industry. She was a strong thinking type. She came to psychotherapy to address what had happened in an interview for a promotion:

Initially I felt pressure in my chest that rose to my face. I probably felt a heat sensation, and I couldn't respond. My mouth was dry. Unable to find words, I hesitated . . . I couldn't articulate a response. When I spoke, I regretted it. I forgot a simple detail and I felt some shame and embarrassment. I just felt worse inside. My boss asked if I wanted to take a break. When we returned, I was more myself. I still felt a bit nervous on the inside but I could think again. And I could breathe.

Had Gia been responding to Jung's stimulus words in the WAE, we could guess that her timed reaction would be high and her galvanic or physical reactions would verify several of the complex indicators by simply asking her about the interview. The complex indicators for Gia were initially somatic, but they also impacted her mind, thwarting her ego and her memory, so her creativity and imagination were blocked. The disturbances denoted the presence perhaps of an inferiority complex associated with her father (father complex), who had been demanding and critical. As "a daddy's girl" she had internalized the father as both powerful and critical. While Gia's boss was an authoritative man, he treated her with respect; yet his role still constellated her father complex that consisted of memories, her projections, and her own unconscious power shadow. Gia realized her job offered an opportunity to confront the autonomous reactions and rather than blaming herself or others for the complex's repetition compulsion, she could become conscious of and claim her own authority.

Jung's clinical knowledge pioneered how the body's expression of energy is intimately connected to the affect-laden material of the complex. While Hillman (1960/1997) amplified Jung's energic and symbolic connections, he also pointed out the importance of bodily location. For instance, is it the brain, the glands, the gut, or is it the muscular or skeletal system where there is psychic functioning and out of which the images arise? Where do bodily symptoms arise? Specific locations in the body may offer us new images. Jung's complex theory and his overall psychology beautifully supports art therapy with the various body-centered techniques such as the combination of Focusing with art therapy (Rappaport, 2009).

The Purpose of Complexes

Complexes have several purposes, but predominantly they challenge the dominant position of the ego to force change. According to Jung, the ego's resistance to change does not support the individual in the long run, but only keeps him rigidly adhered to dogmatic thoughts and expectations. With an emotional reaction from the unconscious, complexes have the potential to alter the attitude of the ego in both positive and negative ways. For instance, we may resist moving our aging parents, but this situation requires us to adapt and meet the challenge by doing what is morally and ethically right. If we wrestle with the tension that complexes constellate, we are doing our psychological work and we have a better chance to integrate shadow material and find purpose and symbolic meaning from what has crossed our path—whether it is through compensation or adaptation. Both ideas lead to individuation but from different directions.

What I mean by this is that as we engage with the collective we are adapting, and as we work with an inner personal journey we are discovering the compensatory unconscious material (individuation). Jung noted this was not an either/or process but one that is deeply intertwined: it's a process of moving back and forth between the internal and external demands of our life. What we know for certain is that an active complex puts our conscious ego state into feeling utter threat, of compulsive thinking and acting, if only for a moment, but it can be long enough to get us into trouble (Jung, 1934/1972, CW 8). What emerges are images that are specific to those memories and experiences in that moment, and that complex then demands our attention.

Progressive and Regressive Complexes

Complexes express both progressive and regressive psychic energy through their autonomous qualities. We are reminded that when a complex arises, it competes with the ego for available psychic energy. The energy of the ego is fueled so that it holds onto its position. This innate teleological essence of a complex is its pathological and shadowy manifestation, especially as it gathers and gains strength in the shadow (Shalit, 2002, p. 9). The progressive and regressive energy is illustrated by Margaret, a 40-year-old woman who suffered from major depression with bipolar features.

Figure 7.2 was a spontaneous drawing that gave light to her depression. As an image her drawing beautifully depicted a map of her psychic energy, which we followed over the several years of our work. It also pointed to areas of failure and defeat. The whole image is reminiscent of Sisyphus and the rock. Margaret's energy moved up and down the hill, from an extraverted more masculine-driven period followed by a depression. She oscillated between states of successfully adapting to the collective, but only temporarily, because then she would tumble back into depression where she would collapse, and retreat from the world. Along with the progressive and regressive flow of psychic energy, the image described the split within the psyche described by her as "success and failure" that preoccupied her. The directionality and placement of the drawing highlighted the opposing masculine/feminine principles (Abt, 2005).

Unfamiliar with Jungian psychology, Margaret described the green figure in the top left (masculine principle) corner as herself, revealing her over-identification with the masculine, like Carol in Chapter 6. The large red circle in the middle was her "balanced self," and the small black and blue circle in the bottom right corner (feminine principle) was what she called her "failed self." This tension revealed a pattern of an extraverted animus energy that enjoyed the world and determined her introverted

Figure 7.2 Margaret #1

feminine energy was failed and broken. She rejected the feminine principle despite her secret enjoyment of being in the darkness of her psyche—she saw it as weak and irrelevant. Shifting her focus in life to care for herself in the ways she longed for meant she would have to become "more selfish" and this was unacceptable to her.

When Margaret was diagnosed with terminal cancer, her images became more circular as she unconsciously searched for wholeness. With her illness, she could justify a bit more attention and care being given to her, but it was measurable and limited in dosages. In Figure 7.3, she worked with torn paper to describe the different complexes in her life. Margaret explained that the square was a place of totality, a place of centering. At the time she was attending a meditation class for cancer patients. The dragonfly wings that she had placed at the center of the image were about "vulnerability and magic" and her desire for "transformation." The two shapes on the right were joined with a pen design. She associated the smaller shape as herself and the larger shape as her mother. As she designed "the bridge between the two," she noted the relationship had changed. Since she had been sick, Margaret admitted that she now enjoyed the attention she received from her mother's visits despite her being overbearing.

The image of Sisyphus and the rock was an appropriate mythic blue-print for Margaret. Indeed, I too was sometimes pulled into the Sisyphean process. The image offered me a way to hold her material. Instead of a treatment plan, the myth guided me with images of the complexes associated with failure, hope, and patience. Using art materials did not

Figure 7.3   Margaret #2

guarantee that Margaret would be free of her complexes, nor would she be cured of her depression. I learned to allow her "predicament to penetrate" my own "repetitive rock-pushing" (Vesey-McGrew, 2010, p. 20) and I grappled with my own feelings of failure, frustration, anger, grief, and unrealistic hope, particularly when she couldn't. She and I tolerated the range of emotional reactions that we both wrestled associated with the difficult pattern to which she was bound (Vesey-McGrew, 2010). I learned not to hold too much hope, particularly as some of the autonomous natures of the complexes were unbeatable.

Complexes and Multiplicity

As discussed before, splitting is a natural occurrence within the psyche. Jung subscribed to the notion that the psyche is made up of many autonomous parts, or complexes. As mentioned before, Jung echoed Janet's use of "fixed ideas" and called complexes "splinter psyches" or "fragmentary personalities" that can be progressive or regressive depending upon their ability to be accepted by consciousness and integrated into the personality as facilitators of individuation while also finding an appropriate adaptation to the collective. Because of this fragmentation that naturally happens, Jung believed:

> [T]he so-called unity of consciousness is an illusion . . . We like to think that we are one; but we are not . . . We are not really masters in our house. We like to believe in our will-power and in our energy and in what we can do; but when it comes to a real show-down we find that we can do it only to a certain extent, because we are hampered by those little devils the complexes.
>
> (Jung, 1936/1968/1989, CW 18, pp. 72–73)

Jung's description is applicable for Margaret, who was severely hampered by not always living as the "master of her own house." Multiplicity was embraced by Jung, who did not view it as pathological in all situations. If we work analytically with the complexes through personification, we become familiar with their range and diversity and their potential to facilitate new consciousness.

Jungian Art Therapy: Olivia's Story

An image of the multiplicity within the psyche is illustrated by the clay figures (Figure 7.4) that represent the various internal "voices" that disrupted and irritated Olivia's consciousness. Each figure contained the energy of a particular complex. Creating the clay pieces helped her become more conscious of these complexes that could sneak up on her and suddenly derail her process. When visible they spoke more distinctly of such thoughts and behaviors (e.g. procrastination or criticism) that gripped

Figure 7.4 Olivia's Clay Figures

her. Olivia used them in creative and interactive ways to facilitate a new attitude towards her life. This is an example of how, as personal complexes, they act like servants or gods on our path of individuation.

Complexes and Trauma

Jung was well aware of the more clinically severe complexes—in fact, his psychology is a natural fit for contemporary trauma work, trauma recovery, or post-traumatic growth.[4] Because Jung's psychology looked towards the future and appreciated the possibilities within the psyche, an individual who has suffered from trauma and begins the inner investigations into the horrors of their life may eventually uncover a tremendous creative reserve waiting to be expressed. In other words, as Schweizer (2017) explained, "there is a far greater spirit that lives behind the darkness of the horror." When the psyche suffers and endures trauma, whether it is in early childhood, ongoing, long-term, or situational, the psyche finds ways to protect itself by forming splinter psyches. More extreme cases of complexes are found with Dissociative Identity Disorder (DID). The complexes behave like individual *siloes,* so autonomous and disconnected from each other that the ego lacks any conscious awareness about their influence for longer periods of time. For instance, someone goes shopping and does not remember the event. This is a severe dissociative disorder.

In some ways we have all suffered traumatic events; however, some individuals have extremely severe trauma histories that require a theoretical model that incorporates ideas on multiplicity and dissociation, which is not discussed in depth here. Oftentimes people will come to therapy and not realize that the multiplicity is running their life, although they may wonder why things are not going well or why they are unable to break certain patterns, suggesting the presence of a protective Self-care system (Kalsched, 1996; 2013).

Jung's conceptualization of complex theory was clinically prescient for the eventual understanding of trauma. It provided what was missing between the traumatic experience and how we react to those borderline states of mind (West, 2016). Some of the early clinical cases at the Burghölzli that were considered *dementia praecox* (*schizophrenic* or *psychotic*) might be viewed today as traumatic grief, early childhood trauma, complex trauma, DID, and/or post-traumatic stress. For instance, Jung told a story of an old woman who presented with catatonic behavior and dementia praecox. She had required a lot of special care, but one unique thing that Jung could never figure out was that she made odd hand gestures and no one understood why. After she had died, Jung learned that not only was she a shoemaker, but the man she had loved was one too. When he did not want to marry her she had gone insane and lived the rest of her life in the asylum (Jung, 1925/2012). When the psyche is unable to handle impingement or intrusion, it creates barriers of protection; these are complexes that act as protectors within the psyche. There are several stories where Jung's interest in the individual led to an open-minded observational process that embraced paradox and the opposites and sought symbolic meaning in distinct behaviors and language.

At the time, Jung was undaunted by the clinical aspect of trauma as he had encountered it on a regular basis. He also was unconcerned with managing *abreaction*,[5] and the highly charged affect that constellates the trauma complexes, but his primary therapeutic issue and question was how to integrate the dissociated parts (Jung, 1921/1928/1985). He explained that:

> A traumatic complex brings about dissociation of the psyche. The complex is not under the control of the will and for this reason it possesses the quality of psychic autonomy . . . Its autonomy consists in its power to manifest itself independently of the will and even in direct opposition to conscious tendencies: it forces itself tyrannically upon the conscious mind. The explosion of affect is a complete invasion of the individual, it pounces upon him like an enemy or a wild animal. I have frequently observed that the typical traumatic affect is represented in dreams as a wild and dangerous animal—a striking illustration of its autonomous nature when split off from consciousness.
>
> *(1921/1928/1985, CW 16, pp. 131–132)*

It is noteworthy that Jung had specific clinical ideas for psychotherapy that were first published in the early 1920s. He was attuned to the difficult issue of trauma and dissociation: he was interested in the various parts, or subpersonalities, and how they take over and cause severe troubles for the personality. His theories on trauma and dissociation were also highly relevant for his time (soldiers arriving back from the two world wars displayed "shell shock" and "combat fatigue" and were triggered by such things as sounds or light). While the explosion of affect or self-harming behaviors may interrupt the dissociation in order to bring a person "back to life" again, or ego-consciousness, Jung noted early on that the dysregulation for someone struggling with severe trauma was difficult on both the psyche and the body.

Jung's observations on how to support the integration of the trauma complex were through images and the helping hand of the psychothera-pist, who maintains human interest and personal devotion towards the analysand (Jung, 1921/1928/1985, CW 16, p. 132). He also intuited from his own lived experiences that no one treatment fits all psyches, which reminds us that Jungian art therapy may utilize various materials and methods depending upon the individual and what she brings to therapy. The therapist's curiosity and flexibility is essential. Alongside the relation-ship is the potential for the organizing center of the psyche, the Self, to be awakened so as to encounter the innate healing effects that often occur spontaneously through such approaches as the art making process.

Jung thought these images became known through the ego's relationship to the Self through metaphor, purposeful images, and imagination. The relationship between the ego and Self may generate greater self-acceptance that becomes necessary when working with certain complexes.

> A symptom of damage to this [ego/Self] axis is lack of self-acceptance. Psychotherapy offers such a person an opportunity to experience self-acceptance . . . this can amount to the repair of the ego–Self axis which restores contact with the inner sources of strength and acceptance, leaving the patient free to live.
>
> (Edinger, 1992, p. 40)

In other words, what analytical psychology treasures far more than the literal rewiring of the brain are the profound events and images that create and reveal the soul and foster an inner relationship with shadow material and the unconscious.

Trauma complexes are no different from other complexes except they are less conscious, feel and present far more distinctive somatic indicators, and occasionally stem from deeper areas of the psyche so their capacity for destruction within relationships is much more profound. A complex that is unconscious causes duress for the ego, but when complexes are completely unconscious, the trauma work may come in fits and starts as the psyche unravels and reconsolidates, giving the internal emotional landscape more definition for the therapeutic work. West (2016) suggested that the complex "embodies both the trauma-related internal working model derived *from* the trauma as well as the primitive defensive reaction *to* the trauma" (West, p. 83), which is why trauma work takes time as it spirals around the same issues. Both the results of the trauma and the defensive reactions to the trauma are simultaneously experienced and form a kind of tension of opposites between the past and the present as together they detangle the threads. When the patient gains enough resiliency to confront the internal complexities, a working pattern of opposites begins to unfold. Before then, the unconscious bits are autonomously played out within the transference/countertransference as much as within the internal psychic world.

Complexes and Transference/Countertransference

As splinter psyches, complexes have the energy to create, influence, or dominate the inter-subjective field, which is traditionally referred to as transference/countertransference. In Jungian art therapy, images can reveal subtleties of the therapeutic relationship, through specific images, colors, lines, or use of space. Certain aspects of a picture may be unconsciously placed in the corner of the canvas or page closest to the therapist or furthest away. When asked to describe in colors what she felt like in that moment, one analysand, Sue, drew in the bottom corner closest to her. She described how she felt small and wanted to hide and how my presence gave her a vulnerable feeling, but she also wanted me to "find her." As we explored this hide-and-seek in our relationship, we also considered times in the past where she felt small, cornered, forgotten, and invisible. She explained how she is good at presenting like she's fine, which is another way of hiding and feeling unseen (Perry, 1970).

In other situations, a Jungian art therapist may be asked to join in to help with an image. This could be seen as a reflection of the working relationship within the visual realm of art therapy. Rather than a verbal exchange, the patient may request that the Jungian art therapist offer a visual comment by making a mark or collaborating on creating a clay sculpture. In a painting where a figure was out at sea, Ellen reflected, "it was imperative that you responded to my request that you add something to the picture. Your addition of the rope with the life raft helped me know I wasn't left on my own to drown."

Figure 7.5 illustrates the dynamic relational exchange felt by a psychotherapist who had been working through some difficult issues with another professional in his suite. The day before he was to meet with his colleague, Dan had a dream of two balls of equal size "in a field" that he pictured in the center of the page. Dan associated the idea of "casting seeds" as nourishment for future discussions. However, his association to the red dust-like material was "contamination," suggesting the relationship was somehow contaminated. The unconscious offered a warning so

Figure 7.5   Dan's Dream

with the picture, Dan began to differentiate his thoughts and feelings before the meeting.

Schavarien (1992; 1995) made significant contributions to analytical art psychotherapy by expanding on Jung's idea of the picture as a bridge that reflects important aspects of the transference/countertransference phenomenon during Jungian work. She built on Jung's notions of the therapeutic relationship by investigating the intricacies of the art therapy image as the scapegoat that holds and carries difficult material (1992, p. 42). Sue (who had felt small) and I worked within a three-way relating process (Schaverien, 1995, p. 149), which enlarged the role of the picture as the *analytic third* in the room and provided us with a psychic representation of her emotional world. The picture communicated first what she was later able to articulate through words.

Complexes and Art Materials

Art materials facilitate, document, and express the quality of complexes; they also encourage and provide a literal space for a *relationship* with complexes and then ultimately can enable an active exploration towards transformation of these "personalities" and "figures" depending upon the focus, space, and interest of the psychotherapy. Using art materials first requires a physical participation from the Jungian art therapist—there is movement within the therapeutic relationship, meaning a willingness to shift to new positions, change focus, or ask for and receive needed supplies that the art therapist responds to. In other theoretical traditions, the requests and movement might be interpreted, but art therapists aim to encourage spontaneity through the use of materials in the room. We imagine this preparation process as part of the emotional "glue" that supports the psyche so it can have a place to express itself as freely as possible. If we are inviting the soul into the room, we need to prepare for its arrival and welcome its entrance. This is not caretaking or simply ego support. Our preparations are subtle interventions that sidestep the dominant persona/ego presentation so the unconscious can venture forth and the individual can be as authentic as possible.

It takes courage to use art materials and then even more courage is needed to make something visible through self-expression. In a classroom space where art therapists and non-art therapists join together to use art materials, we may confront the discomfort of those who are new to the experience. Analysands may be caught by complexes associated with earlier stages of development. Some may be delighted with themselves when they get started, while others may continue to be self-conscious or self-deprecate. A few students have even dropped a class when they realized one of the assignments was to make a mandala in every class using markers. Complexes that block the flow of psychic energy in some people may uncover vitality in others; objectifying and expressing psychic energy and personifying inner figures strengthens our encounters with psyche as mysteriously alive, dynamic, and autonomous.

If clay figures are created from paintings, the tangible quality of the clay represents an interesting shift in psychic energy. It's possible that if the clay figures become concrete anchors, the energy is less likely to move towards dissociation. Ellen described it this way:

> Clay comes when I am in a better place. If I'm having a terrible time, I use the sketch book. When on the other side of the feelings, clay represents some solidity. The ugly difficult images are a reflection on how it had been the day before—it gets the residue out, naming it without words. I sweep the rest of it out by making my images in the sketchbook. With images I see them before I do them. I can't be told what to do—because they are not rooted in my feelings—they rise up from within, sometimes while walking. With clay, I know I want to create something, but I don't SEE the image when I use clay. My knowledge comes through my fingers—the clay process is directed by the picture I have already done perhaps, so for me the clay is more directed as a concept.

For Ellen, the clay was another stage of working with her complexes. We might consider her sketchbook images as immediate expressions of raw personal complexes while the clay expressed the archetypal structures at the core of the painting or images. In other words, as Perry (1970) suggested, Ellen was first getting to know how the archetype was dressed through painting and then through the clay she could find an archetypal image for the deep psychic structure sitting at the core of the complex. Ellen noticed that if she didn't have a connection to the clay, the personality would not reveal itself. She added, "There is something qualitatively different about the clay versus the images. Clay takes more physicality, working it and trying to make it be what it becomes. It's like my hands and fingers have some knowledge."

All art materials naturally facilitate a relationship with the unconscious; they reflect the tension between freedom and structure, which may naturally ignite the transcendent function during the art-making process. Sometimes, however, a patient may give up, and leave the table with their drawing and throw it in the trash. They may squash the clay when they get frustrated. Sometimes destruction is important to find a new attitude, a new beginning. Or sometimes the materials were not quite right and a patient could only know this by trying and then re-choosing. Dry materials like pencils and markers offer intensity, structure, and containment for complexes associated with chaos or uncertainty. But sometimes launching someone into free expression using paints, glue, and tissue paper can be playful and exploratory and interrupts the complex enough for self-reflection to be possible. The fluidity and potential messiness, which constellates more emotion, can soften the ego consciousness and allow for the emergence of imagination that exists behind the persona and ego.[6] Which art materials are used and how they are used depends on the therapeutic approach, art space, and the patient's interest to work within or outside of sessions. These are all possibilities and having this variety again falls under Jung's view that many psyches require many different approaches.

Depending upon the context, Jungian art therapy can calm, redirect, or activate psychic energy (complexes) through movement and expression brought into form and given distance to what feels so deeply imbedded and personal. Eventual relief comes when the unconscious offers its own images from the soul or the deep feminine aspect of the psyche. The use of mandalas, boxes, stitched quilts, stretched canvas, and taped paper, and lots of glue and tape or combining or switching materials may offer enough compensation that the ego is energized and the dissociation is interrupted. An example from the Grail Legends is Parzival, who falls into a trance when he sees three drops of blood on the snow. He is reminded of his beloved. The correct interruption means the therapist stays in relationship with the patient while guiding them back into an emotional connection with the "here and now," the therapist and the community. This is what

Gawain did for Parzival when he arrived and laid a cloth over the three drops of blood. This automatically freed Parzival from the dissociative trance. These archetypal images are compelling because they speak the unspeakable and tap into universal forms of communication while at the same time illuminating the personal complexes.

Jungian Art Therapy: Dahlia's Story

Dahlia was a bicultural student who shared her investigations into issues related to her mother complex. For the class "Red Book" assignment, she worked freely. "Normally I'm analytical about everything. The project was a mirror for myself." Dahlia's spontaneous images unexpectedly invited her to explore her childhood. She used colored markers that were bright but contained and regulated the psychic energy associated with her traumatic memories.

Briefly, Dahlia's mother was in an abusive marriage when she was young and so Dahlia was often in the position of caretaker and protector that formed an internalized self-care structure (Kalsched, 1996). It had been challenging for Dahlia to understand or respect her mother's silence, so Dahlia had spoken her mind, which sometimes put them both in danger. The following is how a cluster of complexes can form around relational trauma.

Figure 7.6 shows a figure whose upper body and lower body are split, rising from a shell that sits on the word "Mother." Dahlia expressed concern about the repetitive split in her drawings. If we had rushed into an interpretation she would have missed the multiplicity of the unconscious message, so instead she patiently noticed it and attempted to be open enough to this pattern so that she could learn from it. Dahlia had been born and raised in another country but was acculturated after living in the United States for many years. Was the image attempting to illustrate these two worlds while simultaneously searching for some reconciliation? How was a new aspect of her psyche emerging through these images, like Venus emerging from the shell? Keeping these questions in mind, the split figure held the unconscious conflict of twos associated with her mind/heart, two countries, extraverted/introverted, or a psychological separation from her feminine body and nature. There were many layers Dahlia investigated during her Jungian art therapy process and these were just a few of them.

Dahlia noted that the transparent skeletal structure in the image was held together by a heart, an important motif for her. The heart carried "the glue of emotion" and repaired interactions. She was pleased how the image expressed her emotional fragility and vulnerabilities. The image was compelling because it touched within her what had remained hidden and

Figure 7.6 Dahlia's Body

unspoken, not unlike her mother who "hid" by remaining silent. The image was a bridge that brought awareness, and Dahlia acknowledged that Jung's idea of the opposites had amplified her internal experience and made sense of what had previously remained unconscious shadow material.

The savior complex, shown in Figure 7.7, was an unrehearsed description of Dahlia's inheritance from her mother and her indigenous ancestors. She explained how the savior complex played out when she worked as a therapist with high-risk children. This was a hook for Dahlia and she realized the savior was what Jung would have referred to as an adaptive approach to dealing with her fear of danger and guilt for wanting independence as a child. "I might repair what felt broken in others" through becoming a therapist. Withdrawing the projection of her own hurt on other children, Dahlia imagined her savior complex could "come home" to focus on her inner work by beginning to make visible what had been cast into the shadow.

The armored knight is an image of a complex that clustered near Dahlia's savior complex (Figure 7.8). This cold protective stance surfaced when she felt too exposed, vulnerable, and overwhelmed with emotion.

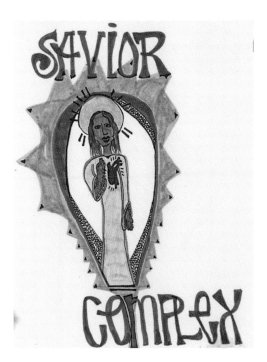

Figure 7.7 Dahlia's Savior Complex

The complex slid over her with a cool analytical mind "and as a kid I knew how to escape into the bushes," Dahlia recalled. Because the complex was both adaptive and compensatory, Dahlia explored how the knight had provided strategies for safety. The knight had two poles—one of protection, but also a side of penetrating clarity and wisdom that she relied upon. The knight was pressing for attention because it could be dangerous to herself or others—it had the skill to cut things in half and hurt people, or it could bring clarity, but it also offered protection from overextending herself (the savior). Working with this image gave Dahlia respect for the complexes, archetypes, and the unconscious process.

In Figure 7.9, Dahlia wrote, "Tear—to rip apart wounds and allow them to breathe." With this image, the unconscious offered a pun (to cry or to rip apart), that invigorated Dahlia's emotional work and reconnected her to the feminine principle. Dahlia noted feeling "torn" as something she had not previously articulated. Alternatively, as an image of a *genius loci*, this sacred place had cleansing elements that arose from the unconscious. Undergoing a radical change within the psyche and outer life, Dahlia was now stitched into the deep well of her soul, and as she cultivated a stronger ego/Self relationship, she found renewal through her emotions.

Figure 7.8   Dahlia's Knight

Figure 7.9   Dahlia's Tear

Whatever the symptom is, it becomes known to us through our complexes. The more we work on our personal psychology, the more we consider the distinctive features of each complex. As we do this work, the psyche is actually seeking out the solution to those complexes—it is like a homeopathic cure where the antidote is the poison. First, we *feel the poison* of the complex and then we discover the hidden tincture that begins to heal the psyche. According to Jung, the solution to the conflict is found by entering *into* suffering our complexes. By remaining as conscious as possible, we tolerate the emotional fires, hold the tension, and wait for whatever might emerge through our personal images. Our actions in the outer world will be responded to by the unconscious—all we have to do is remain awake and listen to the visual voices that deepen our insights into the supporting structures of the archetypes, which will be discussed in Chapter 8.

Endnotes

1. Psychologically, valence is a predisposition to bond or energetically react with any circumstantial data or individual who has an opposite valence or some charge that serves as a key for the lock of the individual, who then responds when the key is present or inserted into the lock. In other words, the complex is unlocked and expresses itself.

2. Jung hypothesized that culture played an important role in the psychological expression of individuals and that memories and cultural patterns from previous generations are found in subsequent generations. His views on complexes and archetypal patterns are now strongly supported by the field of epigenetics, a field within genetics that refers to heritable traits that hold genetic "memory" that is expressed in response to environmental changes. Put another way, what we are exposed to can impact our grandchildren; because traumatic events in older generations have inheritable effects on future generations that are passed down through genetic memory that can be turned on or off. This is why someone in the family may resemble an ancestor they never knew, or why the gene for a physical or mental illness may be present but latent in several generations; it may require specific environmental stressors to awaken the expression of the epigenome.

3. Jung coined the term *psychoid realm* or *psychoid layer* as a description of the interface between psyche/soma. Not only does it give value to both the unknown and the unknowable somatic material within the psyche that is knowable through experiences such as birth, sex, physical accidents, dissociative states, and past-life regressions, but energy and synchronicity play a role. Thus, Jung's complex theory served as an important precursor to somatic psychology especially as he expanded upon some of Janet's key ideas.

4. Trauma is now more widely considered in the field of analytical psychology. The following are a few of the Jungian authors who have specifically focused on the etiology and treatment of relational trauma: Donald Kalsched, John Merchant, Eberhard Riedel, Nathan Schwartz-Salant, Daniela Sieff, Margaret Wilkinson, Marcus West, and Ursula Wirtz.

5. The term *abreaction* is a psychoanalytical term for reliving an experience to purge it of its emotional excesses—a type of catharsis. It is sometimes used as a method of becoming conscious of repressed traumatic events.

6. Art materials and their psychological principles and applications are found in Michelle Dean's art therapy text, *Using Art Media in Psychotherapy* (2016).

CHAPTER 8

Archetypes
Anchors of the Mythic Pattern

Within the field of psychotherapy, Jung's most unique and far-reaching idea was his translation of the archetype into a psychological structure that expresses the universal lived experiences of humanity. Moreover, the clinical consequences and applications differentiated his psychology from other models because not only did the archetype explain significant patterns of human instincts and development, but it also facilitated our understanding of the patterns of human consciousness. Jung's discovery of the collective unconscious revealed the purposive and transformative nature of images and symbols, including crosscultural and transpersonal influences on the psyche. With his theory of archetypes and the collective unconscious, Jung sought to define the underlying "living bedrock of human psychology" (Stevens, 2006, p. 74).

Based on his experience in a dream, Jung (1927/1978, CW 10) used the image of a building to describe the archetypal structure of the psyche and its development. In this building, the upper floors were built in our current time and then as we move down to the "cellar we come upon Roman foundations, and under the cellar a choked-up cave with Neolithic tools in the upper layer and remnants of fauna from the same period in the lower layers" (Jung, 1927/1978, CW 10, p. 31)

The image of a building provided Jung a developmental process of growing up out of what we might call prehistory, or our phylogenetic (evolving out of groups of organisms) as well as our ontogenetic (growth as humans from an egg) development because we have "grown up out of the dark confines of the earth" (Jung, 1927/1978, CW 10, p. 32). In other words, we have evolved from the earth both as a species and as individuals. The child who plays in the mud and uses natural objects as tools is rehearsing both the phylogenetic and ontogenetic principles of her personal ancestors and mankind in general. In fact, research has shown that children around the globe first draw scribbles that shift to circles, then a tadpole formation, which then evolves into a face with arms and legs, and finally the whole body (Kellogg, 1969/1970). This universal progression of drawing falls in line with Jung's formulation of human stages of development, or what he termed the archetype of individuation.

Definition of Archetypes

The etymology of the word *archetype* consists of two root words: *arkhe*, which means "primitive or primary," and *tupos*, which means "model." An archetype refers to the primary or original model or pattern that begins at one point and unfolds over time like a ball of yarn unraveling into the future with a particular pattern and trajectory.

Jung conceptualized archetypes as the inherited psychological structures located in the unconscious that carry psychic energy. As described previously, like a riverbed through which water flows, the archetype provides the necessary form into which the flow of psychic energy animates the psyche. Archetypes express the primordial, instinctual energy within the psyche that is autonomous, unconscious, and undifferentiated. The structure of an archetype connects body and image through dynamic instinctual energy.

The Structure of Archetypes

If we can find images or metaphors that resonate for us, we are better able to grasp how analytical psychology fits together. The images are the doors that we use to enter the house. Jung used several images to describe the archetype and its transformative role within the psyche; the crystal and the light spectrum are chosen and described below.

The crystal, which has an invisible archetypal lattice structure and shape, becomes visible to us as the chemical layers form out of the chaos of solution to complete the crystallization process. The image, and the process of making the image, reminds us that the specific unseen skeletal makeup exists and is retained despite our not being able to perceive it directly—its invisible presence is verified by what grows to form its structure (Jung, 1938/1990, CW 9i, p. 79). This crystallization process is an example of how the instincts assume the form of the archetype. Jung's "assertion that images evoke the aim of the instincts implies that they deserve equal place" (Samuels et al., 1986/1993).

The light spectrum, with its infrared and ultraviolet poles, is a memorable archetypal image of the opposites expressed through warm and cool colors. The infrared end of the pole represents the instinctual somatic and sensory *dynamism* while the ultraviolet pole represents the spiritual *image* that is associated with the soul or spiritual pole of the psyche. Simply put, violet is a combination of red and blue. Jung (1947/1972, CW 8) explained that cool blue is related to spirit based on the color of sky and air while the warm red correlates with instincts and suggests feelings and emotions (p. 211). The light spectrum expresses the energy within colors with the opposites noted by the warm and cool colors. With this metaphor, the archetypal structure becomes partially known through color and light; the *bipolar* aspect of the archetype is noted with its instinctual and spiritual poles, which will be discussed later in this chapter.

The images of a crystal and the light spectrum illustrate the visible and partially unknown elements, which requires us to use our imagination when we address that which is not visible, or what then becomes visible through dreams, artwork, visions, and other images.

Jung and Archetypes

History

Jung's conceptualization of archetypes underwent several stages that paired with the development of his own lived experience, professional development, and theoretical methods. Because he viewed mankind as more similar than dissimilar, his archetypal theory offered him a structure that held his personal experiences as well as his empirical research and interest in the collective unconscious. His formulation of the archetype as a psychological perspective was rooted in the historic Platonic tradition of universal forms being present in the minds of gods, St. Augustine's *ideae principales*, Kant's *a priori* categories of perception, and Schopenhauer's *prototypes*. The philosopher and anthropologist Lévy-Bruhl called them *collective representations* and the archeologists Hubert and Mauss called them *a priori* categories of the imagination. Jung also called archetypes *a priori*, ready for action, as an inheritance of "systems of readiness and at the same time images and emotions" (Jung, 1927/1978, CW 10, p. 31) and used the phrase *primordial images* as inherited potentialities of our imagination. Jung translated these various notions of an archetype into an applied psychological concept.

Jung's Three Developments of the Archetype
Jung developed his theory of archetypes over his professional career in three separate phases, as described below.

1912–1934
Jung's development of the archetype unfolded in three primary stages from 1912 to 1919. The first development was initiated with the publication of *Symbols of Transformation* (1912/1967, CW 5), which set his model of the psyche apart from Freud's model. Jung referred to universal patterns that he noticed in his patients and within himself. He first used such phrases as *primordial images, typical myths*, or *universal human symbols* to describe the idea of the archetype.

Dedicated to his own personal work as well as learning cultural stories, myths, and symbols, Jung sought to understand the deeper structures that were being expressed from the unconscious that signaled both the chthonic and the transcendent nature of the psyche. The motifs are repeated throughout the globe and history; however, according to Samuels et al. (1986/1993), "their main features were their "numinosity, unconsciousness, and autonomy" (p. 26). Jung's early hypothesis suggested a kind of library within the unconscious that contained inherited, historical, and repetitive structures, yet this was controversial and distracted people from understanding his fundamental hypothesis, which is that archetypes are inherited *structures*, but the actual archetypes themselves are not inherited. Instead, the *modes*, or universal patterns of the archetype, are inherited and the images that reflect these structures are made personal by our complexes. In other words, we don't automatically dream about the Greek god Zeus, but we do dream about the modern equivalent structure, perhaps the president or a powerful father figure. Thus, the *archetypal pattern* of the father or Zeus narrative is at the core of our personal lived experiences, but how we express it is personal.

Around 1917 Jung formulated the archetypal patterns of introversion and extraversion based on psychic energy. Jung also referred to archetypes as *dominants*, and in 1919 he became more explicit and used the term "archetype" for the first time (1919/1972, CW 8, p. 133). Jung also used such terms as *primordial image, dominants, archetypes*, and *engrams* during this phase, and he described archetypes as inherited with a certain brain structure that holds a preparedness or *readiness for action* that is awakened by certain psychic situations.

To help prove his point, Jung used the snake to illustrate the presence of the collective unconscious and its instinctual, chthonic nature (1927/1972, CW 8, pp. 139–158). The psychic activity of the instinctual or lower brain stem, the cold-blooded aspect of the psyche, are expressed while simultaneously the image carries references to the healing of spirit and creative transformation. For Jung, the snake (or any other archetype) was a way to explain how individuals who have never seen a snake can dream about them and have strong reactions to them. Jung's "assertion that images evoke the aim of the instincts implies that they deserve equal place" (Samuels et al., 1986/1993, p. 26).

1935–1945

By the time Jung had completed his confrontation with the "spirit of the depths" and had emerged from his work on *The Red Book*, his notion of the archetype had become a lived experience that he would illustrate with his pivotal formulation of typology. Between the years of 1934 and 1946, Jung further distinguished *the archetypal image* from *the archetype as such*, finding evidence within his research on alchemy. This crucial clarification remained until his death and is the most salient description of the archetype for us today. The *archetype as such* describes the channel or structure for preexisting instinctual energy, a path that seeks a relationship with consciousness, like the riverbed ready for the emotional waters of life to flow into its structure.

The archetype of water in motion represents the movement of history, the daily movement of an individual life, the passage of time, the flow of affect, or the vitality of living an engaged life. So we can see how the archetype is partially known through our personal associations that build a multilayered archetypal image. This image, when invested with the personal content, has the potential of becoming a living symbol, although, as noted previously, Jung understood archetypes as lacking human feeling and suffering. Images and symbols from the collective unconscious, such as a wheel, a mandala, or a path, can suggest the individuation archetype. Underneath all motifs are "visual representations of an archetypal character, symbolic primordial images which have served to build up and differentiate the human mind" (Jung, 1935/1985, CW 16, p. 13).

As we can see with the snake and the water, images of archetypes express the instinctual and energic aspect of psychic activity, connecting us to our own glacial nature through the chthonic and primordial portion of our existence. Equally so, the images also hitch us to a mysterious transpersonal aspect of the psyche through numinous expressions, such as creativity, nature's beauty, spiritual music or practices, or important rituals. The complexity of the inheritance within the unconscious did not allow Jung to view it as simply a repository for repressed infantile material— he was compelled to define the unconscious as containing "archetypal conditions" that formed a fundamental framework and "precondition of all consciousness" (Jung, 1929/1985, CW 16, p. 34).

1945–1961

Later Jung used the terms *collective representations, categories of the imagination,* and *elementary ideas.* Several things are important to note in this time period. It seems that the psychological structure of the archetype carried great significance for Jung, partially because it mobilized the development of consciousness, which was his great passion, and the archetype also bridged the co-existing paradigms (energic and symbolic) that Evers-Fahey (2017) explained as the structural foundation for this theory.

To summarize, by the end of his life, Jung had established two clearly defined ideas: the *archetype as such* and the *archetypal image,* which is what we work with today. To clarify, the *archetype as such* refers to the actual invisible structure and form of the archetype itself that contains an *a priori* order within the collective unconscious, while the archetypal image is what we consciously apprehend or perceive about the archetype through the various representational images and symbols. This clarification is emphasized because archetypes are never seen directly, but are only partially known to us through an image or symbol that illustrates the presence of its universal pattern. This conceptualization deepens how we work with images and symbols as art therapists.

The Psychological Development of the Archetype

It took Jung time to name the archetype as a psychological concept, yet we hear how the notion is imbedded in his early and consistent interest in patterns. Freud and Adler also thought that the *a priori* was instinctual, impersonal, universal, and inherited, yet Jung did not stop there (Stevens, 2006). By incorporating this notion into the foundation of analytical psychology, he shifted the unconscious into an innately healing resource of symbolic material that included a dynamic relationship between the personal and the collective unconscious and an explanation for universal patterns that occurred throughout humanity. Later in life, Jung was immersed in thinking about how universal patterns had a powerful, and sometimes devastating, impact on the collective as much as the individual. Having lived through two world wars, a Great Depression, and two heart attacks, Jung saw great personal and collective tragedy at the hands of embodied archetypes that swept over the ego's vulnerable state of consciousness. This seeded his ideas on the relationship between the personal and collective shadow.

How Archetypes Influence Consciousness

Archetypes are recognized by the personality through our complexes. As they cannot be seen directly, but are at the core of every complex and connect the collective unconscious with the personal unconscious, their presence and impact may not be easily or immediately comprehended. Our personal complexes cluster around these innate structural patterns that push to become known and conscious; they dress the non-human archetypes in specific material that predisposes us to uniquely personal images. In other words, the unconscious archetypal energy clothes itself and becomes visible to us through our complexes (Perry, 1970). The archetype changes the psyche's attitude in various ways: through painful confrontations and trials of endurance or feeling inspired or deeply touched. Such transpersonal awakenings can spontaneously follow a difficult period of regression, emotional descent, or dark night of the soul (Corbett, 2011), which is why the hero's journey or patterns of initiation offer rich archetypal patterns that amplify enigmatic states of conciousness.

Jungian Art Therapy: Rebecca's Story

However, like Rebecca's pregnant tree drawing shown in Chapter 2 (Figure 2.10), images also emerge prior to an important event to provide the anchoring needed when transitioning from one state of consciousness to another. Rebecca, who was in her last trimester, drew herself pregnant. As a yoga instructor, she spoke about liminal space and her connection to nature through her growing body, which reminded her of certain yoga principles (tension of opposites). Rebecca's association of her pregnant body to a tree alludes to the unconscious relationship that pregnant women may have with the *anima mundi*, the soul of the world, or the idea that we are all interconnected.

Rebecca struggled to combine the two images (tree and pregnant body). When she was finished she talked about her exhaustion and fears. She was surprised to see such an idyllic image of nature emerge on the paper. The picture spoke of its own consciousness, its own purposive connection to the transcendent qualities of nature. This deep primordial wisdom became known to Rebecca through wrestling with the image.

The archetypal image contains both the instinctual dynamism of the *archetype as such* expressed through her growing pregnant body (rooted in the biological drives of nature), and the spiritual pole of the archetype as a whole picture containing many parts. In particular, the image integrates and unifies two archetypal symbols (tree and pregnancy). Rebecca worked on the profound "twoness" she embodied, associated with herself and the fetus, with her desire to remain connected but separate. A backdrop to the archetypal image is the pattern of psychological yoking, or *syzygy*, and often occurs between the masculine and feminine aspects of the psyche during pregnancy (Swan-Foster, 2012). Rebecca said, "The yellow is intuitive energy reaching up and down—we are held by the yellow. I'm containing and stretching." She also noted she was "held by the blue sky." At the time when Rebecca embodied several archetypal patterns, the unifying image had emerged just as she waited on the threshold of childbirth and the birth of her child.

Jung understood the image bridges both the conscious and the unconscious to produce a condensed representation of a psychic situation. Certainly, the image held the complexity of Rebecca's perinatal journey. The archetype of the tree evokes a wide range of associations: the ancient crosscultural tree of life, the individuation process, or the passage of time and the changing of the seasons. At the end of the session, Rebecca remembered the story of the Bodhi tree, suggesting the transcendent function via the drawing process had unearthed a new attitude. When our noetic wisdom is awakened by archetypal experiences, like it was for Rebecca, we find our personal experience beautifully stitched into a mutual relationship with the collective as well as the collective unconscious and we may remark on the unifying moment.

The Bipolar Archetype: Instinctual and Spiritual Poles

Myth of Psyche: Instinctual and Spiritual

Archetypes are bipolar: there is an instinctual pole and a spiritual pole, but the structure is probably best explained first through images. The myth of *Psyche and Eros* is concerned with several things, but for our purposes the myth expresses the archetype of individuation and how the goddess Aphrodite illustrates two sides of an archetype. Most commonly Aphrodite is an archetypal image of spiritual nourishment through beauty (spiritual pole). Yet when she is rejected by the collective, Aphrodite expresses the archetypal image of rage, jealousy, and the harsh taskmaster mother (instinctual pole). Very briefly, in this myth, society has become disoriented because they no longer honor Aphrodite as the goddess of beauty, but honor the human Psyche for her beauty instead. This angers Aphrodite and her instinctual response is to send her son Eros to fix the situation. Instead Eros falls in love with Psyche, who is brought into a beautiful serene world with him. Psyche is cherished by night and becomes pregnant by Eros, whom she never sees in daylight. After time, her sister's envious comments stir Psyche's unconscious desire for knowledge about Eros wins out and she uses an oil lamp to reveal his identity. When she inadvertently burns him with drops of oil (we might initially think, "how could she be so careless?"), Eros awakens and is infuriated by her disobedience to him. Now, as he warned her, Eros must abandon her.

Psyche is suddenly left alone to face Aphrodite's instinctual revenge, which is illustrated by giving Psyche impossible tasks to complete. Psyche faces her own suffering and hardships but eventually completes them. By the end of the story, Psyche is transformed by her labors—she has wrestled with the effects of the instinctual pole of Aphrodite, and through her suffering Psyche eventually encounters the spiritual pole of Aphrodite when Eros saves her from a death sleep in the nick of time, and she is welcomed into the celestial realm of the gods. The myth ends with the birth of their baby Joy.

Each character in the myth expresses an important aspect of the transformation process that evolved from Psyche's unconscious moment of "failure" through her disobedience, which expressed an underlying teleological drive for consciousness. Moreover, Aphrodite's instinctual rage created an underlying driving dynamic force of individuation throughout the myth. In order to become conscious of her "mistakes," Psyche had to confront the shadow of grief associated with Eros's abandonment, and engage with her suffering brought about by Aphrodite's impossible tasks. The essential steps facilitated an expansion of Psyche's personality. Now let's look more closely at the theoretical aspect of the instinctual and spiritual pole of the archetype.

Instinctual

Expanding upon Freud's idea of the sexual instinct, Jung speculated that the psyche is fueled by five primary instincts: *sexuality, nourishment, creativity, reflection,* and *movement/action* (Jung, 1937/1972, CW 8, p. 118). Because archetypes are *structures ready for action,* they contain, express, hold, and move the instinctual energy within the body fulfilling the archetype's determination to become known and have an impact on consciousness. For instance, the creative instinct, inherent within the art process, flows into an archetypal structure and awakens the soul to bodily desire, which may mean a desire to express, reflect, move, or become nourished. When we experience an embodiment of desire, soulful-longing, and creative expression, we know that the instinctual pole of the archetype is impacting and directing the psyche to move towards consciousness and to incorporate the spiritual pole of the archetype. Jung clarified that the creative instinct employs the instincts of action and reflection and this can be expressed in both constructive and destructive ways (Jung, 1937/1972, CW 8, p. 118).

For example, the creation of nuclear fusion was certainly a creative endeavor and signified a new level of consciousness, but the question still remains as to whether humanity has the necessary consciousness to fully comprehend the power of its archetypal destruction when used against humanity, because once its power was unleashed, the collective confronted the archetype of destruction that had never been seen before. We are again faced with the same issues around how we use our creative discoveries and inventions when it comes to artificial intelligence (AI)—will we use them to benefit humanity or will we use them for nefarious purposes? These are examples of the bi-polar archetypal energies that the collective must confront.

The instinctual drive of an archetype must be consciously worked with and transformed so that the spiritual pole of the archetype can be recognized. Then both poles of the archetype are made conscious within the psyche. Jung believed that when we confront our own personal shadow we participate in this transformative process so as to mitigate and avoid unconscious destruction that is driven by the raw personal complexes and archetypal instincts. On a personal scale we have already heard about the destructive shadow expression of the creative instinct carried out by a negative animus with Carol in Chapter 6, when she impulsively destroyed her box with a hammer. Her process left no space for the instinctual and spiritual poles of the archetype to be consciously considered and assimilated to foster new consciousness.

But what exactly does this mean? Many times we identify with only the positive aspect of an archetype. Our innate lack of consciousness blinds us to the powerful capacity that an archetype has to cause destruction or, at the very least, require from us endless, unrelenting, endurance until we do become conscious. For instance, in the recent hurricanes, individuals who lost their homes in Hurricane Katrina, moved to make a new life, only to lose their homes once again with Hurricane Harvey. Such Biblical storms and floods are experienced as overwhelming forces for the ego and represent the raw energy of the archetype experienced in the personal realm. They signify the moment when we are looking directly at the unstoppable instinctual force of archetypal energy. How an individual is impacted and gains a new level of consciousness (spiritual pole) brought about by such archetypal energy is a deeply personal journey that demands our confrontation with pain and suffering.

So while archetypes bring about liberation, enlightenment, and moments of ineffable beauty and peace, they can also destroy, enchant, or bedazzle us, driving us into an inflation with the desire for control and power. They may trap us in a deflation associated with an identification with a dark aspect of power, self-hatred, vitriol, shame, compulsion, obsession, and if not interrupted, ultimately some form of negative personal and collective destruction as discussed earlier. Without the input of our human feeling and compassion, archetypes have the capacity to constellate a rigid adherence to rules and cultural expectations, such as the extreme demands made by cults where the individual is lost within a group mind.

Consequently, the archetype's bipolar nature—the positive and the negative extremes—require mediation and navigation. To lose our mind, our ego consciousness, to an archetype suggests that we have lost our sense of "I" and the ego is no longer in the seat of consciousness. Sometimes we may believe we can consciously choose this experience (an ego decision), but if the ego is not in the seat of consciousness then it implies that our complexes and archetypal forces are "running the show." In the most extreme situation there is a severe psychological disorientation expressed as mania, depression, addiction, or even psychosis.

Deeply imbedded archetypal issues often require greater support through specific groups that can collectively reflect the depths of the archetypal challenges. However, group process or educational training programs, recovery groups, meditation/prayer groups, creative dance or art groups, or forms of group therapy all have a shadow that has the potential to do harm to the individual. While these groups have tremendous healing powers, the shadow remains with the risk of subjugation and cult mentality (Shaw, 2014).

Margaret's depression was not cured by using watercolor, but the colors in Figure 8.1 provided some temporary vitality. Rather than using a large, overwhelming piece of white paper, Margaret used small trading cards. She then used black pens to create small pictures. This process was Margaret's discovery and developed organically from within, not as a predetermined art therapy intervention; her discovery gave her a sense of confidence and authority within her creative work. Because the pen marks were like black threads that moved around and made a path out of her psychic maze of

Figure 8.1   Margaret's Watercolor

depressed energy, an archetypal reference for her image making might be the ball of thread that Ariadne gave to Theseus so he could retrace his steps out of the labyrinth.

Jungian Art Therapy: Faye's Story

Childbirth is also an example of an autonomous archetypal process that maintains specific nonhuman structures but gathers personal elements (complexes) around its powerful pattern. As chthonic sensory experience, the instinctual and spiritual poles are expressed. Faye, who endured a traumatic childbirth, was left with unresolved grief and impotent rage. Her medical staff was nonchalant about what had occurred and the medical malpractice laws prevented any recourse. Both Faye and her baby survived, but her newborn had numerous medical issues and Faye's body had endured noticeable internal physical harm that impacted her daily life.

Faye used a wet watercolor process for many months (Figures 8.2, 8.3, 8.4), creating one painting a session. As she painted she reviewed and documented the horrific details that included numerous moments of

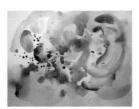

Figure 8.2   Faye #1

Figure 8.3   Faye #2

Figure 8.4   Faye #3

abandonment. Faye articulated her disappointment, rage, shame, and sadness throughout the detailed event. These were important personal complexes. But she also remembered feeling gripped by the archetype of utter pain and terror and not being able to speak.

Initially, Faye needed to consider her personal relationship with her mother and where she got "lost" in the threshold period of childbirth. She also recounted the subtle dismissal and words of blame she encountered from the doctor throughout the medical process, that mirrored her mother's voice. The instinctual wounds had been inherited through the mother-line, suggesting she was vulnerable to feeling irrelevant and small. The pain now lived within her body as much as in her psyche, as both memory and present experience. However, it was too early for any archetypal amplification to heal the excruciating emotions and physical discomfort with which she lived on a daily basis. Instead, Jungian art therapy provided her the time and space to circumambulate around her personal story until she excavated a new language from within. This language emerged by listening to the painful friction between her voiced stories and the unpredictable watercolors.

Although archetypal images arose in my mind, they were not relevant for Faye in the early part of the work. The images were more helpful for me: I thought of Psyche who was given impossible tasks, Persephone who was raped and taken to the underworld, and Demeter who wandered the earth in grief. I also thought of enraged Hera who was betrayed by Zeus and took her rage out on others. These myths provided the potential archetypal images that I might hold to later amplify Faye's archetypal grief and one day help her not feel so alone. But, her awareness of the underlying archetypal patterns would come naturally from within her—if I had fit her story into an archetypal recipe, I would have only deepened the wounds. Faye needed to know that I could sit and listen to her full story; *she* also needed to hear herself tell the full story as there were holes and fragments that needed stitching together. Through painting and telling of the difficult events, Faye was mending herself.

Faye's spontaneous paintings reflected the potent archetypal themes of power, abandonment, and vulnerability she felt during childbirth. The watercolor also expressed the archetypal grief and shame bound up in the wetness of her bodily fluids, tears, and blood. At the same time, the painting process reconnected her to a whole and healthy place in her psyche (Self). The paints and colors reminded her of a sacred and resilient space within her that spoke an inner truth and soothed the torn and ruptured places, both psychically as well as physically. By painting, Faye found distance from the raw emotions as she formulated her memories. She imagined the potential for recovery, a resilient place for her future. Eventually, Faye gained perspective to simply *imagine* medical repair. Corresponding with her development, the colors changed from the early blacks, reds, and purples to brighter colors and more white space. She incorporated pencils (Figure 8.4, Faye #3), which suggested clarification, differentiation, and assimilation of this new identity.

To lose ourselves in the instinctual realm of the archetype or the archetypal process, as Faye experienced during childbirth, means our conscious psyche is overwhelmed and we are impacted or perhaps possessed by an archetypal energy. Such possession by the archetype can be terrifying; we lose relationship to the "I" or ego within the psyche and the post-traumatic stress symptoms (complexes) begin to disturb and destabilize the conscious psyche. In the moment it is impossible to "extract" the complexes from the body and externalize the personal through projecting them into images so we can clarify the archetypal images that dominated the experience of the conscious psyche. That investigation may follow the event. Faye did not fully resolve her situation, but she left our work with new perspectives and a more complete story—she had reconnected to her feminine and made some small peace with the archetypal process that became visible through her painted images.

Spirit

The opposite of the instinctual pole is the spiritual pole. Originating from the Greek word *pneuma* that means "breath" and "wind," *spirit* suggests the invisible, mysterious, and ineffable qualities that may ignite the fires within with a gentle breeze or a swift wind (Jung, 1945/1990, CW 9i, pp. 207–254). Spirit is the energy that leaves the body and exists in infinite space and time, is uncontainable and unknowable through image, and arrives unbidden through positive or negative affect to incite or inspire us (Samuels et al., 1986/1993). In other words, spirit blows in through a moment of reflection or insight, and gives us an eerie feeling (or goosebumps!) that offers a confirmation. Or, we notice a presence from something invisible, either within us or coming from around us associated with the transpersonal or the spiritual pole of the archetype.

Jung also reminded us that spirit is the opposite of matter, which represents stasis and inertia. Bringing spirit into matter is the work of alchemists and it is in the actual visual image that instinct and spirit are united in the emotional work of relating to material from the unconscious. This is most definitely the soulful labor of Jungian art therapy.

Jungian Art Therapy: Claire's Story

Making images also offers an active way to engage the spiritual side of an archetype and support the relational aspect of the ego–Self axis. Claire, an American–Vietnamese woman, wanted to acknowledge the women in her mother's family who had died (mother archetype). While an ego-driven thought, the Self was evident as she explored materials. Eventually she put together a small mobile of important objects like tin stars, a crystal, and a paper flower—all things she had found. She then made a web of origami cranes that illustrated the lineage in the feminine line of her family. Each color brought the mobile to life with Claire bringing the women's spirit into matter.

The mobile hung in Claire's window and moved in the breeze. She imagined that when the cranes moved, there was a "visitation" of these women who, despite their deaths, continued to inspire her. While working, Claire had explored her shadow projections about each woman and how their gifts compensated for the internalized critic that she had inherited through the feminine line. Claire often said, "I have a hard time mothering myself," but through the mobile, she encountered the spiritual pole of the mother archetype. This example illustrates how the collaboration between ego and Self began to repair Claire's wounds within the ego–Self axis.

Self: Archetype as the Spiritual Pole

By 1905, William James had already named, explored, and outlined the beginnings of the transpersonal psyche[1] and Jung, having encountered his own altered states of consciousness and paranormal material, was keen to investigate these observations associated with the transpersonal aspect of the psyche, which he referred to as the Self.

The Self archetype was a pivotal psychological concept that explained the religious psyche, various field phenomena such as synchronicity and paranormal events, and the psychological role of a godhead. However, Jung was skeptical of dogma and rejected religion in the traditional sense—partially in reaction to his own father who was a minister—so for Jung the Self was a psychological structure that provided access to God, but he was clear that the Self was *not* God. Instead, he remained with the transpersonal, transcendent quality of the religious psyche that influences individuation (Corbett, 2011). Jung's reflective instinct, closely attuned to the contemplative attitude, is integral to every religious practice around the world. In Jungian art therapy, the reflective instinct is as essential to the creative process as any emotion. The reflective instinct carves out the space that holds the sacred image, giving us *Kairos* time to gain some distance and call on our imagination.

The archetype of the Self has at times been considered Jung's preoccupation with a religious complex. While this may be accurate, his personal interest in these issues was based on human experiences that connected him to universal patterns, so his investigations furthered transpersonal psychology as well as the investigations into the realms of the irrational psyche. William James was an influential figure for Jung and seeded his imagination regarding the religious psyche. As mentioned previously, James published *The Principles of Psychology* (1902/1912)[2] at the turn of the century and is credited for using the term *transpersonal*, which signified the altered states of consciousness and the healing nature of religion and spiritual experiences. Because James suffered from periods of depression, he had an interest in finding emotional wellness and noticed that whenever he took refuge in a contemplative and spiritual life, he felt relief from his symptoms. As he undertook vast research into altered states, he categorized universal spiritual patterns within the human experience. James (1902/2012) defined four primary components of the transpersonal experience:

1. *noetic*, or arising from an inner knowing, which was a notion originating from the Gnostics;
2. *transiency*, or lasting for a limited time;
3. *ineffable*, which suggests the spiritual experience cannot be described by words or ego;
4. *autonomous*, thus requiring a willingness, passivity, and/or surrender.

Clearly, James's investigations and key definitions of the transpersonal experience were integral to Jung's conceptualization of the collective unconscious and the structure of the psyche, particularly and more specifically the Self. On many occasions, our work as Jungian art therapists might enter the transpersonal realm; it has a quality of being greater than ourselves, with what can spontaneously arrive on the paper, in the clay, or in the room between the therapist and the patient through image making. In this stage of the work, it is helpful to remember that we only have to attend to the moment and remain in relationship with the patient who is touching into this new state of consciousness. We do not have to respond to questions that arise because they often exceed human understanding. It is also helpful to have a willingness to remain quiet and attentive in the face of archetypal emotions and images, to simply listen for the whispers, because in the face of so much information and knowledge, the archetypal field remains mysterious.

I once worked with a five-year-old boy who made small hand-held layered images with torn paper and drawings. When finished, he would lean in close and whisper to me as he revealed the hidden blending of colors covered by small shapes of torn paper he had glued down. While a psychodynamic approach may offer an Oedipal interpretation or focus on his developmental stage, what was also present was this young child's precious connection to the joy and mystery of what he created. The images were like beautiful little jewels that held our attention in those sacred moments when he whispered the stories about what he had made. If we listen closely, children are often intimately and unabashedly connected to the archetypal energy of the Self and are rarely self-conscious when it comes to appreciating what they have made.

The Relationship Between Ego, Complexes, and Archetypes

The ego's relationship to the unconscious and the relationship between the complex and the archetype are both key considerations of Jungian art therapy. Because the archetype is at the core of a complex, it contributes both structure and energy to the complex that becomes constellated. The complex expresses the personal affect, or gives a *personal* face to the universal primordial pattern that is trying to be expressed. For instance, we all have a mother, but the personal details of our own mother form a particular feeling-toned image, thought, or pattern that locates the work in the present rather than in the material of the archetypal mother, or the universal past, present, and future.

The attitude of the ego determines how the complex and the archetype are received; the aim is to maintain a level of consciousness, or relatedness, in the face of unconscious material. Structurally, complexes and archetypes are always in relationship, which is why images and symbols become conscious when psychic energy flows from the archetype into the complex with a particular quality and intensity. Jung's inclusion of the archetype as the theoretical structure meant that within each personal complex is a foundation from which the lived experience is animated and purposeful.

In the therapeutic relationship, archetypal patterns also manifest through the unique quality of the transference/countertransference field phenomenon first noted by Jung, but more specifically by von Franz (1980) as an archetypal field. Subsequently, many Jungian authors have explored the vast archetypal dynamics of this phenomenon. Archetypal material can feel both personal and contemporary with particular meaning for an individual and expand the mutually shared space while it is discussed, explored through art, and found in shared visions or dream images (Cwik, 2011). When we use a myth or fairytale, followed by art materials, the archetypal images may offer helpful underlying structures for personal experiences and emotions. As we have heard from Ellen, using the inherent structures of art materials facilitates a reaction and aids in weathering the winds of the unconscious material that may overwhelm her psyche and, in some cases, potentially the therapeutic container.

When we force the use of archetypal material, we are actually using an ego-oriented approach, which can concretize and trap the archetypal energy just so we have a tidy story. This approach can further abandon individual complexes associated with suffering and pain, but it also overly simplifies the archetypal experience and feels like salt in the wound. Sometimes the therapeutic relationship may endure a compensatory archetypal reaction from the analysand that sets us straight and clears the air. In Faye's case there was no tidy solution. Although she had longed for relief, she knew she was working with complicated grief. Instead, she learned to name and negotiate her individual suffering (complexes) and weather the intermittent archetypal storms (post-traumatic stress reactions) that blew through her daily life. When both Ellen and Faye could gain clarity to piece together a meaningful storyline, then there was imagination and a greater connection to the collective. With imagination, they had endurance to continue on the treacherous paths that run throughout the landscape of grief. Writing our own myth entails imagination, endurance, and the willingness to circumambulate and suffer the unconscious emotional content and our human failures and mistakes that ultimately lead to consciousness, and access to the Self. Step-by-step, we rejoin the world with a new frame of reference, and a new perspective. We participate in the collective with fresh insights, and, importantly, with the capacity to rely on our imagination because it has been fertilized to withstand future archetypal forces.

How Do We Recognize an Archetype?

Without a doubt, archetypes are purposeful—not because they want us to succeed but because *they* want to succeed. As noted, they want to become visible. Jung contended that when we have a psychic reaction to a common situation that is out of proportion to the situation itself, we are probably in the midst of archetypal energy and should at least investigate if what is occurring is partially the expression of an archetype attempting to become known to us through our personal complexes or through contemporary issues within the collective. For instance, an ambivalent reaction to our male boss could be related to our father complex, but at the core of the complex is the Father archetype, which then has ties to growing up in the hierarchy of organized religion and a male-dominated society. Not only is there a religious or spiritual pole, but there is an archetypal power and structure that denotes the instinctual side of the archetype as well as the shadow side, particularly if there was an early interference with the body such as sexual or emotional abuse. Sorting through our personal complexes from the archetypal threads is essential work for Jungian art therapy.

Archetypes also mark major life events. Rather than analyzing or interpreting them, we acknowledge the profound influence that archetypal structures have on our life and how they highlight our humanity. Then we parse out what is personally meaningful. Archetypes take us into the depths of our soul, influence us, move us, touch us, and perhaps destroy us in ways that are catastrophic to the ego, and are ineffable, meaningful, and life changing. However, Jung tells us our ego plays a conscious role in negotiating and regulating how we engage with and mediate these unconscious energies; then the function of archetypes furthers individuation. An individual who was ill and has recovered may need to work with the power of the archetypal experience by sorting through the events to find a meaningful narrative. The understanding may come through dreams, images, and symbols. Jung reminded us that when we are suffering from the powers of an archetype we cannot see clearly—this is one important rationale behind Jungian art therapy. Through our creative instinct we uncover the hidden structure of our story that carries us forward.

Jungian Art Therapy: Ellen's Story

Ellen used her sketchbook because it often deterred her from feeling torn asunder, much like Jung's experience of feeling calmer when he drew mandalas (Jung, 1961). Ellen, who was mentioned in Chapter 6 regarding her use of clay, described how she had to "walk a ridgeline" in her daily life during a period of deep personal Jungian analysis. Several traumatic losses within her family had left her bereft and vulnerable to archetypal forces from the unconscious. When she used her sketchbook to make an image of the ridgeline (initially black and white and then color), Ellen was gripped in a complex of complicated emotions and felt the pull to get something down so she'd feel calmer. Making her images gave her perspective and a sense of relief. When Ellen notified me that she was "walking the ridgeline" we knew she was feeling overwhelmed with unconscious material—the phrase and her sketchbook images were personal expressions and documentations of the fine line she had to walk to steady her conscious mind. Sometimes the destructive forces (archetypal) interrupted her capacity for creative solutions (ego thoughts), while other times a subtle shift in the "climate" through using her sketchbook led to emotional recovery so she could carry on with her day. It was a balancing act for us both as she navigated the path between experiencing her emotions (complexes), but not becoming overwhelmed by archetypal energies. Theoretically, Ellen's emotions indicated how the archetype was clothed—the ridgeline image and metaphor brilliantly described the tension of the opposites unique to her story as well as the danger and alienation that her ego felt as she made her way through the untold emotions associated with events in her life. Her Ridgeline images #1 and #2 (Figures 6.1 and 6.2) illustrate the threshold between the conscious and the unconscious, light and dark, and life and death. Ellen was not privy to Jung's theoretical model, but her images naturally illustrated specific aspects of his map of the psyche.

The burdens Ellen carried on this path were heavy; at times they exhausted her. For protection, complexes had formed around the archetypal grief from a very early age. In order to remain on the "ridgeline" path and not fall to either side, Ellen was learning to mediate the opposites long enough for a new image (facilitated by the transcendent function) to emerge that would reinstate the imagination and a relational connection to herself, and to our work. One of the symbols that took on various expressions was a small home by the sea where Ellen imagined shelter from the precarious path on the ridgeline (Figure 8.5). As she peeled away the old protections of some of her complexes, she was also in need of new images, new metaphors, that could explain her interior world. For Ellen these images had to arise naturally: from walks, active imagination, dreams, or visions.

The home by the sea represents both a complex and an archetypal image. Although the unconscious (sea) takes up most of the page in Figure 8.5, at the top center, in a location of command and consciousness, we find a brown shape that gives the picture a particular location. This was an important point of recovery for Ellen even though it might still look precarious. Could this be an image of her personality, a reconnection to consciousness, a new "emotional home," or an archetypal image of nourishment? The spacious element in the picture was specific to Ellen with its two-sidedness of overwhelming grief and isolation and spaciousness and liberation. The image verified her need for the notion of "home" while the archetypal phenomenon of the existential challenges was left unimpaired.

Figure 8.5 Home

The discovery about her psyche that Ellen made through her images was a powerful affirmation and often liberating, which is why it is important that the images not betray what is authentic and true for a patient. Whatever we may wonder about the image, for Ellen the proportions felt emotionally correct and authentic. When our eyes land on the small home, our focus locates a new *possibility*—the possibility of a place to ground, an emotional shelter from the world. In this moment, what mattered most was that the image pushed up from within Ellen and carried the symbol of home, a deeply embodied archetypal reminder of a certain place of belonging that did, in fact, exist deep within her psyche. Jungian art therapy waits for the healing properties of the archetype as we work with the shadow and splinter psyches (multiplicity) within us. When the instinctual energy is awakened, the paths open to "affective experience which heals splits. Images give form to emotion and emotions give a living body to imagination; the expression of archetypal possibility is both poetic and dramatic" (Salamon, 2006, p. 70). The image gave Ellen a reminder, and a sense of purpose; she had an image of land and belonging amongst the great sea of life and death. The image spoke the truth. Yet it also provided a bridge between the worlds she navigated, and this was deeply satisfying for Ellen. Several months later, Ellen used this image to place selected clay figures on the landscape, which reinforced a sense of ground within her psyche.

Jungian Art Therapy: Janet's Story

The three mandalas in Figures 8.6, 8.7, and 8.8 were painted by Janet, a 53-year-old woman. The profound loss remained undifferentiated for her, so I suggested she tell me the story like a fairytale and make a new mandala for each stage. The first image in Figure 8.6 focused on her initial existential emptiness and paradoxically the new beginning. Figure 8.7 was concerned with her grief and Figure 8.8 was the anger she had not yet considered.

Curiously, the second image (Figure 8.7) seemed to portray the spontaneous image of a fetus. Janet didn't recognize this image until we reflected on all three of the paintings and she suddenly saw it. She associated it to an earlier time in her life when she had a second-trimester miscarriage. The image reveals how the psyche is layered and the archetypal

Figure 8.6 Despair

Figure 8.7 Sad

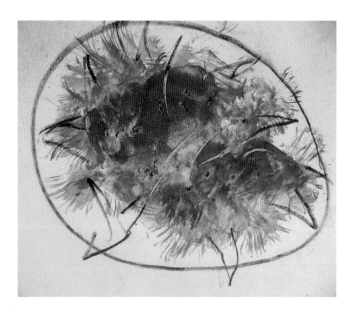

Figure 8.8 Anger

patterns are autonomous structures that remain hidden until they are ready to become known. Archetypal grief was imbedded within her psyche and awakened as she acknowledged her personal memories and feelings associated to her losses. This is an expression of the poetic and the dramatic, or the bi-polar nature within the psyche.

The Archetype of Individuation

Although individuation has been mentioned above, Jung's concept is so pivotal to his theory that it is worth further discussion. Jung saw the archetype of individuation as a circular process that expands beyond the daily development of ego and Self: "There is no linear 'evolution,' there is only circumambulation of the Self. Uniform development exists, at most, only at the beginning; later everything points towards the centre" (Jung, 1961, p. 188). Jung's point remains relevant today, particularly in an age where narcissism is no longer considered a diagnostic category and where a healthy will in life is conflated with ego-driven accomplishments, sometimes to the point of devaluing relationships at the expense of self-aggrandizement and inflation.

According to Jung, the ego has to endure suffering for the Self to express itself. He asserted that the ego is often mistaken for the Self because of how we overvalue the conscious mind and distrust the unknown aspects of psyche. There is tremendous fear of the unknown and the unconscious, but when we become obedient to the deeper and more expansive part of ourselves we undergo a maturational change and pass through developmental stages of life. The ego's ability to endure is not synonymous with the Self or individuation. Jung made great strides in considering human development as a psychological journey with stages. Individuation may begin at some point within the womb and continue until we die. We never become fully individuated, but are constantly engaged in the archetypal process of death/rebirth. The ego can then be of service to the Self so as to facilitate its purpose and realization; otherwise we have only an ego-dominated and ego-driven life. Contrary to popular opinion, Jungian analysis facilitates the liberation of the individual through "Individuation [which] does not shut one out from the world, but gathers the world to oneself" (Jung, 1937/1972, CW 8, p. 226). In other words, Jung reminds us that our individuation cannot occur alone, but must take place within community and with engagement with the collective.

Jungian Art Therapy: John's Story

John was a 26-year-old college student who was well acquainted with Jung's work. His Jungian art therapy unfolded in such a way that he productively accessed his imagination and anchored the archetypal energy through the discovery of stone carving. But first John arrived in my office with a stack of active imaginations and an elaborate dream that focused on a castle with battles in mysterious realms. This alerted us to the profound psychological "event" that was taking place in his psyche and his capacity to consider his inner world with a wide lens. Prior Jungian analysis had opened him to deep psychological work, and now, enchanted by archetypal material and the multiplicity of the psyche, he wished to continue his investigations. I sensed from him some idealization about the material from the unconscious, but his enthusiasm for the work touched me.

John's biracial/bicultural heritage hinted at the fact that he embodied a quality of duality that at times generated internal friction for him and much suffering that had yet to be told. He identified himself as an intro-verted thinking type, although he had already developed a positive respect towards the feminine aspect (anima) of his psyche through his imagination. I initially carried the feeling function and noticed at times I could feel like the simpleton in a fairy tale: I might feel pulled to join his intellectual investigations towards the unconscious material. My work as the art therapist and Jungian analyst was to make sure the feeling in the room was available to us both so the soul was not pinned like a butterfly for our mere fascination and observation.

John arrived on time for weekly sessions. As he made use of associations and symbolic thinking, new parts of his psyche were revealed. Education about Jung's psychological map of the psyche was helpful for John and gave him permission to deepen into emotions he had banished to the woods (shadow). He felt relieved when he unloaded his burdens and shared his emotions; these times produced key shifts in his perspective about the past, present, and future.[3]

During a difficult period when John consciously worked on his relation-ship with his father and the Father archetype, he took a sculpting course. He found and bought a piece of alabaster, a stone with archetypal refer-ence as it was once used to hold special ointments and was mentioned in the Bible. The process of finding the stone, caring for it, and buying excellent tools so "the best of the stone could reveal itself" took John into the creative instinct that relies on Jung's instincts of action and reflec-tion. He was engaged with the stone participating as "other" and he found a new way to listen to his soul. "I let it talk to me. I worked into dusk, working without any conscious thoughts . . . Sanding and polishing it was meditative. It was like cooking." Having worked as a chef, John noticed times when his unconscious was silent and simply tending to the tasks. Other times he was driven into a new psychological process of reaching down into himself to bring life out of the stone. John was pleased by how the slow meditative tasks could give birth to new energy, and a fresh consciousness. It made use of his healthy aggression, and the work satisfied him. John's title *Emergence* was appropriate for both the carving and his emotional process. The archetypal quality of the stone both structured and pushed on John's individuation.

John noticed through carving that he had reconnected to his body and that his dissociation dissipated. In our last session, he reflected upon how his early archetypal material had led to periods of psychological inflation, interfered with his relationships in the human world, and distorted his connections with the unconscious. We noted the paradoxical encounter with separateness while at the same time a greater intimacy with the stone was incredibly expansive for John in an unexpected way. Until John made the carving, this part of his psyche had not yet been recognized because it had been in the grips of the archetypal realm of the parents and their religious practices. He had not yet been psychologically born. The stone literally invited him to use his aggression and be true to his own nature as he engaged in the relationship.

Intuitively, John had found a creative method that expressed his lived duality and acknowledged the internal opposites that lived within him. Every view of his stone (Figures 8.9 through 8.12) elicited a different imaginal space and meaningful associations. Moreover, the multiplicity within the psyche was not split off into separate complexes, but contained in one solid mass of alabaster, which resulted in a psychological emergence. John was fully engaged with this archetypal material, but he was no longer unconsciously possessed by its archetypal forces. Now John had the felt-experience of how the archetypal energies within his psyche were structured, held and expressed by the weight, color, and innate expression of the stone and the stories that accompanied the images therein.

These four different viewpoints of *Emergence* illustrate how John's relationship to the archetype of the Self was a psychological initiation. Each image documents a different archetypal pattern. The first view (Figure 8.9) resembles a body hunched over to one side, coming into its own. The image suggests *The Thinker*, an archetypal statue by Rodin.

Figure 8.9   John #1

Figure 8.10   John #2

Figure 8.11   John #3

Figure 8.12   John #4

John was a logical type, but our work together gave him the opportunity to explore the messiness and painfulness of his emotions. In the second view (Figure 8.10) we see two sides coming together as one, folding over to form an exit/entrance or a place for the "third." This view suggests John's work with the opposites and the shift in consciousness that occurred with the transcendent function. The third view (Figure 8.11) shows the full circle and hints at the archetypal presence of the Self—the transpersonal image of wholeness within the psyche. In the fourth view (Figure 8.12) the stone from above reveals the three-sided triangle. This may allude to the archetypal pattern of change, psychological transformation, and the inherent role of the transcendent function within the psyche. Indeed, John had worked diligently with the psyche to give birth to a new consciousness. By the time John finished Jungian art therapy, he had graduated, was getting married, and would attend graduate school. In our psychological work together, John had cultivated an authentic and generative relationship to the archetype of the Self.

Important Summary Points about Archetypes

Universal patterns are found everywhere from the smallest cells in our body to the most remote areas of space. Jung formulated his ideas of the archetype as a psychological concept based on the research carried out by previous generations and he spent much of his life wrestling with this idea, which was a kind of personal expression of his own individuation. Jung positioned the Self as the centering force that unifies the archetypal structures. The numinous power of the archetypes is enticing and seductive—they feed our soul, but they deserve respect as we step into dangerous territory when in the grips of their nonhuman energy that has the power to both destroy and transform. It is important to remember that archetypes:

1. are at the core of all complexes and exist in the collective unconscious;
2. are not seen directly but are partially apprehended through images and symbols;
3. are bipolar, meaning they contain both a spiritual pole and an instinctual pole, and have positive and negative forces;
4. provide a powerful source of energy that fuels the affect that is felt through our complexes which disrupt the ego's seat of consciousness;
5. are purposeful and our conscious mind is either positively or negatively impacted by their force.

Endnotes

1. William James gave his first lecture using the term *transpersonal* in 1905 at Harvard University, where he had also taught the very first class ever offered in psychology.
2. For further reading consider M. Ryan (2008). The Transpersonal William James, *Journal of Transpersonal Psychology*, 40(1).

3. See the Appendix on Jung's Stages of Therapy. Jung gave as much theoretical consideration to the stages of psychotherapy as to the stages of life and wrote several essays collected in *Volume 16* regarding his ideas. With these stages, Jung used various approaches to psychotherapy, specifically his methods of working with dreams, art, and active imagination within the clinical work. His vast knowledge of religion, myth, cultural anthropology, science, and literature were important contributions not just to his ideas on psychotherapy but to help him verify that image is psyche and that the collective unconscious is a driving force behind human development and consciousness.

Part III

Passage

Engaging with Images

Passage is the final phase of the three-part liminal process associated with the initiation rites. It is concerned with moving forward, taking action, and giving some interpretation and commitment to the unconscious process. It is also a time of rebirth and renewal, but it does not come easily. Dreams and active imagination are methods that, when combined with Jungian art therapy, allow us to put shape and color to the inner landscape of the attending phase. We take action to bring consciousness to our story and uncover some of the riddles of the unconscious. Passages can be tight squeezes, dark alleys of uncertainty, or gushing waters. Suddenly everything can change and we are ushered into a new state of consciousness with a new attitude. This new attitude is born from our dedication and devotion to our psychological work and the subtle respect for the images that can destroy or cure us, but there is always a possibility for transformation.

CHAPTER **9**

Dreams and Art Therapy

The Importance of Dreams

Dreaming is a universal experience. Everyone dreams even though we don't always remember our dreams. In fact, sometimes we might wish we could forget them, or we might ignore them because they are not readily understood, or the images disturb or frighten us. In order to truly learn the language of our dreams, we have to make time to study the specific contents. As a Jungian art therapist and Jungian analyst, I work with dreams on a regular basis because they are the most unadulterated material that comes into the therapy and they offer insight and compensation for the individual interested in consciousness. My approach has structure but is fluid enough to follow the analysand's interests and the needs of the psyche. This means I sometimes work in a focused orthodox way with the dream from start to finish, while other times I encourage analysands to engage with their dreams, to bring them alive by first painting them, sculpting them, or sketching key images so the mind can be affected. Psyche wants us to pay attention, and when we do, the rewards emerge from the collaborative and creative process facilitated by Jung's synthetic method.

The synthetic method (Chapter 5) is an essential tool for unwrapping the deeper meaning of a dream; it provides a structure that we can follow to grasp the underlying tension of the complexes while we circumambulate the images from the dream. Jung's synthetic method used with dreams is clinically therapeutic, relational, and is best used with a dose of spaciousness and curiosity. Much like initial pictures for art therapists, the initial dreams

189

may give a broad perspective on the future of the treatment and the individuation process; however, Jung felt interpretation was not always advisable for dreams and certainly we should not suffocate the imagination by over-defining with our own ideas (Jung, 1931/1985, CW 16). The meaning of a dream can change over time, alongside our own development of consciousness. This is similar to the images we work with, as we'll see below.

Jungian dream analysis is a massive topic that benefits from personal experience and professional training; however, its various perspectives are widely published and selected details will only be mentioned here. Since we are interested in how dreams fit into Jungian art therapy I will provide a brief background and some basic details to orient us. What follows will focus on how dreams reflect the unfolding of the psyche and its various key concepts. Building on the previous chapters that emphasized the role of complexes and archetypes within the psyche, the following vignettes will illustrate the powerful influence that these have on the individuals who work with their dreams in Jungian art therapy.

Freud and Dreams

As we know, Jung was greatly influenced by Freud's pioneering ideas on dreams and his work with the unconscious. In order to fully understand Jung's view of dream work, it is illustrative to again consider the contrast between their views. Without a doubt, Freud's *Interpretation of Dreams* opened the door in psychoanalysis to see dreams as a useful psychological method. For Freud, dreams were the royal road to the unconscious, meaning the *personal unconscious*. Freud viewed dreams as expressions of either the previous day's events or of repressed childhood content that was made available for analysis. His attachment to the sexual drive theory led Freud to conclude that forbidden sexual wishes were expressed through the images, or manifest content, in the dreams, which pointed to repressed latent feelings and wishes that were typically of a sexual nature. Freud also thought the mechanism of a censor, or superego, protected the ego from disturbances and preserved the ability to sleep. These disturbances could be analyzed in a reductive way, meaning the content was taken back to its original meaning through a process of free association until the essential latent meaning of the dream was found. At this point the psychological neurosis could be resolved. The original image in the dream was overlooked or bypassed in the search to find the infantile latent fantasies through this method of reductive analysis.[1] This simplistic explanation is only an introduction and is not meant to minimize Freud's discoveries and significant contributions.

Initially, Jung mostly agreed with Freud's ideas that dreams were significant expressions of the unconscious. He concurred that dreams included wishes and fears; he also thought they were purposeful but felt they were presented without hidden meanings and that we needed to understand the picture language of the unconscious. Jung devised his synthetic method to analyze dreams because it incorporated personal associations to events and mythic images as a way to "triangulate" potential archetypal content. In developing his own method, Jung was explicit about *not* narrowing his dream method down to a technique or a doctrine (Jung, 1931/1985, CW 16, p. 148). Contrary to popular opinion, Jung valued the phenomenology of dreams and reinforced that both pictures and dreams were baffling to him—that interpretations were limiting. He did not believe that symbols should be confined by simple interpretations, but he was incredibly knowledgeable about many subjects and, as a result, could easily provide references and amplifications to dream images that some perhaps misunderstood as a reductive model of working with dreams and their symbols.

Jung realized that we are all prone to investigate, define, differentiate, and, at the worst, potentially fall into the trap of confining the psyche with empirical rules by simply aiming to better understand its mechanics (energic paradigm). These Jungian concepts may guide us at first, but they are only markers and do not fully define a lived experience. Rather, through our dreams and Jungian art therapy, we are liberated by the expression of psychic energy that moves from one image or symbol to another. When the symbol has lived its purpose, its *energy* becomes an assimilated lived experience. The approach to the psyche requires a taste for a creative, dialectical, and collaborative process associated with a death/rebirth pattern, as well as an appreciation for aesthetics, culture, phenomenology, images, symbols, and amplification (symbolic paradigm), all of which unearth and revitalize the soul and transform the psyche. As Harding (1961) said so well:

> [a]ll down the ages the religions have called symbols *revelations* . . . Symbols having this kind of numinosity are, of course, expressions of the archetypes which exert such a powerful influence not only on the life of the individual but on that of society as well.
>
> (pp. 2–3)

Amongst many things, symbols have been known to unite individuals and communities by providing hope, inspiration, focus and direction, and some relief from the pain and suffering of being human.

Jung's Approach to Dreams

Jung's approach to dreams was not dogmatic, but he did eventually reject Freud's reductive ideas and establish his own principles regarding dream analysis (Stevens & Storr, 1994, p. 82). A notable difference was that Jung maintained a position of "not knowing" when settling in to work with a dream alongside his tremendous knowledge of symbols to support the amplification process (Jung, 1931/1985, CW 16). Rather than repressed or disguised expressions of unfulfilled sexual wishes or a primary intent to preserve sleep, dreams were "more likely . . . natural products of the psyche . . . they perform some homeostatic or self-regulatory function, and . . . obey the biological imperative of adaptation in the interests of personal adjustment, growth, and survival" (Stevens & Storr, 1994, p. 83). Jung's work with dreams to encourage the health of the psyche was a notable and creative shift in the psychoanalytic work with the unconscious.

For Jung, dreams offered specific details and elements that we attend to, and at the same time, a whole complete image. They are "physiological facts: if sugar appears in the urine, then the urine contains sugar, and not albumen or . . . something else that might fit in better with my expectations. . . . I take dreams as diagnostically valuable facts" (Jung, 1934/1985, CW 16, p. 143). Both the details and a complete image in a dream reveal the inner truth of the psyche. Once Jung recognized that dreams could be completely and utterly independent of the conscious mind, he was obligated to investigate more deeply how the dream impacted the development of consciousness. His recommendations for working with dreams gave a beautiful formulation for the art of psychotherapy that remains applicable today (Jung, 1934/1985, CW 16, pp. 139–161). Unquestionably, working with dreams is a craft that improves with professional clinical proficiency, exposure, and ongoing personal involvement with dream imagery.

Jung's dream method can also be explained by his own individuation process. After his separation from Freud, Jung became more fluid and expansive towards the role of dreams. There are several events that informed and influenced him during this time. One was when Freud refused to allow Jung to analyze his dream in 1909, on their way to America, because he would lose his authority over Jung. This moment is noted as a turning point for Jung, who realized that Freud valued authority over the discovery of the unconscious. In addition, Jung recognized how authority interfered with the expression of the unconscious (Jung, 1961). He recognized that the unconscious tells the unavoidable truth. Even though Jung thought the ego may prefer to deny the contents in the unconscious as an outright rejection of becoming conscious, he viewed dreams as offering the gifts for psychological transformation through unadulterated and truthful unconscious material. According to Jung, the complex was the royal road to the unconscious, not dreams as Freud had said. But within dreams both personal complexes and archetypal material are discoverable and offer magnificent and unexpected psychological insights.

Perhaps Jung's separation from Freud allowed him to be more creative with dreams. It may have also influenced his preference for a collaborative relational process in analysis. He chose a face-to-face model, or what we might refer to today as a two-person relational analysis, over a couch model, or one-person analysis, and encouraged an openness and a willingness not to know what the dream meant:

> We must renounce all preconceived opinions, however knowing they make us feel, and try to discover what things mean for the patient. In so doing, we shall obviously not get very far towards a theoretical interpretation . . . But if the practitioner operates too much with fixed symbols, there is a danger of his falling into mere routine and pernicious dogmatism, and thus failing his patient.
>
> (Jung, 1934/1985, CW 16, p. 157)

With this attitude in place, the therapeutic pair could dive into the dream and rely on emotions, associations, and imagination.

Throughout his life, Jung had many dreams that were significant to him and influenced his theoretical relationship towards the unconscious (Jung, 1961). He recognized that most dreams were about daily events, but beneath that content was rich material associated with complexes and archetypes; these details require concentrated investigation by an engaged psyche, particularly as assimilation was key to individuation and moving towards psychological wholeness.

Since most people's dreams are about everyday topics and material, Jung pointed out that rarely do people have archetypal dreams (or big dreams, as he called them) about unfamiliar topics. When these arise they are markers on the path. In most cases the analyst or Jungian art therapist works to sort through the everyday images in the dream to determine the complexes, and then consider the archetypal elements. This is not an easy task. Particularly, Jung reminded us, because interpretations are only based on an hypothesis. As he worked with the dreamer, he found that she gradually began to have her own interpretations, something Jung supported as an important result of analysis. However, he acknowledged it as a later stage of the analytic work that emphasized the individuation process and the activation of what he called an *inner agent* (Jung, 1930/1985, CW 16). From the beginning of Jungian art therapy, the analysand is supported in listening for and knowing the language of her own psyche.

Overall, Jung insisted that we must remain open to each new dream. When we sit down and face a dream, we might have a reaction or a thought, but we do not know what it means. A dream demands that we work on it, and that we circumambulate, picking apart and putting together. Sometimes it might feel as though we are working on a large puzzle, holding many images at once, but have no idea where the pieces belong. Jung noted that if we don't know what the dream means, it is not the dreamer's problem nor the problem of the unconscious, but our inability to see it correctly, which simply means we have more work to do with the dream. More often than not, the dream needs to work on us until we have time to circle back and try again. Some dreams take time to simmer. We stir and mull and stir some more. Other dreams hold meaning for an entire lifetime. The unconscious likes attention. When we deny its existence and relevancy in our life, it becomes louder and more forceful.

How to Catch a Dream

We first have to "catch" our dreams by writing them down. Dreams are as slippery as fish and so if we hook a fish (dream) from the unconscious, we often struggle to figure out how to "land" it, how to reel it in. One way is to keep paper and pencil by our beds. Before going to sleep, we can ask the unconscious for dreams and then when we have even a small image or word, we can write it down. As we all know, as soon as we get up or begin walking around, the dream can be lost. Having a special ritual or place to put our dreams offers an important message regarding our commitment to the unconscious. Sometimes people type their dreams and keep them logged on the computer. Getting them off our phones and into a place where they are truly honored is often a challenging task for today's culture. I still prefer to hand-write my dreams so I can also draw or add other elements that are important to the dream content. Whatever way we choose to catch our dreams, dream work requires that we take the unconscious seriously, which means making the time and attending to its message so we can move its contents to consciousness. That is often a primary reason why people come to Jungian art therapy—they want a regular sacred space to mull over the contents from their unconscious whether it be dreams, images, or visions. Furthermore, the space to actively create images has become rare in our modern world.

The Structure of a Dream

According to analytical psychology, dreams have an important structure (often compared to the dramatic structure) that is a useful map for navigating them. The first stage is the setting or *exposition* where we consider time, place, and the characters who open the drama of the dream. The second stage is the development of the plot or *peripeteia* where we learn about the ups and downs of the story line that lead to the ensuing conflicts or trouble. The third stage is the *crisis*, where there is a decisive action and the dream shifts and speaks to the problem or the complex.

The *lysis* is the final event or message in the dream that offers a solution or is the result of the dream work. Or it may leave the question open for the dreamer to wonder about, suggesting a tension of the opposites and indicating where the friction of psychic energy must be felt to ignite or activate the transcendent function. Using our imagination about any stage of the dream highlights ways in which we can access the message of a dream, particularly if the dream details are translated into a picture where a dreamer can work with her complexes.

Types of Dreams

While dreams are probably the best possible expression of content that is still unconscious, Jung was adamant that "the values of the conscious personality remain intact, for unconscious compensation is only effective when it co-operates with an integral consciousness. Assimilation is never a question of 'this *or* that,' but always of 'this *and* that'" (Jung, 1934/1985, CW 16, pp. 155–156). Jung's synthetic method with dreams allowed for a mutual dialogue within a shared experience of the unconscious imagery and helped uncover what attitude may be too one-sided in the self-regulating system of the psyche as it seeks balance.

Jung thought dreams compensated for a conscious attitude by either opposing the conscious psyche or by confirming the conscious attitude. When we have a dream we ask: what conscious attitude needs compensation? And what type of compensation does it suggest? Or, what wants to become known by way of these images? There are other types of dreams as well, but *traumatic* dreams or nightmares can feel frightening or destructive, and are highly affect laden. They may not be the immediate focus of the therapy simply because they disorient and overstimulate. It is often helpful to first search for equilibrium before poking further into the dream's content. The dream may have served its purpose to bring something of importance to consciousness that is worked on within a therapeutic setting; if need be the psychotherapist can circle back around to the dream at a later date. Other times an image in the dream is a critical point of illumination and numinosity. The use of materials to express the contents of the dream is of tremendous help in not just documenting or concretizing the dream, but furthering the experience and expanding the important qualities of the dream. But each individual works differently so there are no hard and fast rules.

An example of a non-compensatory dream is the *prospective* dream. These give us warnings. Dan's dream from Chapter 7 is a good example. Dan was working through some issues he had with another colleague in his suite when he had a dream of two equal-sized balls or seeds in a field

(Figure 7.5). Dan associated the image to a meeting that was going to happen. The image looks safe enough with two red seeds in a green field, but the red color (anger, heat) and the association of contamination to the dust near the object gave Dan a warning that things might not be as they seem. In reality, the meeting was difficult and things were said that could have potentially "contaminated" the relationship, but because he had consciously prepared himself, the result of the meeting was successful.

Basic Notes on Dreams

When we are presented with a dream, the first thing we might notice is the mood of the dream and what it does to us inside our body—our somatic reactions to the dream. We may notice what draws us in, what is peculiar or out of balance or what is left unsaid. These all refer to shadow content and lead us to images of defensive structures or complexes. Sometimes dreams have missing pieces and other times they have sudden shifts, while still other dreams are long, rambling, and sometimes chaotic. As people work on their dreams, the dreams can become more condensed and organized. No one dream is like any other. Each needs to be held as a unique treasure from the unconscious. The images that are experienced first when the person has the dream, when they write it down, and when they share it is an emerging process in and of itself. Catching a dream by using art materials can be incredibly powerful as it promotes a visual relationship with the unconscious, and, as mentioned above, expands and highlights particular qualities within the dream. Of course, whatever is made conscious inherently leaves something else unconscious or as shadow to be uncovered at a later time.

If dreams are internal psychic experiences that are real, and unadulterated truths, then our job is to soften enough so as to allow them to impact our attitude and shift our perspective. According to Jung their symbolic potential is meant to have an effect on our psyche. We cannot translate dreams into literal or concrete messages, such as the fantasy about "getting back together" or meeting someone new. While some dreams may lead to real human events, initially, we stay close to the dream imagery and work diligently with our own unconscious associations—shadow and complexes—regarding the dream as whole story. Also, when the unconscious compensates with "faces" of familiar people in our life we are challenged even more so to not become literal but to work symbolically. We rely on projection, differentiation, and the subjective and objective associations to uncover what these figures might express or represent within the psyche rather than only who they actually are in real life.

Dream images carry the energy of the transcendent function, which presupposes that dreams are propelled by an unconscious psychic energy flowing out of (progressive) the collective unconscious to fill archetypal structures and constellate complexes that are made visible and more conscious. Our reactions may propel us to paint or draw. The energy within a dream presents specific elements and details of the psyche's condition and at the same time may suggest ways to engage or move that energy forward, especially when the symbol is given concrete form in a picture, painting, carving, or other art product. Stevens and Storr proclaimed that "Human beings owe their pre-eminent status in the world to the fact that they are symbol-making animals" (1994, p. 86) and the clinical case below offers an example of how this flow of energy moves forward into an innate process of symbol formation. With this in mind, let's move to some ways in which Jungian art therapy works with dreams.

Dreams and Jungian Art Therapy

"Dreams are the guiding words of the soul. Why should I henceforth not love my dreams and not make their riddling images into objects of my daily consideration?" (Jung, 2009b, p. 132). When we attend to our dreams using journals or visual journaling practices we are circumambulating the *imaginal* realm. In a small and intimate format, we can begin simply with markers and soft pencils or water pencils to document feeling-toned aspects of the dream or illustrate details of the dream. The picture will naturally take on its own character that may not exactly duplicate the dream, but that is an essential step of the dream unfolding into an art therapy process where we get more information about the dream. We may shift our choice of materials to capture certain images of beauty or aspects that terrify us or we may create a picture of the whole dream. With traumatic dreams we can deliberately create an image that compensates for the dream content before we begin further investigations into the dream. For instance, Marion brought dream images that reminded her of her childhood abuse. Marion knew that before she could discuss the dream she needed to first make an image of her adult self protecting her child self. It's also important to consider what the dream is asking of us—or what it might want or need from us. Perhaps it wants a larger format than our journal. If the dream had a lot of movement, we could document it in a comic strip or storyboard format. Using the mandala circle, we can make a spontaneous image as soon as we wake up so as to visually record our raw response to the dream. Jungian art therapy encourages the dream images to continue to live and express themselves through us. It's important to let go of all egoic expectations because the dream is its own entity and the images that follow begin a life of their own if we give them a visual voice. As Jung reminds us: ". . . dreams pave the way for life, and they determine you without you understanding their language" (Jung, 2009b, pp. 132–133). In fact, each time I am faced with a dream, I am also confronted with my own incapacity to know what it means until I begin to engage with the images.

Dreams Carry Energy, Memory, and Emotion

Jungian Art Therapy: Anna's Story

Sometimes dreams express a structural quality of the psyche with the movement of psychic energy, but we may have to wait for further clarification from the psyche. Anna, a 62-year-old woman, had the following dream: "*There were two green snakes, one in the house and one on the porch. My black cat ran inside to escape the big snake on the porch. My husband helped with the snakes.*" Without personal associations, the dream illustrates the instincts as "typical modes of action" and a possible tension within the archetypal field between the two poles of energy defined by two snakes: one in the house and one outside—alluding to one in the conscious and one in the unconscious. The dream images of the snakes express the instinctual and spiritual poles of the archetype as they are understood as both dark and cold-blooded and as transformers of psychic energy through the archetypes of initiation and individuation. Anna associated her black cat with her soul; we might imagine the cat carried some energy as it ran away from one snake. We might also imagine the psychic energy was retreating, or the energy was moving between the poles, back and forth, to facilitate a transformation through an integration of opposites. Much of this is speculation until we gather associations from the dreamer that can verify in which way the dream is offering compensation.

When Anna drew the dream (Figure 9.1) she noticed that in that moment she was emphasizing the green color. "The green new growth aspect felt more present than in the dream," she said. She had also experienced a loss of idealization as she reclaimed some shadow projections. An important decision in her life had unearthed a transformational process deep in her psyche illustrated by the dramatic energy within the dream with the two snakes and the cat and the help of her husband.

Jungian Art Therapy: Dawn's Story

Dawn was a 40-year-old professional woman, artist, and mother. She was pregnant when she had the following dream (abbreviated):

> We all go to a house and there are lots of creative supplies. On the wall is a picture of a castle with a white horse in front of it. The horse was glowing. Then I looked around and saw that we were going to the

basement. There was a beautiful green banister on the stairway. I love that green. There were even more art supplies and I feel this need to have some of them. I think how they are all fresh. But, I'm so angry with my husband.

In Jungian art therapy, when we have a relationship with an image it means that it too is living and has the capacity to be transformed. Dawn thought that her dream was about her mother complex (house). Aspects of the dream revealed her shadow projection of her own creative instincts, and the biological longing she had to find a *genius loci* (horse and castle) for her own maternal body (pregnancy and childbirth), her soul's desire for creative work. Dawn's dream was both a confirmation of available creative psychic energy stored in her unconscious (basement) and a compensation that encouraged her to maintain time for herself. Her longing for more art supplies may suggest a longing for her own creative play, time for reflection, or increased resources and concrete space.

Creating an art space in her actual basement required fortification as well as flexibility. Childbirth would also require some of the same qualities. The various details and images within Dawn's dream expressed the work of the transcendent function and reflected her connection to the feminine initiation journey through pregnancy into motherhood. Might the green railing illustrate both the process and the method of the transcendent function through its utilitarian element and its guidance for moving "objects"?

Dawn and her husband decided to make a pregnant belly cast and then together they painted the dream castle (Figure 9.2). As a creative project, it influenced Dawn to step into the next stage of her life. The colors represented the growth that comes from the darkest dwellings in our psyche. Dawn discussed her pregnancy, including the feminine separateness, anger, love, and uncertainty she felt as the major change of childbirth drew near. The shared creative work of the belly cast led Dawn to find light within the dark. She could finally reconcile the interior process that was taking place by bearing the tension that opposing forces invariably bring: "a new synthesis will follow between conscious and unconscious, persona and shadow, ego and Self" (Stevens & Storr, 1994, p. 86). Stevens asserted that "such reconciliations are attained neither rationally nor intellectually, but symbolically, through the *transcendent function of symbols*. Creative work with symbols is, therefore, the key to successful personal development and therapeutic practice" (Stevens & Storr, 1994, pp. 86–87). We have touched on this in the various vignettes thus far. In other words, symbols are not chosen by the ego, but arrive spontaneously and are nourished through the relationship with the unconscious. Digging into her feelings about the irreconcilable opposites (masculine/feminine, dark/light, known/unknown, inside/outside, love/anger) eventually constellated a renewal of psychic energy for Dawn. She cleared a space for painting. From the symbol of the white horse and castle, Dawn had opened the psychological gate to attend to her inner emotional life in a more devoted way. And from the dream she indeed found a new path.

The Bridge Dream

A couple years later, Dawn separated from her husband and was living in a new home where she could easily live creatively, and share the parenting of her two children, yet she was still passing through what Jung called "the valley of the shadow" (Jung, 1946/1985, CW 16, pp. 198–199), or mid-life. She dreamt the following:

> I'm in my car driving to the beach. I reach an inlet and I'm driving over a long bridge that stretches over the ocean and I can't see where it is going. Out my window I see a fisherman with a green hat in a little wooden boat. I can see his hands holding a large piece of bait at the top of his fishing pole as if he is getting ready to cast his line. I recognize him and call out his name. He calls my name back, loud and clear. He recognizes me. We are both surprised to see each other. He anchors his boat and comes onto the bridge. We are together and embrace in love and longing. I can feel his flannel chest against my cheek. We are one. He says he has to go back to work, but "Come Friday, I want you to meet someone," he tells me. When he got back to his boat I watched as he pulled up a huge rainbow fish and ate it whole.

Specifically, the dream has several images. There is the long bridge and Dawn (dream ego) was on the bridge. There is also a man in a green hat and flannel shirt who joined her on the bridge. He offered the dream ego a moment of oneness, or wholeness and the potential for someone new at a specific time. There was a specific time. He then returned to his work in the boat where he caught and ate a rainbow fish whole.

While Dawn's dream is rich with imagery ready for personal associations (bridge, man, green hat, rainbow fish), the images will be used to illustrate aspects of the psyche according to Jung's model. What follows are the subsequent paintings that were inspired by this vibrantly textured dream; Dawn's painting process illustrates one path that Jungian art therapy can take.

In terms of Jung's model of the psyche, we can play with the images and hypothesize that the man could be a complex associated to a past relationship (objective) or he could represent a well-needed unification with the masculine principle in Dawn's psyche (subjective). As the furthest thing from the ego, the man could also be an image for the animus that navigates the edges of psyche and retrieves necessary material through "work" that, in this case, may allude to stages of psychic development. The green hat was the same color as the banister in the earlier dream, so he hints at special knowledge about time, transition, death/rebirth, and the symbolic skill of fishing. The green may hint at the transcendent function, but this color green is probably a positive complex indicator because Dawn was attracted to this green.

During times of transition, vivid or numinous figures may arrive to hint at the unity within the psyche. We might assume this man is skilled at navigating the levels of consciousness including the darkness because he baited the hook, caught the fish, and then ingested the fish (incorporation of the sacred material). Psychologically he also demonstrated the pattern of transformation related to the work with the unconscious.

For Jung, the fish was a Self symbol so the lysis of the dream carried the suggestion of wholeness. There was also a contrast between the bridge as a healing symbol that propels the psyche forward while at the same time the rainbow fish reminds us of the symbolic nourishment that arises from the slow contemplative work of digestion and assimilation.

Dawn travelled deeper into her personal work with the unconscious; in response, her unconscious offered an animus figure that knew how to work symbolically and could be a successful fisherman on the waters of the unconscious. She was compelled to work with the symbol of the bridge in her painting practice. We might say that her complexes provided the energy for her to paint several renditions. Each painting expressed a different tone, focus, and aspect of the bridge. What is noticeable is that Dawn actively worked the opposites—precision versus expressiveness, dark versus light—and in so doing she wrestled with her complexes and channeled the psychic energy into her painting.

The bridge may be an image for how symbols convey potential within the psyche—they bridge two sides that need connecting. In some cases, the sides are incompatible, but the symbol joins them together like the earlier pregnant tree image. Dawn was seeking compatibility and connection with herself during a time of transition. "I'm finding my own handwriting" by painting several pictures of the same image. The first image of the bridge (Figure 9.3) was realistic, and captured the exact dream space, the movement as well as the darkness of the shadow. Dawn was captivated by the bridge and wanted to paint it as precisely as she knew how. The second bridge painting (Figure 9.4) was "the opposite to the first painting" as a compensation for the first: it was loose, expressive, and more colorful. Dawn used the paint in a manner that was more playful. She had taken a painting class to develop her painting technique. This was part of her animus development in the backdrop of her psyche.

Dawn had to hold the tension of how to remain expressive but also acquire confidence through new skills, a process that was also reflected in her daily life.

The next two images of the bridge appear to be in contrast to one another. The bridge in Figure 9.5 seems sunken into the gentle sides of soft pillow-like paint, while the bridge in Figure 9.6 is bright and spacious, reaching straight into the distance. While each bridge reaches out into the unknown, "I'm trying to get somewhere, but I'm feeling more and more okay with the unknown." Figure 9.6 is clearly linked with the red horizon straight ahead. Was this Dawn's conscious attempt to confront her suffering or reach her passion, or both? Traditional Jungian picture interpretation (Abt, 2005) might consider the bridge reaching out from the unconscious (bottom of the picture) towards consciousness, denoting the teleological movement of individuation and a psychological drive and trend towards integration of archetypal content.

In the final painting (Figure 9.7), the bridge is moving towards the left corner once again. The top corner has been associated with the father in traditional Jungian picture interpretation, but it may also reflect the movement from the bottom to the top of a picture as an expression of an archetypal reality behind the symbol (Abt, 2005, p. 35). While the top corner might open a discussion around the father complex for some, as Jungian art therapists, we might find interest in the changing shift in mood and direction of the curving bridge that cuts through the light orb back into the darkness to form a circle. As we follow the bridge, we move from the *prima materia*, the original place of darkness, up towards light and into darkness again. The two intersecting circles form the symbol of a *mandorla*, an almond shape at the center. Found in ancient religious iconography, the ancient image could suggest sacred archetypal moments associated with the light found in darkness, suggesting that consciousness for Dawn may push up from an emotional indwelling within the dark archetypal soil of the psyche. This is common for women who have repressed their connection to the dark feminine and its healing properties in favor of the collective.

Figure 9.7 was a spontaneous painting that revealed the eternal opposites of light and dark that live constantly in the background of our human existence, and yet through the expression of a symbol, we can find reconciliation and a fleeting transcendence of oneness. Dawn's painting dialogues with the bridge explored the unfolding relationship with complexes associated with her individuation. Her engagement with the bridge symbol exposed the embodiment of the psychological labors modeled by the fisherman. In addition, if the objective psyche is real and has a life of its own, then we can consider that the bridge also has its own innate metaphysical properties associated with the archetypal energies of individuation, but also the universal principle of opposites associated with conscious and unconscious, subjective and objective, and masculine and feminine.

Alternative Approaches to the Bridge Dream

Had Dawn not been compelled to paint the bridge on her own, we might have worked in session with the color green. We might have gathered into one place as much of this particular color as we could from different sources (paint, textured papers, found objects, or art postcards) alongside personal associations so as to understand the complexes associated with this color. We could have worked deliberately with each image in the dream by drawing the scenes, or capturing through lines, shapes, and colors the most dominant moment of the dream. This too would have circumambulated the complex and uncovered symbolic material. Or, we could have worked with the archetypal and symbolic material by simply painting spontaneously to capture the overall feeling quality of the dream and then discovered the personal associations constellated by the dream imagery such as the fish, bridge, or boat. There are many paths to facilitate the imagination and unearth the unconscious content associated with the mid-life transition, but one thing is obvious: it takes a concerted courageous effort and interest from the patient in order to remain actively involved with unconscious content.

Jungian Art Therapy: Louisa's Story

Louisa was in her twenties and was healing from an abusive relationship. She used her own "Red Book" making process to explore her memories and behaviors. She started with a powerful dream she had as a teenager coming into womanhood, and wondered if she might be able to go back to the beginning to find answers. After creating her "Snake Lady" image (Figure 9.8), she explained, "The snake image was a means to re-channel some of the femininity and sexuality I had in the past before accruing challenging intimate relationships." The figure wrapped in the snake described the powerful transformation that Louisa undertook as a young woman; she was now returning to review the dream. She realized she had made painful sacrifices to some patriarchal attitudes and had disavowed her feminine nature.

Louisa found mandalas helpful for handling her trauma reactions (what she labeled as PTSD) and shifting the energy that came in a repeating dream. Each time, she recorded her emotions in response to the dream and then spontaneously drew or painted a mandala. She often used active imagination to glean more insight and reflection about her reactions.

One of Louisa's last mandalas (Figure 9.9) came in response to the repeating dream. In this mandala she used watercolors with the idea that she could create openness and compassion for the recurring emotions: "It has been a many-layered process." The confrontation from the unconscious was apparent in the repeating dream so Louisa worked to access the self-regulating aspect of the psyche and find the balance between her conscious and her unconscious. This mandala looks as if it is held by "hands" outside consciousness; the colors in the circle intersect and blend to create new and unexpected colors and shapes, yet the vibrancy expressed both the intensity of the pain as well as the potentiality held by the archetypal pattern of the circle. Perhaps Louisa, like Lucinda in Chapter 6, was also beginning to unlock the paradoxical meaning that lay behind her journey through an *amor fati*, or an appreciation for her fate.

Dreams that Dance and Sing

Dreams express the instinctual pole of the archetype through such things as food, movement, music, or animals. The coalescing or "circling" of energy shows up in archetypal patterns such as Dervish or ballroom dancing, a team sport, or a game like "duck-duck-goose" that circles and gathers energy. Music and melodies can also emerge to denote numinous and "noteworthy" information that wants to be heard as in Lucinda's dream in Chapter 6. Animals are precise descriptions of the instinctual energy of the archetypes as we saw with the two snakes and the black cat in Anna's dream or Dawn's white horse. As symbols, they unify the instinctual and spiritual poles of the archetype and invite us to become more conscious. Learning the language of these types of dreams requires time. The animals, movements, and melodies live within us in mysterious ways. Jungian art therapy offers another doorway through which the unconscious can express its unadulterated truth and we can respond with an image, but also with the way we live our life in relationship with psyche.

For example, when I began my educational program in art therapy, I had the following dream: *There is a mole and a female mentor told me to sing the mole's song.* This dream continued to live through me like music as I grappled with how to understand it, often asking myself what it might mean to sing the mole's song. What was the mole's compensatory role? This dream expresses how the unconscious has its own peculiar and mysterious language. This dream continues to live within me as I unearth new meaning in it over time. Periodically I have had other dreams of moles. Many years later, I had the following dream: *the large fat mole was on a velvet red cloth.* The black and red colors were stark. I drew the mole and did some associations to the dream to honor its return (Figure 9.10). The dream came a week before attending my first analytic training meeting (another threshold of education).

On the day of my arrival at the meeting, I took a walk through a nature area. I came across a small dead mole on the side of the path. I was stunned. I had never seen a mole in daylight; this one was dead. Sitting by the dead mole I considered the synchronicity[2] of the moment. I remembered Jung's dream that carried the manifestation of Philemon with kingfisher wings (Jung's guide and image of the Self) which was followed by him finding a dead kingfisher (Jung, 1961, p. 207). My association to the dead mole was Jung's story of the dead kingfisher that affirmed that I was at another defining moment in my own journey. There was both terror of the unknown and awe of the synchronicity. Seeing the dead mole, I recognized a sacrifice had been made and I was on the threshold of yet another one of life's initiations.

Throughout my training years I was asked to use my voice and speak about why I wanted to be in Jungian training, where the meaning was for me, and what was surfacing psychologically from the unconscious. The mole was a living symbol that was expressing the instinctual innate rhythms and stages of my life, of death/rebirth, and of initiation; the dream suggested there was alchemical significance in the black and the white and the red (velvet). I would have to endure and be transformed by my complexes (devils) and archetypal forces, the passion and the suffering that is unavoidable with deep initiations and sacrificial rites. Once again, this would not be a song of the ego, but it would be the reverberating song from the dark, chthonic realm of the autonomous, creative, and rhythmic unconscious. Perhaps this is what psyche meant by "singing the mole's song."

Jungian Art Therapy: Naomi's Story

Naomi was in her late fifties and had recently finished a graduate program. She was a mother of two adult children. Naomi had two dreams around the same time period. In the first dream she *was driving and noticed a small mute black boy by the side of the road with his arms reaching up towards me. I went to him.* In the second dream, *I was in a car and was shot, but the bullet only grazed my head. I was unscathed, but was worried about the boy in the back of the car watching me get shot.*

During this period Naomi was engaged in a series of process paintings that took place in our sessions together. She had lost contact with her own work through graduate school and wanted to reacquaint herself with painting. Naomi used the paints spontaneously without knowing what might emerge and then we worked together to consider the images. In one of the images she saw the boy from her dream by the side of the road, so she embellished the image further, giving him shape and color. As she painted it was as if he was being "born" on the page. There was a spontaneous golden globe behind him that gave him a sacred quality; this indeed was an emotional quality that she had taken from the dream, but it was the painting that visually expressed the dream's numinosity (Figure 9.11).

Naomi discussed her regret and lost time associated with her art. She expressed sorrow about her father's lack of mentorship and support, and how her brother "got it all." She wanted to shift this attitude. The unconscious suggested the rejected, disavowed shadow masculine that had been "found on the side of the road" had some unique and unfamiliar answers. The compensatory images encouraged her to have "another look" at what had been rejected and how to reclaim that psychic energy for her own road ahead. It meant some differentiation around the masculine so she could assimilate its dual nature. Following the painting, Naomi made a clay figure of the boy for her "spirit house." The spirit house was a gradual unfolding of a sacred space (*genius loci*) for her inner dream figures made from clay. The project required her to use power tools and materials that engaged different parts of her artist-self. The figure she created from her dream image was the seed that led to the gradual growing animus figures that "came knocking" in various ways in subsequent dreams.

These two dreams led to a series of concentrated sessions that compelled Naomi to consider the importance of the emerging potential of this new masculine principle. Perhaps if she worked to repair the links between her body and mind, she would find greater balance within her psyche. The progression of the dreams suggested that she had "picked up" the boy from the side of the road and was now working on the ensuing complexes. There were "shots" to her ego attitude (grazing her head) but she was unscathed (she could survive) the event—Naomi thought the original event perhaps being the first moment she realized girls were treated differently. The dream ego was concerned with how the young boy would handle this event, suggesting that an inner relationship was forming because she was actively attending to her dream images and responding to the unconscious by using her hands.

Jungian Art Therapy: Ellen's Story

Ellen had a dream that initiated work with the father complex and animus. *I was digging up a grave and discovered a man who had been buried, but he was still alive. He had on a suit from the 1940s.* Ellen had done significant work on the mother complex, but now the unconscious was suggesting that the work needed to pivot to the father, whom she knew only briefly. From the dream she had an image of a "picture negative" of his face. In response to her imagination, Ellen cut out a shape of a head and then placed it under a piece of paper. She rubbed over it with a black crayon like the rubbings made on graves. Ellen left the image as complete, but then found herself pulled back to make marks in the opposite direction, "to make the face darker . . . It's like I'm trying to get to him, unearth him," she said. This force was similar to Dawn who painted bridges as a way to find her path forward. Both Ellen and Dawn were assimilating profound feelings of grief; painting offered images that compensated and confirmed their paths. "This magical effect of creating pictures is the first step in transforming an emotion" (Abt, 2005, p. 33). It is through the painting and drawing that the emotions (complexes) find their form and evolve in unexpected ways. Jung was calmed by painting his emotions:

> Had I left those images hidden in the emotions, I might have been torn to pieces by them. There is a chance that I might have succeeded in splitting them off; but in that case I would inexorably have fallen into a neurosis and so been ultimately destroyed by them anyhow. As a result of my experiment I learned how helpful it can be, from the therapeutic point of view, to find the particular images which lie behind emotions.
>
> (Jung, 1961, p. 177)

Jung warned that we should not overvalue the unconscious or the images that arise if we are consciously engaged in individuation. Images are not art; they are simply nature (Jung, 1961, pp. 185–187). Yet, very early on, Jung placed tremendous value on the *relationship* between dreams and the making of pictures:

> Such pictures spring from, and satisfy, a natural need. It is as if a part of the psyche that reaches far back into the primitive past were expressing itself in these pictures and finding it possible to function in harmony with our alien conscious mind. . . . However the mere execution of the pictures is not enough . . . an intellectual and emotional understanding is needed: they require to be not only rationally integrated with the conscious mind but morally assimilated. They still have to be subjected to a work of synthetic interpretation . . . we are dealing with life outside consciousness, and our observation of it is indirect . . . some kind of centring process, for a great many pictures which the patients themselves feel to be decisive point in this direction. During this centring process what we call the ego appears to take up a peripheral position. The change is apparently brought about by an emergence of the historical part of the psyche . . . the change heightens the feeling for life and maintains the flow of life . . . it is animated by a peculiar purposefulness.
>
> (Jung, 1931/1985, CW 16, p. 51)

As we have seen through the various examples, behind our dream images are the archetypal patterns and complexes that structure, guide, and heal the psyche. These images reflect not just the personal qualities of our personalities, but also the grand blueprint of individuation that is the backdrop for our lives. Jung was explicit: use the art materials to express the contents of the unconscious, but try not to overvalue the images. Let them have their voice, let them be seen, and let them die when their job is finished. If we hold too tightly, these images are idealized or suffocated and are not allowed their authority. If we hold them too loosely, we miss their messages. Finding the right balance that allows our imagination to transform through the experiences that they bring to us is the best way to respect the life of the soul's images. When they lose their energy, like everything in nature, they fall into the unconscious until the next image takes shape. If nothing else, Jung was steadfast in his belief of the innate healing rhythm of the unconscious—just like any environment, it has its own weather, its own seasons of expression. It is our duty to discover our individual graceful path of loving relatedness to the *mysterious tremendum* that lives both within us and around us.

Endnotes

1. Freud made significant discoveries and contributions to psychoanalysis and psychotherapy. This simplistic and brief summary is meant to highlight the early theoretical differences between Jung and Freud regarding how dreams and their symbols are used.
2. Jung was interested in synchronicity, by which he meant two unrelated non-causal events that come together in a meaningful way. In addition, with these meaningful coincidences the collective unconscious becomes visible as it is experienced by the individual, and even more so when the images are created in response to the unconscious.

CHAPTER 10

Active Imagination and Art Therapy

Active imagination is Jung's method of holding the conscious and unconscious in dialogue around an image, theme, or cluster of ideas to gain further insight from the unconscious. It was one of Jung's innovative approaches for working with unconscious contents that arose from his research, experience, and reflections with his own unconscious material. In fact, Jung referred back to these personal investigations as the foundation for analytical psychology, a time that gave him the seeds for his ideas on typology, archetypes, the collective unconscious, aspects of the masculine and feminine, the Self, and individuation. Active imagination also emphasized his ideas on the ego's relationship with the unconscious, psychic energy, and the image and symbol formation.

Jung's method is often used in a natural way by artists or in art therapy through internal dialogues with psyche's images that further the creative process. However, active imagination is sometimes confused with witness writing, monologues, fantasies, or intuitive insights. Active imagination is not about the ego unfolding fantasy stories, nor is it an intuitive and imaginative "hit" regarding the image. Instead, active imagination is an *experience* that arises from a deliberate dialogue with the unconscious. It is a conscious undertaking to cultivate a relationship with the unconscious.

Jungian art therapy uses active imagination in two ways. Sometimes the actual process of making the response image itself is an active imagination. A dialogue is carried out with the forming and shaping of an image. We step back and redo or repaint through a silent conversation with the emerging life of the painting as we listen for its voice. This is an important way to attend to the image. The second way is by dialoguing with the image once it has been created using art materials. I believe active imagination takes place in both of these stages of image-making as long as there is a conscious engagement from a softened ego to allow the unconscious to be heard. In both situations, the image becomes more enlivened and there is a mutual relationship that develops from listening to the voices within while at the same time listening to the voice of the image that is placed in front of us. Jung's primary aim was to make the unconscious conscious and then to have a dialectical encounter.

Active Imagination and the Pregnant Symbol

Chodorow referred to Jung's use of the German word *betrachten* ("to make pregnant") in active imagination. And, if something is pregnant, it is alive. Something will come out of it in due time because it produces and multiplies (Chodorow, 1997, p. 7). Jung's method of active imagination attends to an image or a felt sense with an openness and curiosity. We offer it the breath of life (spirit). Jung reminded us that an image does not become a symbol until it is attended to through meaning-making, where it becomes "pregnant with meaning" (Jung, 1921/1990, CW 6, p. 474). *Making pregnant* is also Jung's phenomenological description of the arche-typal pattern of transformation, the sexual and creative instincts that lie beneath the method of active imagination. When we commit to the work of the *pregnant imagination* (Swan-Foster, 2012), we can have a shift in attitude. We nourish and deepen our associations through relating to the image by using our imagination and symbolic thinking, which expands beyond rational facts to include the irrational elements. This shift in atti-tude allows the image to become a living symbol. Indeed, the psychologi-cal activity requires a focused presence, investment of psychic energy, and emotional care for transforming an image into a symbol much like the process a pregnant woman undergoes (Swan-Foster, 2012).

To make an image pregnant and to nourish the living symbol high-lights Jung's poetic and Romantic roots that fed his imagination. Active imagination opens the door for us to listen to what seems like the whispers from the creative unconscious, separate from the ego's rational knowledge. Unlike a sign, which has a definite meaning, a *living* healing symbol is difficult to imbue with energy unless we are reflective and observant and appreciate the unfolding of psychological meaning. We consciously attend to the presenting image and this compensates for any dominance of our rational side of the psyche associated with the ego's direction to override what may arise organically in its own time.

The alchemical vessel or *vas* (often shaped like the uterus) suggests an imaginal container for a symbolic conception, incubation, and eventual birth of an image that carries the potential to become a symbol. For instance, the alchemical process of washing and rewashing the material elucidates the circular and repetitive psychological work that is necessary for the transcendent function to gather enough energy for the symbol to become imbued with life force and aliveness within the psyche. When it does come alive, Jung explained that the symbol is a transformer of psychic energy from a lower level to higher level:

> It carries conviction and at the same time expresses the content of that conviction. It is able to do this because of the numen, the specific energy stored up in the archetype. Experience of the archetype is not only impressive, it seizes and possesses the whole personality, and is naturally productive of faith.
>
> (Jung, 1912/1972, CW 5, p. 232)

Jung further reminded us that legitimate faith relies on experience, which grows from our relationship with the unconscious along with the *compensatory striving* within us for an attitude that expresses the totality of our psyche (Jung, 1912/1972, CW 5, p. 232). The creative instinct is reliant upon the transcendent function and nourished and mobilized by active imagination; our soul is fed through a deeper purpose and meaning, which is illustrated by the symbol and results in a change in consciousness. When we use active imagination, we participate in what Jung often referred to as a great interdisciplinary enterprise.

Active Imagination: Experiencing The Psyche

Active imagination emerged from Freud's free association method, but most clearly stated, "free association is an interpretative technique. Active imagination is an experiential technique" (Taveras, 2015, p. 26). As a dialogic process, Jung was interested in the background of psychic energy that mobilized the psyche through the ego's relationship to the images and other content from the unconscious so as to expand the psychological experience. Consequently, Jung's idea of the transcendent function and the energy ignited by working with the opposites led to the discovery of active imagination. In 1941 Jung said active imagination was a method of introspection and he had specific directions to observe the flow of the inner images. He recommended choosing one image that is of interest, from a dream, vision, or picture, and observing the changes that may occur. All critical voices must be suspended and we are to remain objective but attentive. Any dismissal of the contents is simply the ego interfering with the unfolding of the unconscious (Jung, 1941/1990, CW 9i, p. 190). Jung's method consciously engages with material from the shadow, seeking to discover what we don't know: "I realize that the unconscious is a *process*, and that the psyche is transformed or developed by the relationship with the ego to the contents of the unconscious" (Jung, 1961, p. 209).

Jung's method of active imagination allowed him to come to terms with the powerful effects of the unconscious for himself and his analysands. He found that by directing psychic energy into productive images or "personified emotions" and symbolic forms, the psyche could become known, and thus unified. While psychoanalysis was still fraught with the notion that the powerful all-knowing doctor dictated interpretations and directed patient treatment, Jung's method promoted an alternative and highly modern approach. In particular, he made a pioneering pivot when he encouraged the analysand to be independent by learning how to do active imaginations or what Mary Watkins (1984) later called "waking dreams" or "imaginal dialogues" in order to engage with the unconscious outside of analysis, and after analysis had ended.

Jung thought his method allowed for the full expression of individuation, particularly because he advised his analysands to take breaks from analysis in order to integrate the experience back into their daily lives. Jung was steadfast that analytical psychology must be experienced, and that whatever happens in the imagination must also be lived by us (Jung, 1961). Incredibly innovative for the time, Jung's active imagination exposed his analysands to the discovery of their inner direction and psychic energy that revealed psyche's purpose by not just letting the negative or destructive voices in the unconscious to rail on their ego, but by actually coming to terms with its content through a dialectical and constructive method.

Initially, active imagination was viewed as a strict process that someone does alone, much like a meditation practice but with some differences. When active imagination naturally occurs within an art therapy session, we might ask a patient to dialogue with an image by asking, "Can you listen for what it might have to say to you?" and "What do you have to say back?" These questions educate and prompt the analysand to begin to learn to listen in a new way to "voices" outside the directions of an overly conscious or dominant ego. When we collect associations for an image, we will automatically shine light on disavowed material, undoubtedly found in our complexes or archetypal images. Just as art therapy brings the image into space and time through making the unspeakable visible, active imagination offers a few specific handholds that facilitate a deepened relationship with the unconscious.

Jung's *The Red Book*: The Discovery of Active Imagination

Jung refined his method of active imagination through his process of working on *The Red Book* (2009a), yet we know he was deeply connected to the creative and reflective instincts throughout his life (Jung, 1961). When *The Red Book* was published, Jung's intimate visions and active imaginations as well as his paintings and calligraphy of these experiences became available for the first time. The book is an expression of one man's journey into his own psyche and back. In it, Jung recorded his dialogues with figures from the unconscious, and at times his difficulty with the anima, the feminine aspect of his psyche. Such accounts of great minds are rarely, if ever documented, let alone illustrated, and then so widely shared with the world. The visibility of one man's intimate conversations with his unconscious deserves respect and recognition. In *The Red Book*, Jung took himself into a deep descent that he described as a *cosmic abyss* or a *voyage to the moon* (1961, p. 181). In this landscape Jung met the figures of Elijah and Salome, the old man with a white beard and the beautiful young girl who was at first blind:

> I caught sight of two figures, an old man with a white beard and a beautiful young girl. I summoned up my courage and approached them as though they were real people, and listened attentively to what they told me. The old man explained that he was Elijah, and that gave me a shock. But the girl staggered me even more, for she called herself Salome? She was blind. What a strange couple: Salome and Elijah. But Elijah assured me that he and Salome had belonged together from all eternity, which completely astounded me ... They had a black serpent living with them which displayed an unmistakable fondness for me. I stuck close to Elijah because he seemed to be the most reasonable of the three, and to have a clear intelligence. Of Salome I was distinctly suspicious. Elijah and I had a long conversation which, however, I did not understand.
>
> (Jung, 1961, p. 181)

In order not to lose himself in the unconscious during these descents, Jung explained that he held a binocular vision of both observation and engagement, holding both conscious and unconscious in mind. It is an acquired task for Jungian art therapists, psychotherapists, and psychoanalysts alike, but at this time, Jung was charting new territory in his self-analysis.

Jung had a specific process in making *The Red Book*. His active imaginations were faithfully conducted and recorded through the years of 1913–1930 when he dedicated himself to his own analysis with the help of Toni Wolff. Shamdasani (2009, p. 33) noted that there were three levels to Jung's psychological process. First he recorded the images and inner dialogues precisely as he had experienced them. He then stepped back and provided a conceptual review, and then he offered interpretation in the third level (Shamdasani, 2009, pp. 30–33). Then when he transferred the material from his black books to *The Red Book*, he added embellished paintings and mandalas (Jung, 1961). The paintings at first were directly related to the text, but as time passed, the images became more archetypal responses or perhaps "[t]hey are active imaginations in their own right" (Shamdasani, 2009, p. 33). Jung enjoyed focusing on the aesthetic qualities for a time, but he never finished *The Red Book*; instead he was drawn towards new intellectual landscapes, to what he called a "rigorous process of *understanding*" (1961, p. 188) found in alchemical texts.

Jung straddled the tension between a romantic imagination and an empirical scientific mind (Shamdasani, 2009), but this process relieved his unconscious of what lived not just deep within him but was expressed through him from the collective. Moreover, Jung became more conscious of the dual personality that lived within him, which he called personality Number 1 and personality Number 2. Despite how others may have judged him, he recognized that his discovery was not just the material "which is the stuff of psychosis . . . and . . . the insane. . . . But is also the matrix of a mythopoeic imagination which has vanished from our rational age" (Jung, 1961, p. 188). Specifically, *The Red Book* introduced the myth-opoetic story of Jung's subpersonalities that emerged as images from his psyche. He noted that imagination is available everywhere but both "tabooed and dreaded, so that it even appears to be a risky experiment or a questionable adventure to entrust oneself to the uncertain path that leads into the depths of the unconscious" (Jung, 1961, p. 188). With this departure, Jung's active imagination process remained influential for his future work and continues to influence those clinicians and analysands who follow aspects of his theoretical methods. Consequently, Jung's personal work was invaluable for Jungian art therapy methods and applications, and substantiated a heuristic research model with a creative therapeutic approach. From this body of work, Jung's method of active imagination has evolved yet it has proven to be a prescient and sturdy clinical tool.

Jung's Method of Active Imagination

Jung's method has two primary stages: letting the unconscious arise and then coming to terms with it—the second part being much more important (Chodorow, 1997; Cwik, 1995). In coming to terms with the unconscious, not only is the standpoint of the ego justified but the unconscious is granted the same authority, as Jung explained: "The ego takes the lead but the unconscious must be allowed to have its say too" (Jung, [1916]/1957/1972, CW 8, p. 88). Jung also thought that when someone worked extensively on their active imagination, the dreams would decrease and lose their energy (Jung, 1936/1937/1990, CW 9i, p. 49). It was from this observation that he concluded that dreams have content that longs to become conscious through a relationship with us.

An active imagination always begins with the *prima materia*, or the raw material, such as a compelling thought or feeling, a disruptive affect or situation, or an image from a dream that grips us. Jung eventually refined his method to have three basic stages or steps that reflected his notion of directed and non-directed thinking:

1. lowering of consciousness
2. bringing in consciousness
3. taking action.

The first step requires us to settle down, quiet the mind, and soften the ego in order to allow something to happen with non-action or non-doing (Chodorow, 1997). In his *Commentary on 'The Secret of the Golden Flower'* Jung referred to this step as *Wu Wei* or *Abaissement*, which allows the unconscious contents to become known (Jung, 1929/1983, CW 13). Sitting quietly, turning inwards, and allowing the *abaissement* is similar to meditation, but it is not the same because we don't let thoughts and feelings go, or flow "down the river." However, Jung reminded us that the alchemical *meditatio* is a familiar process for psychotherapists who regularly use an "inner dialogue" to attend to the unconscious, which is not meditation, but a dialogue between the subject and the object (Jung, 1944/1993, CW 12, p. 274).

Jung thought the second step was far more important, which was to *bring in* consciousness. Bringing in consciousness encourages an internal process and dialogue so the image can then take shape through external approaches such as art, movement, or sandplay (Chodorow, 1997). As the affects and images flow into awareness, the ego now enters actively into the *experience* through a dialogue. The third step includes taking action so as to live our experience of the active imagination. The dialogues are not meant to be left dormant and/or remote from conscious life, but brought alive through engagement and action. We are familiar with volunteer or service work in our community, but this is work that serves the autonomous healing potential of the unconscious. All three of these steps can occur through the methods and applications found in Jungian art therapy.

Jungian Art Therapy: Lisa's Story

Lisa, who endured abuse as a child, drew an image of her child-self stuck in a room. As she drew, she had tremendous feeling that came over her although she rarely cried as an adult. The active imagination process was at work, so we slowed the process down and explored the emotions that were arising, the images she saw, and the conversation that was happening with the voice from within. For the first time, she decided to listen to the words of this inner child part of herself. "She tells me she needs me." She wrote the words in the picture as she drew the room. "I am mad. Don't forget about me," said the image. "But, I'm not sure how to take care of you—what do you want from me?" Lisa asked. "I need you. I'm scared, no, terrified. Can you get me out of here?" the child-self responded. Lisa was working with a terrified and isolated splinter psyche or complex, but it was actually a real part of herself that needed to be retrieved. Hearing the child part of her psyche articulate feelings through this dialogue was at first uncomfortable for Lisa, but it gave her a reason to intentionally cultivate a relationship with this frightened, vulnerable child complex. What she later noticed was the negative pole of this complex with its desire to hide in a deeply entrenched place of self-destruction. When she said: "I can feel you wanting to push me away," the truth was at last spoken aloud for Lisa and her continued work eventually brought an insight that changed her life.

Jung's third task of active imagination, taking action, is essential to complete the process. In Lisa's case, she collected photos of herself at that particular age and photocopied them. She then created a collage of herself with all the words she never got to say. She framed the collage and put it near her desk so that she remembered the little girl every day. This active imagination ended up being very deliberate and solution oriented, but it still cracked the door open for Lisa, who could test the waters of working with psyche in a new way. In doing so, Lisa also recognized that she had overlooked her creative needs and desires. This single art process gave her the inspiration to register for a poetry class.

Psychologically, the raw instinctual energy of unmet needs was now being attended to by the adult Lisa. Rather than suddenly erupting like a child when she felt unseen, Lisa acknowledged the needs that had been denied and the potential found in this divine female child. These needs had remained in the shadow in the form of a difficult inchoate child. Through the action of confronting the raw feelings and dialoging with the images, Lisa found a way to accept and work with the parts of herself that had been neglected, rejected, and shamed.

The notion that the empty page has the potential to hold the unconscious contents is particularly important for art therapists. Sometimes the page remains empty for a long time, yet the emptiness is a complicated place of waiting, perhaps protection or fear, but also possibility all at once. What is being expressed through the emptiness cannot be forced but needs to be revealed in its own time. This silence can also occur in active imagination. In this exploratory process that requires patience, curiosity, tenacity, and faith, we may draw from both an aesthetic interest in beauty and an analytic view that seeks greater meaning and purpose from the unconscious. In the mix is the messy material of our humanness.

Another way of thinking about dialoguing with art is to talk *with* rather than *about* the images, with a mindset to listen rather than defend and explain (McNiff, 1992, p. 105). This is an important jumping-off point that establishes a mutual exchange between the conscious and the unconscious, the rational and the irrational, the maker and the image. We are reminded once again of Jung's notion that the purpose of directed and non-directed thinking is to hold both sides of a conflict at once, and accept that our images bring to us that which is needed should we be willing to investigate the content.

Von Franz's Method of Active Imagination

Marie-Louise von Franz (1983) expanded upon Jung's method in the following way:

1. Empty the "mad mind" of the ego: this is a place of relaxation yet attentiveness.
2. Let an unconscious fantasy image arise: this is where we welcome whatever image arises, attending to its presence with a lightness of being, not grasping too tightly yet not letting it fade.
3. Give it some form of expression: this is where art or rituals are taken up and where matter becomes playful and expressive. Jung thought this was an efficient way to deal with inner material.
4. Ethical confrontation and apply to ordinary life: von Franz felt this was an important step that is often overlooked in modern techniques (von Franz, 1983; Chodorow, 1997).

The fourth step of giving form to our active imagination in the world is valuable; art therapists do this naturally. The unconscious appreciates reflection and acknowledgment even if the product does not accurately reflect the original image. The art product becomes a process of dreaming the dream forward or carrying the active imagination forward and giving it life. This might also include hanging the image on our wall, or sharing it with others. Furthermore, von Franz reminded us that integrating our inner work into everyday life is revitalizing because it sponsors the new attitude by giving it a place to flourish and fulfill its purpose, which is to impact the collective (as cited in Keyes, 1983). For instance, Ellen used her personified clay figures from her active imaginations to carry forward scenes from dreams or her analytic sessions. Placing the figures in relationship to each other in specific ways, and using clay structures, she created her own *genius loci* that protected her from the personified negative complexes that were placed at a distance. Ellen followed her imagination and this process unfolded naturally as a way to have ritual and bring her inner imagination into the outside world. Similarly, if we dream of baking a fancy cake, we could decide to bake a cake for a gathering instead of buying one. In this way, the energy from our dream is shared in the world.

If we reject the unconscious, it shows us a frightening or negative face through shadow content, such as intrusive frightening figures. But if we embrace the unconscious, it provides us with energy and insight for individuation. Jungian art therapy is not just about attending to the individual's inner world, imaginations, and embellishing aesthetic images. The inner world sponsors energy for us to be transformed and then we can return to the collective with gifts. Then as Jung suggests, adaption to the collective occurs in a way that also honors individuation and the fullness and authenticity of the individual's personality.

Post-Jungian Reflections and Methods

Active imagination is an integral method for art therapy and aspects of it are found in contemporary techniques that rely on the imagination for healing complexes and trauma.[1] Although it is one of Jung's most primary and exceptionally creative methods alongside his work with dreams, this method is often neglected even by Jungian analysts or Jungian-oriented therapists. On the other hand, active imagination has been considered from various perspectives as described below.

Active Imagination and Transitional Space

According to Fordham (1967), Jung used active imagination to develop transitional objects that expressed and handled his separation anxiety during his frightening descent into the unconscious. In other words, Fordham considered the creative process from an early relational model based on Winnicott's ideas of transitional objects. Another way of looking at Jung's process is that active imagination is a key that opens the door to a "play-space" (Cwik, 1991) where a dialectical process ensues. This honors Jung's original ideas on regression as a source of renewal for the psyche. In *Playing and Reality* (1971), Winnicott had explored the development of creativity evolving from the transitional space or the space between the mother and the infant/child. He theorized that we learn to play and develop our imagination both in relationship and alone. Cwik

(1991) considered Jung's idea of the "third element" and the transcendent function and compared active imagination to Winnicott's psychoanalytic idea of creativity, which encompassed a capacity to be amused within our own play-space or to delight in our own solitude without persecutory anxiety. This capacity originated from the support of the "good enough mother."

In this transitional space where possibilities become known, Jung noticed the tension that arose between an artistic aesthetic pursuit versus an intellectual search for meaning. His aim was to have the psychic tension push the edges of consciousness and force the analysand to prioritize the dialectical process, which requires both the needs of the ego as well as the needs of the unconscious. This means there is neither a perfect image nor a perfect intellectual brilliance. "When the principle of understanding predominates, the individual struggles to comprehend the meaning of the unconscious product and has little interest in the aesthetic aspect. Both principles have inherent dangers and lead the individual astray" (Cwik, 1991, pp. 103–104). With Jungian art therapy, we are mindful of one-sidedness that can surface in patients who may emphasize their artistic skill over their intellectual understanding, or they emphasize their intellectual understanding and neglect their artistic engagement—becoming one-sided and reinforcing a certain ego-oriented attitude. While this may be necessary for early stages of Jungian art therapy, the aim is to make room for what is pushing to become visible in that moment. We do this by investigating the complexes that hang out in the shadows cast by the ego's brilliance. Everything has a shadow and can be used defensively, including image making, dreams, and active imagination. As a Jungian art therapist, it's our task to consider and hold whichever side is not yet ready to become conscious and to listen and look for ways that this material might become known.

Active Imagination and Transference/Countertransference

Others view Jung's process as a way to cultivate a deep relationship with the transpersonal psyche or the Self, while still others note that active imagination occurs within transference/countertransference relationships (Davidson, 1966; Cwik, 2011; Schaverien, 1992). Schaverien (2005) recommended that we embrace both the process as well as the product, particularly as the shared image influences the transference/countertransference relationship. This suggests that working in the transference, that is, conversations about how the work appears between the therapist and artist, can elicit valuable insights and meaning related not just to the past and present, but also in shifting how one engages with future events. Cwik (1995) also encouraged using common sense with active imagination.

Sometimes it can be used successfully to help contain persecutory voices, while other times an overly positive or idealized view of the method can be intimidating for someone beginning this work, particularly as most early active imagination consists of differentiating complexes associated with mundane and neurotic issues of daily life and there is a lack of archetypal material. Cwik (1995) offered an important reminder that archetypal figures and numinous material may slowly arise as we deepen our relationship with the unconscious, but this may not always hold true, particularly if someone has a major life event that immediately constellates archetypal images—then the process is different. Maintaining clinical awareness in case there is a need for a more regulated process may also present itself so the ego is not overwhelmed or the therapeutic relationship is not destroyed. In other words, the Jungian art therapist is cautioned when working with this method within certain clinical situations. In some situations, the natural resistance and containment of using art materials can serve to redirect psychic energy or compensate for what might be missing.

Whether we view Jung's method as a creative descent into the unconscious, as grief and loss associated with resigning from his professional roles within the psychoanalytic community in Vienna, or as severe depression and "separation anxieties at losing Freud as a mentor and father figure" (Cwik, 1995, p. 140), Jung's individuation required that he turn away from the expectations of the collective and "return home" to attend to his soul.

> My soul, where are you? Do you hear me? I speak, I call you—are you there? I have returned, I am here again. I have shaken the dust of all the lands from my feet, and I have come to you, I am with you. After long years of long wandering, I have come to you again.
>
> (Jung, 2009b, p. 127)

No matter the reasons, we know the path taken for his individuation journey required the courage to listen to the suffering, and we have greatly benefited from Jung's willingness to listen deeply to the irrational psyche, and to follow his discoveries found in his inner landscape. This too becomes our responsibility.

Creating a Personal "Red Book"

I recommend that students and analysands create their own visual books for dreams and images and make a commitment to their psyche by having one place where content is collected. People rarely make time for their inner process today, but when students develop a relationship with the unconscious through the creation of their own "Red Book" they tell me that they are amazed by what unfolds. They are especially appreciative of how they created the time to attend to their inner life, and can now reflect back on where they have been and what has grown within them as well as around them.

The process of making their own book reveals the shadow of their creative process. Students sometimes struggle with whether or not they want their images attached within the book because this can feel like it is too final, too fixed. The book might be shelved and perhaps one day lost, or their feelings about loss, preservation, and years of feeling invisible will be made too vulnerable. On the other hand, by not attaching images within the book, the images are untethered and may literally fall out, perhaps a sign of the unconscious process not being fully respected or by the lack of intense concentration. These examples highlight neglected feelings, lack of a container, or perhaps even a fear of digging deep to honor the work of the unconscious. Other art therapy students are exploratory and messy for the first time. They discover a different side of themselves by using their books as a place to play and to experiment. But this too can be terrifying. Whether students affix their images or not, the actual process becomes the lived experience that is infused with complexes that encourage them to listen to the irrational psyche or the unconscious. Most importantly, the "Red Book" creates a mutual space for their images and self-reflection:

> Unlike visualization and dreams, art has a tangible and material existence. It records traces of the imaginal activity that produced it. Moreover it holds, and fixes, at once moving and limiting the flow of the unconscious. In art therapy there is a public manifestation and a shared viewing: both people see the same thing: there is an object for the shared gaze of the spectators.
>
> (Schaverien, 2005, p. 144)

This shared gaze is terrifying for some, particularly if they are in a group setting or training program. Creating a "Red Book" elicits both personal and archetypal problems; within the tension of opposites, there is a confrontation of self-reflection with the fear of criticism; visibility versus privacy; ambivalence around intimacy versus violation; attachment styles related to images or techniques versus concerns about artistic skill; or simply the tension between emotional wellbeing and the fear of "going crazy." The alchemical phrase "fix the volatile and volatilize the fixed" speaks to the tension that is felt and worked with through a creative engagement of being open while also not becoming lost to the creative powers. Certainly, our approach to the creative process reflects our typology.

When the Jungian analyst and art therapist Sondra Geller (2013) uses active imagination with elders she suggests a quote from Jung: "Now, really, what are you about?" (1961, p. 174). Her questions are applicable for anyone using this technique because they spark essential questions:

"What have you come to tell me?" "Why have you appeared?" The dialogues that ensue become touchstones—a place to revisit. It is heartening to find out that even though one is aging and perhaps losing independence and mobility, there is still an inner source of knowing. You grab hold of the tiger's tail and hold on tight. It will take you this way and that, and at the end of the time, you will find a thread of connection.

(Geller, 2013)

In Figure 10.1 Ellen painted how powerfully the psychic energy pulls on her when her imagination takes on a life of its own. In her active imaginations, she metaphorically held tight to the tails of the tigers as she learned to negotiate and mediate the powerful images from her unconscious.

Jungian art therapy is concerned with the flow of psychic energy, but more specifically the process of how best to attend to the movement of energy inherent within the psyche as internal opposites. How do we find middle ground or live the middle path as Jung recommended? The serpentine path is one approach, while a spiral or circumambulation is another. Either way, as we engage with the shadow we discover our own means to relate to the unconscious contents that surface. Some images we make are familiar or comforting, yet they also open us to deeper self-exploration and realizations, not all of which are easily accepted as part of our psyche. However, if we allow the images their space through a meditative or contemplative presence, we may engage and appropriately attend to what is being presented to us.

Jungian Art Therapy: Alyssa's Story

In our last class, students share images from their "Red Book." It's common that initial images alert us to repetitive implicit patterns found within our picture-making process. This familiar or habitual pattern eventually softens to include more spontaneous work. Alyssa's "Red Book" began with a layered mandala (Figure 10.2), which she offhandedly introduced as a "defensive image." Her description seemed to be more of a judgment that dismissed the image rather than an attempt to listen to its purpose as Jung encourages us to do. Alyssa was like most of us who have been exposed to more Freudian theory and language than Jungian ideas, where there is an automatic and initial reliance on reductive statements to describe an image. Alyssa's layered circle of many colors could be classified as an "embodied image" that allows for a change or transformation in attitude towards the unconscious (Schaverien, 1992).

Figure 10.2 may illustrate an ego-oriented image that offers a support-ive anchor prior to a descent into the unconscious realm of images. It is reminiscent of the "Layered Woman" (Figure 1.3) that ushered in a process of uncovering and discovery. Alyssa's mandala has layers that lead to a center point of focus. From a Jungian perspective, images reflect both complex-laden and archetypal patterns within our psyche. Comments such as "defensive image" prematurely judge psyche's message and circumvent the investigation of personal complexes and the poten-tial message of the image. Alyssa admitted that she created this image to comfort herself and then quickly added, "Is that such a terrible thing?" Repetition in images is not just a stuck perseveration, but could also be the psyche "washing" through material over and over again as a way to "cleanse" and redeem the soul by "washing away the sin" so that psycho-logically we can open to new understandings. As we do this work on our complexes, we draw around a center, we become focused, more embodied.

The layering that we do to comfort ourselves is also related to the layers we travel to find our center. The deep gray center in Alyssa's picture might represent an aspect of the Self as an organizing aspect of her experience. Alyssa referred to her image as a reaction to the abyss from her dreams. The abyss is a place where we call out for images but find emptiness. While this was frightening for her, she was determined to proceed. What followed was several weeks of working on snake images, which enhanced Alyssa's understanding of her ego's relationship to her persona as well as her ego's relationship to the unconscious. The psychic energy ebbed and flowed.

Alyssa said, "The art in my book is a container for emotion—using the 'Red Book' allowed me to meet the emotion without it engulfing me." She used active imagination and art work as catalysts to enter further into the abyss from her dreams. It was a relief to her unconscious and a bit frightening for her ego as she confronted the elemental archetypal symbol. Snakes are coldblooded and have deep instinctual purpose associated with death/rebirth and profound transformation. To compensate for the abyss and the snake symbolism, Alyssa had a first touchstone image that retained familiarity. In the feminine initiation process, when we are in the descent, we are not who we were and not yet who we will become, as the pregnant woman archetype reminds us (Swan-Foster, 2012). The psyche makes a wise choice to have a known landmark while simultaneously a woman plunges into the darkest parts of her psyche. The depth renews her desire to share, through the synthetic method, her creative content with the world, which furthers her individuation. Although discouraged by the collective, traveling into the dark also may be a natural path based on biological, evolutionary, and emotional rhythms.

In her therapy outside of class, Alyssa took leaps into the unknown and let psyche speak to her through the snake. What she discovered was a powerful new dimension within her psyche that she described as the movement of psychic energy associated with her "creative feminine being and expression." The snake helped her navigate the new territory in her daily life. This was both exhilarating and frightening. She reported that through continued image making and somatic movement therapy she held the tension between inflation/deflation, and attraction/repulsion, as she experimented with some aspects of the snake energy. Alyssa reported that she uncovered what felt to her like hidden ancient knowledge in the darkness of her psyche; within the darkness lost parts of herself (positive and negative) were illuminated.

Alyssa used paints and markers to work on early images of the snake (Figure 10.3) that was not quite an infinity symbol, suggesting the initiation of a psychical process. The two heads imply that the opposites were at play. Alyssa deepened her knowledge about the energy of the snake as it lived within her body; she used directed and non-directed thinking, and differentiated her complexes in her personal therapy. The more she dialogued with the images, the less energy the complexes had over her. Alyssa felt this image working on her, deepening her connection to her body and facilitating her individuation as a woman who could speak her mind. Out of the initial abyss there was a growing trust in the archetype of feminine transformation.

Eventually the infinity snake symbol found its true form within a circular container (Figure 10.4), suggesting Alyssa was connecting with her own true nature. Emptiness is a natural jumping-off place (Wallace, 1987, p. 125). It's a natural occurrence where one either waits patiently in the emptiness or goes against nature and takes the leap into the darkness. Under either circumstance, a guide, such as a Jungian art therapist, is important, says Wallace (1987). We hold space for psyche, provide witness to the process, but also maintain a kind of faith and dedication to psyche's rhythm. The relationship between the analyst and the analysand holds a particular "in-between space" for waiting, gazing, wrestling, and having a shared experience of delight when the transforming symbols comes into the light by way of the transcendent function. However, while waiting, the liminal, or "in-between space" is available for the active imagination method to be used.

In Figure 10.5, the snake skeleton suggests that Alyssa was touching the emptiness and getting to the crux of a psychological issue. We might say she was touching the bones of her experience. Alyssa shared the following:

> It seems to mark a turning point in my process . . . I see it as an image
> reflective of my work to strip the snake of the negative . . . identity . . .

it becomes an even greater metaphor for my work to accept my shadow qualities with myself that had been pushed down into the unconscious —through my own self-shaming, and through cultural values telling me such "wild woman" tendencies are shameful. . . . On the other hand, the image is reflective of feeling stuck, without much to go on, during a time when I was not receiving much from the snake in dreams or imagination.

Stripping away projections can feel like the death of an image, particularly if we over analyze it, or in other words, analyze it to death. Jung named the pictures:

baffling, if only to stop myself from framing, on the basis of certain theoretical assumptions, interpretations, which I felt were not only inadequate but liable to prejudice the ingenuous productions of the patient . . . I always took good care to let the interpretation of each image tail off into a question whose answer was left to the free fantasy-activity of the patient.

(Jung, 1947/1972, CW 8, p. 202)

Alyssa was pulled by the energy of the unconscious when the following spontaneous image came from working with tissue paper (Figure 10.6). Alyssa used Wallace's (1987) art therapy method of tissue collage to facilitate spontaneous imagery and active imagination. She noted, "What started as an abstract tissue image quickly showed itself to be a snake eye." This startled her "but I was no longer . . . surprised by the synchronicity . . . around images related to the snake." When she did an active imagination with the snake eye, she learned that it depicted an "inner wisdom—an inner sight" that was intricately connected to the dark feminine principle. Through the dialogue with the images she let go of the fear of the snake. In other words, Alyssa became conscious of her own shadow projections and could withdraw them. There were ideas she had about the snake that needed to be revisited, important aspects to be integrated. Alyssa noted that she had more energy and felt an expansion of her personality that seemed to follow her psychological work and active imaginations.

Sometimes at a very deep level there is an archaic fear that we will not survive the impact of our unconscious images or that we will magically create more problems for ourselves—might the images somehow annihilate us? Will we be strong enough to handle their truths? Images do have an effect on our psyche so our instinctual reactions are real. While this arises from an ancient protective instinct, how the images transform us depends upon the attitude of the maker (Abt, 2005, p. 33). If we partake in the idea that the unconscious is real and the images have a life of their own, then our engagement with the power of our images releases psychic energy, and when there is a surrender there is also a return of vibrancy within our personality through an ego/Self connection. These sparks of aliveness brought about by Jungian art therapy Jung would have associated with the transcendent function that is constellated by making visible both diversity and wholeness as well as the relationship that vibrates between our psyche and the world that cannot, at times, be easily discerned because of its inseparability as much as its permeable and enigmatic qualities. Indeed, no matter how much we make conscious, the mystery remains.

Through the use of active imagination and art, we learn how Alyssa experienced the chthonic archetypal movement of the snake as the psychic energy that transformed her psyche/soma relationship as well as her attitude towards the world. She also used movement and writing to facilitate these conversations with her therapist. The gathering energy of the transcendent function forced her to wrestle with both sides of psyche's images of snakes, such as vulnerability versus spontaneous expression. She knew that Jung wrote extensively on the snake as an image of the unconscious and found it helpful that he also referred to the snake as the instinctual primitive brain. As an image for kundalini energy, the snake connected her to what had been rejected as it can symbolize the rejected dark feminine wisdom reclaimed through relationship with psyche as well as the world. At the core of her inner process, Alyssa was working with many layers, but the archetypal themes of initiation, death/rebirth, and transformation were predominant.

Alyssa's images illustrate what Cwik (1991) named "Self-relatedness" or "the establishment of the ego–Self axis," which is expressed as a complete process with all the images. As bookends to the process, Figure 10.2 (an embodied conscious ego) and Figure 10.6, "Snake Eye" (an embodied unconscious Self structure), provided visual bookends for Alyssa's psychological initiation process that carried her through the semester.

We can speculate how these two circular images share similarities in their mandala shape but carry unique differences and expressions of psyche's innate complexities that are further noted with art materials (markers/ego versus tissue paper/Self). The layered mandala in Figure 10.2 allowed Alyssa to venture into a dialogue with the unconscious from a firm foundation, her psyche becoming prepared for the subsequent inner process of the attending phase. What unfolded was a deepening into a relationship with the unconscious and a newfound relationship with the Self (passage phase), spontaneously expressed in the tissue paper process (Figure 10.6). She worked around a focal point that suggested the presence of an organizing aspect of the psyche, that emerged as the snake's eye (Self). Alyssa's encounters with the unconscious are an example of how "[a]ctive imagination designates one of the most mature forms of the capacity to be alone in its highly conscious and concentrated focus on being present to, and in active encounter with, the unconscious" (Cwik, 1991, p. 110). In other words, it is not one attitude or the other, but both/and that must collaborate within the psyche for deep changes to occur.

Questions to consider when using the method of Active Imagination with art therapy:

- What do you feel in your body as you sit with the image?
- What do you notice first about the image?
- What area speaks loudest to you right now?
- What are you (image) truly about?
- What have you (image) come to tell me?
- What do you (image) want or what would help you feel better?
- Dialogue with the emptiness and the tension in the picture?
- Dialogue with a line, shape or color: what do these want from me?

Conclusion

Image making is a messy psychological process that is associated with emotions and suffering our fate. In fact, it stretches far beyond Aristotelian logic into the ineffable and irrational psyche by bridging these interminable dichotomies of the opposites that live within us. The offering is a whole image, and vivid, living symbols that unify and transform. What might not fit together in our minds can co-exist through compensatory images, or revelatory symbols that express and hold psychic energy, the suffering that arises from the paradox of life through these internal opposites. Images and symbols give form to the past, present, and future. In contrast to Freud who looked mostly backwards, Jung and analytical psychology distinctly looked to the future (Schweizer, 2017). The image making then reveals what was not previously known, gives the unspeakable a voice, and shines a light in the dark as we step onto our path of individuation.

Concepts are only brief handholds and theory is not definitive but alive and developing. Now, our inner work begins. The images that arise document the past yet at the same time they lead us forward; they hint at what may still be lurking and they open the gate to the inevitable changes, and rich possibilities. Jungian art therapy liberates the ego to be both solid and flexible as it confronts and engages with the shadow, wrestles with complexes and navigates the powerful forces of archetypal material, all of which is made possible through our dedication to the creative nature that lives within us. In this process we must not forget to acknowledge the importance of the destructive forces if we are going to honestly grapple and endure the painful suffering that comes with the creation of the new and an enigmatic fleeting connection with the Self.

Jungian art therapy is a natural yet specific method of action mixed with a reflective visual container that reveals the *hidden places*, the *genius loci*, or sacred, protective places for our healing. This is reminiscent of the caves of Asclepius, where people went to heal their ills and hear the guiding messages from the gods through their dreams. A non-poisonous snake was an important remedy as was milkweed, or the lick of a dog. These antidotes are some of the archetypal symbols from our Western inheritance. Without a doubt the *imaginal* thread of the psyche leads us to the creative "solution," unearthed through the mysterious connection to the darkest part of the psyche. Paradoxically, this transpersonal flicker of the creative psyche is found not in the glorious light and elevation, but deep within the chthonic mud of our raw, deep, and utterly personal existence. As Jung wisely noted in *The Red Book*, "The knowledge of the heart is in no book and is not to be found in the mouth of any teacher, but grows out of you like the green seed from the dark earth" (Jung, 2009b, p. 133). Jung did not proclaim a theory, but hypothesized his whole life about the potentiality of the psyche. He encouraged us to work with our shadow and tend to the inner process and follow our own heart, to our own center of knowing.

While many remain blind to analytical psychology and are unable to appreciate Jung's sensitivity and dedication to the relational and irrational psyche, his attitude and his psychological methods used with unconscious material and the depth of suffering within the individual as well as humankind were vastly ahead of his time. They continue today to be profound sources of support and illumination. He did not anticipate that he would change the world with his life work, but trusted that those who recognized his efforts would begin their own journey into the shadow. Most importantly, Jung fell into art therapy through his own process as well as having his analysands use his methods clinically, so he most definitely comprehended the depth with which the creative process impacted the darkest parts of our soul. As the first psychoanalyst who eagerly established the arts as a credible and profound method of expression and treatment, Jung not only inspired the field of art therapy (and the expressive arts), but his ideas and transparent personal investigations had a significant influence on the pioneers of art therapy, their creative ideas, methods, and their innovative clinical applications. It is my hope that this small contribution will inspire you to open the gates to learn more about Jung and analytical psychology, and continue on the path seeking future possibilities waiting to be found within. "If your creative force now turns to the place of the soul, you will see how your soul becomes green and how its field bears wonderful fruit" (Jung, 2009, p. 142).

Endnote

1. EMDR, Brainspotting, and Focusing methods are all structured contemporary techniques partially formulated from Jung's original work on active imagination, particularly when they facilitate a relationship between the ego and the unconscious and rely on the imagination for amplification and healing.

Jung's Four Stages of Therapy

In his essay *Problems in Modern Psychotherapy* (1929/1985, CW 16), Jung divided psychotherapy into four stages: Confession, Elucidation, Education, and Transformation. Archetypal patterns and alchemy formed the basis for analytical psychology; as a researcher, Jung gave tremendous consideration to clinical methods and applications, but he was also imaginative and innovative with his ideas on the psychotherapeutic process. He considered all psychotherapy an offshoot of early initiation rites, with its dynamic and transformative properties.

Jung saw psychotherapy and analysis as an art and didn't want his four stages to be taken literally. Thus, the process of any therapy, including Jungian art therapy, might be accurately viewed as a circumambulation. As in the art of alchemy, we work with the *prima materia* or the raw material of our personality. In addition, Jung's consideration for the opposites (in alchemy, to separate and then synthesize and consolidate) was paired with the importance of the therapeutic dyad, in which the analyst undergoes a transformation through the willingness to sweat and suffer the unconscious material that is ignited by the work:

> Psychological induction inevitably causes the two parties to get involved in the transformation of the third and to be themselves transformed in the process, and all the time the doctor's knowledge, like a flickering lamp, is the one dim light in the darkness.
>
> (Jung, 1946/1985, CW 16, pp. 198–199)

When we embark in a mutual analysis, we are changed as much as our patients. Jung also thought the individual had responsibility for his or her own life and that it was beneficial to take occasional breaks from analysis after about 10 weeks. The reason behind this was to give the analysand time to incorporate the inner work and take it out into the world, and live life. This does not mean that Jung dissuaded individuals from regular and intensive psychotherapy. He sometimes encouraged analysis more than once a week, particularly if the unconscious was working and there was material that needed digesting.

Jung explored the range of reactions to emotional content and discovered that there are individuals who are willing, and there are individuals who avoid relating to the unconscious. Jung understood that the individuals who avoid relating to the unconscious benefit from various techniques (Jung, 1929/1985, CW 16, p. 60). The use of dream images, active imagination, and spontaneous painting in Jungian art therapy can disturb the secure position of the ego and ignite the psychological process.

Jung's method of active imagination encouraged analysands to work with the unconscious outside of the therapeutic container. Some might abhor his thinking today, but individuation and the facilitation of the *inner agent* was at the heart of Jung's analytic philosophy and suits Jungian art therapy and the creative process. Jung was adamant that individuation is not only about the analysand but also requires the analyst or Jungian art therapist to ensure that the path forward is a collaborative one, created through mutual discussion and construction that includes material from the unconscious to guide the way. This means the analyst must be willing to change as much as the analysand. Many of Jung's ideas remain in use today, such as in the relational models of psychotherapy.

Confession or Catharsis

In his first stage of therapy, *confession*, Jung explained that at certain points we are asked to give up what we have in order to receive something new. This stage is a purposeful concealment that reflects the hidden place in the psyche where we store our secrets; it is related to both our process of differentiation as much as our sense of moral virtue. We come to psychotherapy because the hidden material has become too much, and whatever has been withheld now seeks relief. It pushes beyond the threshold of consciousness in various unpredictable ways with unusual symptoms and conflicts that disturb and distort the conscious mind. We share our secrets with the analyst or Jungian art therapist, revealing the truths we've told to no one. Jung explained that the "holding back" of sharing until this point is beneficial because restraint is often seen as a virtue.

In the first days of therapy, Jung noticed that the confession period was a time when we finally put our burdens down in front of us, and, more importantly, in front of someone else. At the root of confession is the archetypal pattern of initiation, which has a distinct and purposeful pattern associated with individuation. Furthermore, Jung elucidated the importance of emotions in therapy because through the initiatory process of confessing our emotional truths, our burdens will be lighter, and we will feel less isolated or inferior. While the confession may appear to be a cure in itself, Jung warned us that if there is an abrupt ending of the therapy, there will be a relapse.

Elucidation

Jung denoted the second stage of therapy as *elucidation*, which includes the onset of symptoms and the transference phenomenon. When dreams, images, and stories are gathered and a therapeutic alliance or attachment is formed, Stevens and Storr explained that

> [T]here is what Jung called a fixation that needs to be examined or areas of failed development, ruptures within the therapeutic dyad . . . . Major transformation rarely happens in this phase, but it is a time when there is a quickening of the work.
>
> (Stevens & Storr, 1994, p. 104)

With the help of the analyst, the shadow aspect of the personality becomes knowable in the therapeutic relationship, through reflection, particular questions, direct feedback, and unconscious content. As unconscious material is gathered, there is increased commitment to the therapeutic process through the transference to the therapist. Jung noted that there may be an entanglement as the analyst and analysand work together with complexes, and recommended that the analyst "submit what scraps of fantasy he can obtain from the patient to analytical interpretation" (Jung, 1929/1985, CW 16, p. 63). His words planted the seeds for the two-person therapeutic relational model that we have today. There will be a great temptation to turn away from the difficulties and despair and this is when the third stage of *education* is helpful.

Education

Psycho-education was and still is an important part of analytic and psycho-therapeutic work, for Jungian psychotherapy as well as various other psychotherapies, to educate someone about his or her symptoms, condition, and treatment of difficulties such as trauma. Education about Jung's model of the psyche allows someone to work more effectively with unconscious material and to not dismiss images from the unconscious. After the first two phases, an adaptation to the collective is required to take one's inner life out into the world, so it is imperative to have the necessary education. In other words, the first two stages have been turned into the soil of our lives and there are slight changes in how we live and view life (Stevens & Storr, 1994, p. 105).

Transformation

The fourth stage of *transformation* emerges after diligent and deliberate work with unconscious content. This stage includes the assimilation of shadow content, engagement with complexes, and mediating archetypal images and patterns. The ego shifts and softens its view so that life is larger and has new purpose. Giving birth to consciousness brings powerful symbolic material found in dreams, artwork, and other unconscious material to the surface, including images found within the transference/countertransference. Jung advised us that this phase is not the final stage of attainment or the only truth.

Ego adaptation to the collective is not the only purpose of psychotherapy; Jung reminded us that non-adaptation may be more suitable when he said: "What sets one man free is another man's prison. So also with normality and adaption" (Jung, 1929/1985, CW 16, p. 70). For Jung, individuation was a lifelong endeavor.

References

All website URLs accessed on August 30, 2017.

Abt, T. (2005). *Introduction to picture interpretation according to C. G. Jung*. Zurich, Switzerland: Living Human Heritage.

Archetype. (n.d.). In *Merriam-Webster's online dictionary* (11th ed.). Retrieved from www.merriam-webster.com/dictionary/archetype

Ayto, J. (1993). *Dictionary of word origins: The histories of more than 8,000 English-language words*. New York: Arcade Publishing.

Baynes, H. G. (1940). *Mythology of the soul*. London, UK: Rider & Company.

Berk, van den, T. (2012). *Jung on art: The autonomy of the creative drive*. New York, NY: Routledge.

Bruner, J. (1960/1977). *The process of education*. Boston, MA: Harvard University Press.

Cane, F. (1951/1983). *The artist in each of us*. Craftsbury Common, VT: Art Therapy Publication.

Celaya, E. M. (2010). *Collected writings and interviews, 1990–2010*. Lincoln, NE: University of Nebraska Press.

Chodorow, J. (1995). Dance/movement and body experience in analysis. In M. Stein (Ed.), *Jungian analysis* (2nd ed.) (pp. 391–404). Chicago, IL: Open Court.

Chodorow, J. (Ed). (1997). *Jung on active imagination*. Princeton, NJ: Princeton University Press.

Corbett, L. (2011). *The sacred cauldron: Psychotherapy as a spiritual practice*. Wilmette, IL: Chiron Publications.

Corbin, H. (1969/1989). *Alone with the alone*. Princeton, NJ: Princeton University Press.

Corbin, H. (1972). *Mundus imaginalis or the imaginary and the imaginal*. Paper first delivered at the Colloquium on Symbolism in Paris in June 1964. Retrieved from https://archive.org/stream/mundus_imaginalis_201512/mundus_imaginalis_djvu.txt

Cox, C.T. (2016) The creative encounter and the theory of formation. In K. Madden (Ed.), *The unconscious roots of creativity*. Ashville, NC: Chiron Publications.

Cwik, A. (1991). Active imagination as imaginal play space. In M. Stein (Ed.), *Liminality and transitional phenomena* (pp. 99–114). Wilmette, IL: Chiron Publications.

Cwik, A. (1995). Active imagination: Synthesis in analysis. In M. Stein (Ed.), *Jungian analysis* (2nd ed.) (pp. 137–169). Chicago, IL: Open Court.

Cwik, A. (2011). Associative dreaming: Reverie and active imagination. *Journal of Analytical Psychology, 56*(1), 14–36.

Davidson, D. (1966). Transference as a form of active imagination. In M. Fordham, R. Gordon, J. Hubback, & K. Lambert (Eds.), *Technique in Jungian analysis* (pp. 188–199). London: Karnac Books.

Dean, M. (2016). *Using art media in psychotherapy: Bringing the power of creativity to practice*. New York, NY: Routledge.

234

Dissanayake, E. (1988). *What is art for?* Seattle, WA: University of Washington Press.

Doidge, N. (2007). *The brain that changes itself.* New York, NY: Penguin Books.

Dougherty, M. (1998). Duccio's prayer: Mediating destruction and creation with artists in analysis. *The Journal of Analytical Psychology, 43*(4), 489–492.

Dougherty, M. (2010). On making and making use of images in analysis. In M. Stein (Ed.), *Jungian psychoanalysis: Working in the spirit of C. G. Jung* (pp. 134–140). Chicago, IL: Open Court.

Dougherty, M. (2011). On articulating affective states through image-making in analysis. *ARAS Connections: Image and Archetype, 4*, 1–15. Retrieved from https://aras.org/sites/default/files/docs/00048Dougherty.pdf

Edinger, E. (1992). *Ego and archetype.* Boston, MA: Shambhala.

Edwards, M. (1987). Jungian analytic art therapy. In J. Rubin (Ed.), *Approaches to art therapy: Theory and technique* (1st ed.) (pp. 92–113). New York, NY: Brunner/Mazel.

Edwards. M. (2010). *A Jungian circumambulation of art and therapy: Ornithology for the birds.* London, UK: Insider Art.

Ellenberger, H. (1970). *The discovery of the unconscious: The history and evolution of dynamic psychiatry.* New York, NY: Basic Books.

Evers-Fahey, K. (2017). *Towards a Jungian theory of the ego.* New York, NY: Routledge.

Finch, S. (1991/2010). *Creating mandalas: For insight, healing, and self-expression.* Boston and London: Shambhala.

Fordham, M. (1967). Active imagination: Deintegration or disintegration? *The Journal of Analytical Psychology, 12*, 51–66.

Franklin, M. (1999). Becoming a student of oneself: Activating the witness in meditation, art and super-vision. *American Journal of Art Therapy, 38*, 2–13.

Frey-Rohn, L. (1990). *From Freud to Jung: A comparative study of the psychology of the unconscious.* Boston, MA: Shambhala.

Furth, G. M. (1988). *The secret world of drawings: Healing through art.* Boston, MA: Sigo Press.

Geller, S. (2013). Sparking the creative in older adults. *Psychological Perspectives, 56*(2), 200–211.

Hannah, B. (1976). *Jung: His life and work.* New York, NY: G. P. Putnam's Sons.

Harding, M. E. (1961). What makes the symbol effective as a healing agent? In G. Adler (Ed.), *Current trends in analytical psychology* (pp. 1–17). London: Tavistock.

Hauke, C. (2006). The unconscious: Personal and collective. In R. Papadopoulous (Ed.), *The handbook of Jungian psychology: Theory, practice and applications* (pp. 54–73). New York, NY: Routledge.

Hillman, J. (1960/1997). *Emotion: A comprehensive phenomenology of theories and their meanings for therapy.* Evanston, IL: Northwestern University Press.

Hillman, J. (1977). An inquiry into image. *Spring, 39*, 62–88.

Hogan, S. (2001). *Healing arts: The history of art therapy.* London, UK: Jessica Kingsley Publishers.

Jacobi, J. (1942/1973). *The psychology of C. G. Jung.* New Haven, CT: Yale University Press.

James, W. (1902/2012). *The varieties of religious experience.* Createspace Independent Publishing: Renaissance Classics.

Jung, C. G. (1912/1967). Symbols of transformation. *Collected Works 5.* Princeton, NJ: Princeton University Press.

Jung, C. G. (1912/1967a). The concept of libido. *Collected Works 5.* Princeton, NJ: Princeton University Press.

Jung, C. G. (1912/1967b). Two kinds of thinking. *Collected Works 5.* Princeton, NJ: Princeton University Press.

Jung, C. G. (1912/1972). Symbols of the mother and of rebirth. *Collected Works 5.* Princeton, NY: Princeton University Press.

Jung, C. G. (1913/1970). The theory of psychoanalysis. *Collected Works 4.* Princeton, NJ: Princeton University Press.

Jung, C. G. ([1916]/1957/1972). The transcendent function. *Collected Works 8.* Princeton, NJ: Princeton University Press.

Jung, C. G. (1919/1972). Instinct and the unconscious. *Collected Works 8.* Princeton, NJ: Princeton University Press.

Jung, C. G. (1921/1928/1985). The therapeutic value of abreaction. *Collected Works 16.* Princeton, NJ: Princeton University Press.

Jung, C. G. (1921/1990). Psychological types: Definitions. *Collected Works* 6. Princeton, NJ: Princeton University Press.

Jung, C. G. (1925/2012). *Introduction to Jungian psychology: Notes of the seminar on analytical psychology given in 1925*. Revised edition edited by Sonu Shamdasani. Princeton, NJ: Princeton Press.

Jung, C. G. (1927/1972). The structure of the psyche. *Collected Works* 8. Princeton, NJ: Princeton University Press.

Jung, C. G. (1927/1978). Mind and earth. *Collected Works* 10. Princeton, NJ: Princeton University Press.

Jung, C. G. (1928/1966). The relations between the ego and the unconscious. *Collected Works* 7. Princeton, NJ: Princeton University Press.

Jung, C. G. (1928/1972). On psychic energy. *Collected Works* 8. Princeton, NJ: Princeton University Press.

Jung, C. G. (1929/1970). Freud and Jung contrasts. *Collected Works* 4. Princeton, NJ: Princeton, University Press.

Jung, C. G. (1929/1983). Commentary on "The Secret of the Golden Flower". *Collected Works* 13. Princeton, NJ: Princeton University Press.

Jung, C. G. (1929/1985). Problems of modern psychotherapy. *Collected Works* 16. Princeton, NJ: Princeton University Press.

Jung, C. G. (1930/1985). Some aspects of modern psychotherapy. *Collected Works* 16. Princeton, NJ: Princeton University Press.

Jung, C. G. (1931/1985). The aims of psychotherapy. *Collected Works* 16. Princeton, NJ: Princeton University Press.

Jung, C. G. (1934/1972). A review of the complex theory. *Collected Works* 8. Princeton, NJ: Princeton University Press.

Jung, C. G. (1934/1985). The practical use of dream-analysis. *Collected Works* 16. Princeton, NJ: Princeton University Press.

Jung, C. G. (1935/1985). Principles of practical psychotherapy. *Collected Works* 16. Princeton, NJ: Princeton University Press.

Jung, C. G. (1936/1968/1989). The Tavistock Lectures. *Collected Works* 18. Princeton, NJ: Princeton University Press.

Jung, C. G. (1936/1993). Individual dream symbolism in relation to alchemy. *Collected Works* 12. Princeton, NJ: Princeton University Press.

Jung, C. G. (1936/1937/1990). On the concept of the collective unconscious. *Collected Works* 9i. Princeton, NJ: Princeton University Press.

Jung, C. G. (1937/1972). The psychological factors determining human behavior. *Collected Works* 8. Princeton, NJ: Princeton University Press.

Jung, C. G. (1938/1954/1990). Psychological aspects of the mother archetype. *Collected Works* 9i. Princeton, NJ: Princeton University Press.

Jung, C. G. (1938/1990). On the concept of the archetype. *Collected Works* 9i. Princeton, NJ: Princeton University Press.

Jung, C. G. (1941/1990). The psychological aspects of the Kore. *Collected Works* 9i. Princeton, NJ: Princeton University Press.

Jung, C. G. (1943/1966). The problem of the attitude-type. *Collected Works* 7. Princeton, NJ: Princeton University Press.

Jung, C. G. (1944/1993). The psychic nature of alchemical work. *Collected Works* 12. Princeton, NJ: Princeton University Press.

Jung, C. G. (1945/1983). The philosophical tree. *Collected Works* 13. Princeton, NJ: Princeton University Press.

Jung, C. G. (1945/1990). The phenomenon of the spirit in fairytales. *Collected Works* 9i. Princeton, NJ: Princeton University Press.

Jung, C. G. (1946/1985). Psychology of the transference. *Collected Works* 16. Princeton, NJ: Princeton University Press.

Jung, C. G. (1947/1972). On the nature of the psyche. *Collected Works* 8. Princeton, NJ: Princeton University Press.

Jung, C. G. (1949/1990). The psychology of the child archetype. *Collected Works* 9i. Princeton, NJ: Princeton University Press.

Jung, C. G. (1952/1993). Introduction to the religious and psychological problems of alchemy. *Collected Works 12*. Princeton, NJ: Princeton University Press.

Jung, C. G. (1953/1975). *Letters Vol. 2: 1951–1961*, G. Adler (Ed.) (Trans. R. F. C. Hull). Princeton, NJ: Princeton University Press.

Jung, C. G. (1954/1975). Psychological commentary on "The Tibetan Book of the Great Liberation." *Collected Works 11*. Princeton, NJ: Princeton University Press.

Jung, C. G. (1954/1990). Concerning the archetypes, with special reference to the anima concept. *Collected Works 9i*. Princeton, NJ: Princeton University Press.

Jung, C. G. (1961). *Memories, dreams, reflections*. New York, NY: Vintage Books.

Jung, C. G. (1973). *Letters Vol. 1: 1906–1950*, G. Adler (Ed.) (Trans. R. F. C. Hull). Princeton, NJ: Princeton University Press.

Jung, C. G. (2009a). *The red book: Liber Novus*, S. Shamdasani (Ed.) (Trans. M. Kyburz, J. Peck, & S. Shamdasani). New York, NY: W.W. Norton.

Jung, C. G. (2009b). *The red book: A reader's edition*, S. Shamdasani (Ed.) (Trans. M. Kyburz, J. Peck, & S. Shamdasani). New York, NY: W.W. Norton.

Junge, M. B. (2010). *The modern history of art therapy in the United States*. Springfield, IL: Charles C. Thomas.

Kalsched, D. (1996). *The inner world of trauma: Archetypal defenses of the personal spirit*. New York, NY: Routledge.

Kalsched, D. (2013). *Trauma and the soul: A psycho-spiritual approach to human development and its interruption*. New York, NY: Routledge.

Karier, C. (1986). *Scientists of the mind: Intellectual founders of modern psychology*. Chicago, IL: University of Illinois Press.

Kellogg, J. (1969/1970). *Analyzing children's art*. Palo Alto, CA: Mayfield Publishing.

Kellogg, J. (1978/2002). *Mandala: Path of beauty*. Belleair, FL: ATMA, Inc.

Keyes, M. F. (1983). *Inward journey: Art as therapy*. La Salle, IL: Open Court.

Lincoln, B. (1981/1991). *Emerging from the chrysalis: Rituals of women's initiation*. New York, NY: Oxford University Press.

McGuire, W. & Hull, R. F. C. (Eds). (1977). *C. G. Jung speaking: Interviews and encounters*. Princeton, NJ: Princeton University Press.

McNiff, S. (1992). *Art as medicine: Creating a therapy of the imagination*. Boston, MA: Shambhala.

Milner, M. (1950/2010). *On not being able to paint*. New York, NY: Routledge.

Naumburg, M. (1950). *Schizophrenic art: Its meaning in psychotherapy*. New York, NY: Grune & Stratton, Inc.

Naumburg, M. (1966/1987). *Dynamically oriented art therapy: Its principles and practice*. Chicago, IL: Magnolia Street Publishers.

Ogden, T. H. (1994). The analytic third: Working with intersubjective clinical facts. *International Journal of Psychoanalysis, 75*, 3–19.

Otto, R. (1923). *The idea of the holy*. London, UK: Oxford University Press.

Papadopolous, R. (2006). Jung's epistemology and methodology. In R. Papadopoulous (Ed.), *The handbook of Jungian psychology: Theory, practice and applications* (pp. 7–53). New York, NY: Routledge.

Perry, J. W. (1953). *The self in psychotic process: Its symbolization in schizophrenia*. Berkeley, CA: University of California Press.

Perry, J. W. (1970). Emotions and object relations. *Journal of Analytical Psychology, 15*(1), 1–12.

Potash, J. (2014). Archetypal aesthetics: Viewing art through states of consciousness. *International Journal of Jungian Studies, 7*(2), 159–153. DOI: http://dx.doi.org/10.1080/19409052.2014.92 4984

Potash, J. and Garlock, L. (2016). Unconscious compensation and integration: Art making for wholeness and balance. In K. Madden (Ed.), *The unconscious roots of creativity*. Ashville, NC: Chiron Publications.

Rappaport, L. (2009). *Focusing-oriented art therapy: Accessing the body's wisdom and creative intelligence*. New York, NY: Jessica Kingsley Publishers.

Ruff, E. (1988, May). *Sacrifice and initiation*. Paper presented at the Pastoral Psychology Guild [MP3 file]. London, England.

Ryan, M. (2008). The transpersonal William James, *The Journal of Transpersonal Psychology, 40*(1) 20–40.

Ryan, R. (2008a). The father of all: splitting, and the philosophical assumptions of depth psychology. Pacifica University Dissertation. http://pqdtopen.proquest.com/pubnum/3666848.html

Ryan, R. (2016). Personal conversation.

Salamon, S. (2006). The creative psyche: Jung's major contributions. In P. Young-Eisendrath & T. Dawson (Eds.), *The Cambridge companion to Jung* (pp. 57–75). Cambridge, UK: Cambridge University Press.

Samuels, A, Shorter, B. & Plaut, F. (1986/1993). *A critical dictionary of Jungian analysis.* New York, NY: Routledge.

Schaverien, J. (1992). *The revealing image: Analytical art psychotherapy in theory and practice.* New York, NY: Routledge.

Schaverien, J. (1995). *Desire and the female therapist: Engendered gazes in psychotherapy and art therapy.* New York, NY: Routledge.

Schaverien, J. (2005). Art, dreams and active imagination: A post-Jungian approach to transference and the image. *Journal of Analytical Psychology, 50,* 127–153.

Schweizer, A. (2017). C. G. *Jung and the red book.* A seminar lecture given to the Boulder Jung Seminar on September 16, Boulder, Colorado.

Sedgwick, D. (1994). *Wounded healer: Countertransference from a Jungian perspective.* New York, NY: Routledge.

Sedgwick, D. (2012). *Before and after Jung's "descent"—some outer images* [PDF document]. IRSJA Lecture Presentation, Dallas, TX.

Shalit, E. (2002). *The complex: Path of transformation from archetype to ego.* Toronto, Canada: Inner City Books.

Shamdasani, S. (2003). *Jung and the making of modern psychology.* Cambridge, UK: Cambridge University Press.

Shamdasani, S. (Ed.) (2009). Introduction. In M. Kyburtz, J. Peck, & S. Shamdasani (Trans.), *The red book: A reader's edition* (pp. 1–113). New York, NY: W.W. Norton.

Shamdasani, S. (2012). Introduction. In R. F. C. Hull (Trans.), *Jung contra Freud: The 1912 New York lectures on the theory of psychoanalysis* (pp. vii–xxi). Princeton, NJ: Princeton University Press.

Shaw, D. (2014). *Traumatic narcissism: Relational systems of subjugation.* New York, NY: Routledge.

Sherry, J. (2015). Carl Jung, Beatrice Hinkle, and Charlotte Teller, the New York Times reporter. In M. E. Mattson et al. (Eds.), *Jung in the academy and beyond: The Fordham lectures 100 years later* (pp. 65–73). New York, NY: The Spring Press.

Singer, J. (1994/1972). *Boundaries of the soul.* New York, NY: Random House.

Stevens, A. (1986). *Withymead: A Jungian community for the healing arts.* London, UK: Coventure Ltd.

Stevens, A. (2006). The archetypes. In R. Papadopoulous (Ed.), *The handbook of Jungian psychology: Theory, practice and applications* (pp. 74–93). New York, NY: Routledge.

Stevens, A. & Storr, A. (1994). *Freud and Jung: A dual introduction.* New York, NY: Barnes and Noble.

Swan-Foster, N. (1989). Images of pregnant women: Art therapy as a tool for transformation. *The Arts in Psychotherapy, 16*(4), 283–292.

Swan-Foster, N. (2012). Pregnancy as a feminine initiation. *Journal of Prenatal and Perinatal Psychology and Health, 26*(4), 207–235.

Swan-Foster, N. (2016). Jungian art therapy. In J. Rubin (Ed.), *Approaches to art therapy: Theory and technique* (3rd ed.) (pp. 167–187). New York, NY: Routledge.

Swan-Foster, N., Foster, S. J., & Dorsey, A. (2003). The use of the human figure drawing with pregnant women. *Journal of Reproductive and Infant Psychology, 21*(4), 293–307.

Swan-Foster, N., Lawlor, M., Scott, L., et al. (2001). Inside an art therapy group: The student perspective. *The Arts in Psychotherapy, 28*(3), 151–174.

Taveras, M. (2015). A Jung aesthetic: Art, active imagination and the creative process. *Quadrant, Fall XLV*(2), 23–35.

Vesey-McGrew, P. (2010). Getting on top of thought and behavior patterns. In M. Stein (Ed.), *Jungian psychoanalysis: Working in the spirit of C. G. Jung* (pp. 14–21). Chicago, IL: Open Court.

von Franz, M.-L. (1980). *On divination and synchronicity: The psychology of meaningful chance.* Toronto, Canada: Inner City Books.

von Franz, M.-L. (1983). On active imagination. In M. F. Keyes (Ed.), *Inward journey: Art as therapy* (pp. 125–133). La Salle, IL: Open Court.

Wallace, E. (1987). Healing through the visual arts: A Jungian approach. In J. Rubin (Ed.), *Approaches to art therapy: Theory and technique* (1st ed.) (pp. 114–133). New York, NY: Brunner/Mazel.

Watkins, M. (1984). *Waking dreams.* New Orleans: LA, Spring Publications.

Wertz, F. (2015). Jung's break with Freud revisited: Method and the character of theory in psychoanalysis. In M. E. Mattson et al. (Eds.), *Jung in the academy and beyond: The Fordham lectures 100 years later* (pp. 15–35). New York, NY: The Spring Press.

West, M. (2016). *Into the darkest places: Early relational trauma and borderline states of mind.* New York, NY: Karnac Books.

Wickes, F. (1927/1966). *The inner world of childhood.* London, UK: Coventure Ltd.

Winnicott, D. W. (1971). *Playing and reality.* London, UK: Tavistock Publications.

Zabriskie, B. (2015). Energy and emotion: C. G. Jung's Fordham declaration. In M. E. Mattson et al. (Eds.), *Jung in the academy and beyond: The Fordham lectures 100 years later* (pp. 37–49). New York, NY: The Spring Press.

Zeller, M. (1975/2015). *The dream: The vision of the night.* Cheyenne, WY: Fisher King Press.

Index

Note: page numbers in *italic* type refer to Figures.

Abaissement 215
Abraham, Karl 59–60
abreaction 147, 158n5
Abt, Theodor 18
active imagination 61, 109, 209–210;
  experiencing the psyche 211–212; Jung's
  discovery of 212–214; Jung's method of
  214–217; personal "Red Book" process
  220–227; and the pregnant symbol
  210–211; and transference/
  countertransference 219–220; and
  transitional space 218–219; von Franz's
  method of 217–218
Adamson, Edward 70
adaptation *84*, 84–85, 85
Adler, Alfred 70, 164
affect: definition 19; *see also* emotion; feeling
AI (artificial intelligence) 167
"Aims of Psychotherapy, The" (Jung) 66
alchemy 76–77, 108, 172, 210–211
alcoholism 55
altered states 174
ambivalence 55
American art therapy, development of 52,
  64–70
amplifications 98–99, 120
analysands: definition 19
analytical art psychotherapy 18
analytical psychology 2, 9; as Jungian art
  therapy framework 52–63; origins of,
  1900–1912 54–58; *see also* Jungian
  psychology
anima (soul) 20, 44–47, *46*
anima mundi 165
animals: animal transference 90–91, *91*,
  92; and dreams 204; Lion image 90–91,
91; snake images 120, 162–163, 203,
  223–225, 226–227
animus (spirit) 20, 44–47, *46*
Aphrodite myth 166–167
Approaches to Art Therapy (Edwards) 10, 53
a priori 161, 164
archetypes 12, 14, 23, 43–44, *44*, *45*, 53, 77,
  78, 97, 98, 157n2, 159–160, 209, 220;
  archetypal image 163, *164*; *archetype as such*
  163, *164*, 165; definition 160; destructive
  potential of 168–169; development of
  Jung's theory 161–164; and dreams 193;
  ego and complexes 164–165, 175–176; of
  individuation 160, 181; instinctual and
  spiritual poles 166–175, *169*, *170*; Jungian
  art therapy examples 165–166, 169–172,
  170, *171*, *172*–*173*, 177–179, *178*, *179*,
  180, 181–185, *183*, *184*; key points 185;
  psychological development of 164–166;
  recognition of 176–179, *178*, *179*, *180*,
  181; structure of 157, 160–161
Ariadne myth 140, 170
armored knight image 154–155, *156*
Artist in Each of Us (Cane) 63, 68,
  102–103
art materials, and complexes 150–155, *154*,
  155, *156*, 157, 158n6
art therapy 33–34; American 64–70; British
  70–73; history and development 62–73;
  see also Jungian art therapy
associations 96, 97, 100
"associative dreaming" 87
associative thinking 74
attending stage 16, 113
autism 55
automatic writing 119

240